LOYALTY TO GOD

LOYALTY TO GOD

The Apostles' Creed in Life and Liturgy

THEODORE W. JENNINGS, JR.

Abingdon Press
NASHVILLE

LOYALTY TO GOD

Copyright © 1992 by Abingdon Press

This book is printed on recycled, acid-free paper.

Library of Congress Cataloging-in-Publication Data

JENNINGS, THEODORE W.
  Loyalty to God : the Apostles' Creed in life and liturgy / Theodore W. Jennings, Jr.
  p. cm.
   Includes bibliographical references.
ISBN 0-687-22821-2 (pbk. : alk. paper)
1. Apostles' Creed. 2. Liberation theology. I. Title.
BT993.2.J46   1992
238'.11—dc20   91-28450
                                                                     CIP

Quotations are from the Revised Standard Version of the Bible, copyright © 1946, 1952, 1971 by the Division of Christian Education of the National Council of Churches of Christ in the USA. Used by permission.

Quotations marked KJV are from the King James Version of the Bible.

Quotations marked NRSV are from the New Revised Standard Version Bible, copyright © 1989, by the Division of Christian Education of the National Council of the Churches of Christ in the USA. Used by permission.

MANUFACTURED IN THE UNITED STATES OF AMERICA

To Ronna Lynn Case
my beloved, my friend

CONTENTS

ACKNOWLEDGMENT/PREFACE

T hese reflections on the Apostles' Creed derive from lectures given at the Seminario Metodista de Mexico in Mexico City and at the Candler School of Theology in Atlanta, Georgia in the years 1983-85. This double origin had the benefit of forcing me to consider the Creed from the disparate perspectives of "third" and "first" world issues, questions, and concerns. Thus I owe a considerable debt to the students in each of these settings, not only for their willingness to engage in serious theological reflection, but also for the enthusiasm which they generated for the perspectives and interpretations that emerged from our work together.

It was necessary to set this material aside for a time to work on other projects. But the encouragement (not to say nagging) of Rex Matthews at Abingdon and of Ted Runyon at Candler drove me back to the task of turning lecture notes (in two languages) into a publishable book.

The appearance of the book also marks my return, after a thirteen-year absence, to Chicago Theological Seminary. During the years of this sojourn I have been able to continue theological work because of my wife's unfailing support and encouragement. It is to her that this book is dedicated.

CHAPTER ONE

CREDO

W hen we come together as the people of God, we do a number of things that mark us as the Christian community. In the midst of the somewhat more familiar activities of calling and sending, of praying and praising, of hearing and proclaiming, of confessing and pardoning, we also, at least some of the time, affirm our faith using the words of an ancient creed. What is the meaning of this recital of a creed?

For many, perhaps for most of us, this question arises when we notice that although the words of the Creed have become familiar through usage in the worship of the community of faith, they have by no means become self-evident. Phrases like descended into hell, ascended into heaven, born of the Virgin Mary, or the resurrection of the dead, may suddenly strike us as odd, as speaking in a way which is unlike the natural or spontaneous declaration of our own beliefs, our own faith.

We may then shrink from the use of these terms, and so from the use of these ancient creeds. We may seek to find another, more congenial creed, a formulation that seems less mythological and more modern. Or we may find the Creed inadequate for other reasons, often not so much for what it says, as for what it doesn't say. Why speak of the virgin birth and not of the life of faith and hope and love? Why speak of Jesus' ascension but not of his ministry of healing or teaching? Why speak of the descent into hell instead of prayer or of loving our neighbor?

Thus many of us approach the moment of the confession of faith with a certain amount of suspicion and reserve. And in many of our orders of worship it is one of the things that may often simply be left out in favor of an anthem from the choir or a reading from the Psalms, or more announcements.

In spite of this, the Creed has an undoubtedly important place in the life of the church. It has often been used as a summary of doctrine in order to teach what Christians believe. It is a part of our tradition, a connection with the centuries of Christian faith always and everywhere. Perhaps then it belongs not in the liturgy of the gathered community, but in the classroom or in the catechetical instruction of the young in the heirlooms of their tradition.

It is one of the odd features of many interpretations of the Creed that its setting in the worship of the community is seldom taken into account. It is simply taken as a summary of some of the doctrines of the community of faith, without asking why a summary of doctrine should find its way into the order of worship. Yet it is precisely in its place in the order of worship, somewhat endangered with the passage of time, that most of us encounter the Creed at all.

In the pages that follow I have undertaken a reflection on the Apostles' Creed. This is the oldest of the creeds that we use and the one that is most often encountered in the worship of the congregation. Later creeds, including the Nicene Creed, are based upon this one. But later creeds often have a somewhat different character as the needs of the church have changed and the original function of the Creed was supplanted by other considerations. Interpretations of those creeds would have to take these altered circumstances into account. For this reason I have generally postponed consideration even of similar clauses from other creeds to a later study. In this way it will be possible to give full attention to the character of the most ancient and most widely used of the creeds of Christendom without being misled by the sometimes quite different character of other creeds.

The following reflection on the Apostles' Creed attempts to take seriously its place in the worship of the Christian community.[1] I believe that if we begin with the Creed in worship and pay attention both to the liturgical action and to the questions that arise in the midst of this action, we may gain important insight into the nature of this confession and affirmation.

I will argue that the Creed functions not as a recitation of "beliefs," but as an affirmation or avowal of loyalty. This will become clear first by comparing what we do with the Creed in worship to the more familiar actions of pledging allegiance to a flag and of vowing fidelity in marriage.

The hypothesis that the Creed is to be understood as such a vow of allegiance or loyalty will then be verified by attending to its relation to early Christian baptismal practice. It will become evident that for the early church the Creed served as the means of vowing loyalty in life and in death to the God whom we meet in Jesus Christ.

THE AFFIRMATION OF FAITH AND
VOWS OF LOYALTY

The way in which the Creed is said or recited is itself illuminating. The congregation stands, facing the altar. The words they say are said in unison. Yet they do not say "we believe . . . " but rather, "I believe . . . " What is going on here? Why this corporate action in which, nevertheless, the singular pronoun is used? Who is the "I" who speaks in unison with so many others?

The action here is formally like certain other actions that we encounter outside the community of faith. In the United States the most similar action takes place above all in schools when young people recite the Pledge of Allegiance to the flag. There too, it is as a corporate body that we stand together and recite together words learned "by heart." There too, the words begin not with the plural "we" but the singular "I." There too, there is a common focus of attention, not on the altar, but on the flag.

The Pledge of Allegiance is obviously an oath or vow of loyalty. We do this in order to affirm that we will be loyal to the flag, and therefore, to the nation for which it stands. The further words of the pledge serve to specify what nation is meant: one nation, under God, with liberty and justice for all. It is to this nation, and not some other, that we pledge our loyalty.

If we use this illustration to clarify the significance of reciting the Creed then we may at least wonder if the use of this "I" in the Creed implies that we pledge our loyalty, or vow to be faithful. This would explain why it is impossible to say "we" here, for an oath of loyalty or a vow of allegiance is something that a person can do only for her or himself. It entails a personal commitment of the will. This is not something that can be done on behalf of another, but which must be undertaken for oneself. It is in this way that I venture into the sphere of promise and commitment in which I may prove to be faithful or treasonous. This is something I can do in community, but only for myself and in my own name.

We also noticed that the remaining words of the declaration serve to indicate to whom we are determined to be loyal; that is, they serve to specify the object of this loyalty. In the terms of the pledge to the flag, my loyalty is not to just this nation whatever it may do but to its founding principles or basic character, described as liberty and justice for all. Those who say this pledge may or may not believe that the United States really does embody the ideals of liberty and justice for all. Perhaps on this point some may have real reservations without this making it impossible to pledge this loyalty. For example, one may undertake to actualize these values as a mark of one's loyalty and so be committed to realizing this liberty and justice not only for some, but for all. Indeed, that is probably what the author of the pledge (a Christian Socialist) had in mind. But in being loyal to this nation, I could wind up betraying it if I were to seek to restrict the extent of this liberty and justice. That would be a betrayal of the pledge in the name of misguided patriotism.

The Pledge of Allegiance is not the only place where we encounter such a loyalty oath. We encounter it in the oath of office of government servants (to uphold the Constitution), in organizations like the Scouts and, above all, in military organizations. This last is not without significance for the meaning of the Creed, as we shall see when we discuss its historical setting.

Another sort of action to which the Creed seems comparable is the wedding vow. Of course these vows are not said by a group in unison, and so in that respect are quite different in setting. But in the wedding vow we encounter an avowal of loyalty to another person that may also illumine what we do in the affirmation of faith.

In the wedding vows we say that we will be loyal to this other person, renouncing all competing loyalties as well. This is evident in the way in which we agree to "forsake all others" to adhere to just this one. Of course this does not mean that we may have no other friends, nor does it mean that we are licensed to be disloyal to other pledges and vows. But it does mean that we will not abandon this one for another, that no other person will have the same claim on us. This exclusive claim of loyalty is also found, though less explicitly, in the Pledge of Allegiance. There we implicitly renounce loyalty to other nations in favor of this one. That is what occurs when this pledge is recited, for example, by those who are altering their nationality. They affirm that this nation and not some other will claim their allegiance.

In both cases what we claim is not belief in certain propositions about the object of our loyalty but that we will be faithful to this object of loyalty, whether nation or person. Certain propositions or opinions may be involved: this is a free nation, its laws are just or at least capable of being made so; this person is trustworthy, we will be happy together, I can't live without him or her, and so on. But the promise is, in any case, one of loyalty and faithfulness, for better or worse.

And it is this sort of promise and pledge which no one can make for another. I alone can commit myself in this way. I alone can be faithful or faithless.

Now if we return from this excursion into the world of pledging and vowing to a consideration of the Creed, we can say as a sort of hypothesis that the Creed is a way of pledging our loyalty to the one who is identified as "God the Father Almighty . . ." That it is a pledge of loyalty would certainly explain the place of this "I" which begins the Creed; it is the "I" of one who pledges or vows loyalty or faithfulness. The faith with which the Creed is concerned is not mere belief or assent to propositions, but the faith of faithfulness: I will be faithful to this one.

At this point this is only a hypothesis derived from reflection on the character of the action as we observe it in worship, and taking into account apparently similar actions in other contexts. It remains to test the hypothesis.

THE CREED AND BAPTISM

It is now generally agreed and understood that the Creed is a reflection of the baptismal practice in the early Christian community. When we reflect upon this practice and its relation to the Creed, we will see that the guess we have made about the Creed as a vow of loyalty is correct.

In Latin, the opening word of the Creed is "credo." This was the response to the questions put to candidates for baptism. They were asked: "Do you believe in God the Father Almighty, maker of heaven and earth?" and they answered "credo." "Do you believe in Jesus Christ, his only Son, our Lord?" To which they again replied, "credo." "Do you believe in the Holy Spirit?" and a third time the reply came: "credo." This threefold credo corresponded to the threefold "name" in which the candidates were to be baptized: The Father, the Son, and the Holy Spirit. The three articles of the Creed then appear as the elaboration of the baptismal vows, which were the elaboration of the threefold name into which candidates were to be baptized.

In baptism the positive meaning of the credo was underlined by the negative act that preceded it; a threefold renunciation of the devil and all his works. In many early communities this was accompanied by a form of exorcism to drive the demonic from the one who was to be baptized. The vow "I believe" was accompanied by "I renounce" or "I abjure."[2] Many of the revised liturgies for baptism in the last few decades have recovered this practice.

It is already clear that far more is at stake here than a set of beliefs. For in renouncing the devil, the candidates did not mean that they ceased to believe in the devil's existence. What is at stake here both positively and negatively is not belief, but loyalty. I repudiate the one in order to adhere to the other.

The Creed then, is like the vow that forsakes all others to be loyal only to one.[3] But the avowal of the Creed implies far more than the selection of a marriage partner or loyalty to a particular regiment or flag or nation. What is at stake here is the ultimate object of loyalty. This ultimacy is expressed as a choice between God and Satan.

In recent times this understanding of the Creed as a vow of loyalty has been emphasized by W. C. Smith in his comparative study of belief in major religions.[4] He notes that the word "credo" comes from the roots *cor* (heart) and *dare* (to give or render).[5] This etymological evidence suggests that the Creed is a giving of the heart (in the sense of will or loyalty) to another. Despite the importance of this argument for an understanding of the Creed, it has been largely ignored by theologians (who tend not to read much comparative religion in any case).[6]

The supposition that the Creed is a vow of loyalty is strengthened by additional considerations as well. The Creed itself is known to us from the early centuries only on account of the preliminary instructions given to those who were to be baptized. For centuries it was forbidden to write the Creed. It was to be learned by heart by those who were to be baptized, but it was withheld from writing lest there be some who would feign membership in the community who had not actually undertaken these vows.[7]

The fact that the Creed was not to be written derives from the time of persecution through which the community passed for the first three centuries of its existence. So strong was this need for care and secrecy that Augustine, long after the passing of the time of danger, could still refer to the importance of not writing out the Creed.[8] For the most part, this veil of secrecy is regarded only as a frustrating obstacle by scholars seeking to establish the words of the Creed in early periods. But it is far more than an obstacle; it is also a clue. In this requirement of secrecy the Creed reminds us of a password: a word or phrase shared by those united in a common cause that is viewed with suspicion by the authorities.

Indeed this is precisely what was understood by the Creed. It was also called a "symbolum": a secret token or password shared by members of a closed society.[9] In the days of the Roman Empire this was primarily a military regiment. A password or symbolum could assume critical importance as allegiances shifted with the intrigues that brought new emperors to the throne from the ranks of military commanders. The symbolum indicated that allegiance for which, as a soldier, one was prepared to live and to die.[10] That is, the symbolum was a marker of loyalty.

Of course this need for secrecy implies danger, and this is the climate in which early Christianity found itself. Their loyalty to Jesus as Lord marked them at once as potentially subversive. The titles of honor that belonged to Caesar were instead attributed to one who had been crucified, executed as a rebel against the empire. It was Jesus rather than Caesar that the Christians called Lord and Son of God. They refused to participate in the imperial cult that held the empire together. From the standpoint of the imperial state, they were obviously subversive. For they were pledged to live and die for a different sort of empire, the empire of justice and generosity, of love and joy.

This subversive character of Christian identity is regularly obscured by the supposition that what was at stake was simply a question of idolatry. We are often told that the early Christians refused to give divine status to Caesar and for this were persecuted. But the Christian assertion of the lordship of Jesus comes into opposition with Caesar not because of abstract reflections about divinity, but on the basis of incompatible loyalties. The Christians were loyal to one who was marked by the empire as its enemy. They would not acknowledge Caesar's lordship because it seemed to contradict their loyalty to Christ.[11]

That is after all why the Creed is also called a "confession." Christian commitment was labeled a crime of subversion. Those who were suspected of being Christians were hauled into court. They could easily escape by denying their loyalty to Christ, or they could "confess." To confess was to admit that they were loyal to Christ, and thus subversive of the empire. The penalty for this confession was often death. Those who paid this full price of loyalty were called martyrs (witnesses), just as those who publicly admitted to Christian identity were called "confessors."

It is striking that baptism was always linked to martyrdom. On the one hand, martyrdom was held to be a substitute for baptism, an idea that goes back to Jesus' words to John and James when he asks them if they will share his baptism (Mark 10:38-39). The question is whether they are willing to be delivered up to death as he was. This is the true "Christian baptism." On the other hand, baptism could be understood as a preparation for or anticipation of martyrdom. During the times of persecution this was a fairly direct connection, for baptism meant swearing loyalty to Christ in such a way as to be marked, in the eyes of the Roman authorities, as an enemy of the state. In less dangerous times it was nevertheless regarded as a participation in the death of Christ (Romans 6:3-11) who had, after all, been executed by agents of the empire.

The relation of the Creed to baptism serves to underscore its character as a vow of loyalty. The faith of which it speaks is not belief or trust, but faithfulness. Those who undertook instruction in the Creed prior to baptism were those who were prepared to seal their loyalty with their own life's blood.[12] They were not parading a set of beliefs, still less opinions about dubious matters. Rather, they were committing themselves to a cause, the cause of the one whom they identify in the clauses that follow this fateful "credo." This loyalty was a matter of life and death, a loyalty that entailed renouncing ties to the devil and all his works, a loyalty that would mark them as subversive in the eyes of even the most enlightened emperors. In this context the recitation of the Creed clearly becomes far more than a sleepy ceremony. It is a pledging of one's life to the cause of one for whom one is prepared to die.

FAITH: BELIEF, TRUST OR FAITHFULNESS?

With this background in mind we may now consider the meaning of the belief that is indicated by the Creed. What is at stake here is not a set of assertions of greater or lesser plausibility, but a commitment for which one is prepared both to live and to die.

For many Christians belief is primarily a matter of assent to certain propositions. For many it is assent to the authoritative teaching of the community of which they are a part. For others it is assent to a book of propositions, the Bible, regarded as a compendium of statements whose correctness is to be accepted without question.

Such a model of belief is not restricted to religious bodies. Assent to a more or less detailed set of propositions may also characterize philosophical schools or political parties. For example, one may believe that the market economy is the best way of ensuring the growth of national wealth, or that justice is best achieved in a democracy, or that the best foundation for law is to be found in the Koran, or that the state ownership of property is the only way to ensure social and economic justice, and so on. Much of what we do in the world depends on a more or less clear set of beliefs about how things are and how they are best arranged.

This is the model with which many of us approach the Creed. We suppose that what is at stake is a set of propositions to which we claim to give assent. Thus we suppose that to recite the Creed with integrity is to claim to believe that Jesus was born of a virgin, that he ascended into heaven, that he will come to judge the living and the dead, and so on.

On this view, a reflection on the Creed should help us believe these odd propositions and enable us to make these words our own way of describing reality. But, of course, for many of us this seems a hopeless task. How could we be expected to believe these things literally, expressed in a language and world view so different from the one in which we customarily live and think?

A fatal gap begins to open between belief and thought. Some may continue to insist that they believe these propositions to be true without being able to say what they mean. They are regarded as beliefs that one must simply accept, repeat, and swallow without question or thought. For others who are not able to divide thought from belief so readily the Creed becomes a moment of embarrassment, as we stand to say we believe, we do so not with our hand on our heart but with our fingers crossed behind our back. In time the whole business of belief becomes somewhat unreal; participation in worship becomes a charade, an odd sort of entertainment that is increasingly easy to replace with other diversions. The notion of faith as belief separates belief from reality so as to make it trivial, ready to be replaced either by more "serious" activities (like politics) or by more diverting ones (like Sunday spectator sports). Thus faith as "belief" prepares the way for the disappearance of faith.

A recognition of the inadequacies of this view of faith as assent to authoritative teaching has produced a view of faith as something like subjective feeling. According to this view faith is equivalent to trust, a willingness to be dependent on another and to repose one's confidence in the other. The Protestant Reformation coincides with the recovery of this view of faith on the part of Martin Luther. For him faith was not assent to propositions, but a childlike trust in the goodness and grace of God. In commenting on the first commandment Luther maintained that "faith alone creates both god and idol" (*Larger Catechism*) by which he meant that the passion and power of this personal trust is such that if it is misdirected it leads us to worship false gods. Yet it is only by this passion of faith that we have any relation to the true God. Thus Luther placed faith as an unqualified trust and reliance upon another at the heart of theology.

In the course of time, Protestant theology often returned to a more objective and rationalistic view of faith as belief, as assent to propositions. But Luther's view of faith was reasserted by those who were called the Pietists. They rejected all dry speculation in favor of a religion of the heart and the fostering of a personal relation to God through disciplines of prayer and meditation. Some of the heirs of Pietism developed an anti-intellectualism that opposed faith to reason. But others, like John Wesley and Friedrich Schleiermacher, were deeply influenced by Pietism without surrendering the importance of giving a reasoned account of the character of Christian faith. More recently, the philosophical perspectives of Kierkegaard and Heidegger have provided an intellectual framework of great importance for the clarification of the inwardness of faith, of decision and passion, of the orientation of the person to that which is ultimate or the unconditioned. Bultmann and Tillich are two of the best known and most helpful theologians who have appropriated aspects of existentialism for an understanding of faith as a matter of ultimate concern, of decision, and of inwardness.

The strength of pietistic and existentialist views of faith is that they free the believer from anxiety over the propositional content of faith. Yet they, too, lead to difficulties.

A danger that is always present in these subjective views of faith is that they may lead us to rely not upon God but upon our faith itself. What begins as a personal relationship to God becomes a personal relationship to oneself. In place of God we are tempted to rely upon our own feelings, our own passions, our own decision. When we believe in our own belief, God disappears or becomes merely the projection of our own feelings, aspirations, depths, and yearnings. Thus Ludwig Feuerbach could claim that in faith we have to do only with ourselves; God is a projection of our own deepest feelings and aspirations. It is important to note that Feuerbach established the truth of atheism precisely by appeal to Luther's own view of faith![13]

This understanding of faith has another liability as well. By concentrating attention upon the individual and the inward it becomes an escape from the world. Like ancient Gnosticism it turns against the world, dismissing it as the realm of matter, sin, and inauthenticity, seeking meaning only within the interior of the enlightened, or pious, or authentic, self. But when faith does this it enters into an unholy alliance with the world it rejects. The institutions that rule the earth—corporations, governments, principalities, and powers—are only too happy to support this sort of religion, for it pacifies the people and keeps them in their place. Karl Marx thus called religion the opiate of the people.

Tyrannies of both the right and the left say to faith: your business is to pray, ours is to manage the world; you take care of people's spiritual needs, we will take care of reality. Trust in the one who is called the creator of heaven and earth and the savior of the world can result in the surrender of both the world and God, and in being left with only the interior and hidden "cave" of feeling and inwardness.

The alternative views of faith as either belief or trust seem to leave theology in a dilemma. To the extent that trust is emphasized (or the passion of inwardness) theology seems to lose its object and to become a form of anthropology or psychology. But when belief is stressed in order to gain a certain objectivity for theology, the subject becomes increasingly disengaged and theological propositions lose their bearing on "real" life.

In this dilemma the interpretation of faith as faithfulness or loyalty has important advantages. It holds together faith's object (to *whom* we are loyal) with faith's subject (we who are loyal or false) in such a way as to overcome the aridity of an emphasis on "beliefs"[14] and the subjectivity of an emphasis on inwardness.

Moreover, the emphasis on faith as faithfulness enables us to overcome a difficulty common to both emphases on belief and emphases on passion. For both of these traditional views of faith it is difficult to overcome the dichotomy of faith and works. The presence of this dichotomy makes it difficult to say how it is that faith entails an actual transformation in one's form or manner of life. The result is a bifurcation between theology and ethics. But the interpretation of faith as faithfulness unites theology and ethics, demonstrating that faith entails a transformation of one's form, manner, or style of life.

This understanding of faith as faithfulness clarifies how faith leads us out of the lofty tower of speculation or the hidden cave of inwardness and into the world as the sphere in which we are called to be loyal to the way of God articulated in the ministry and mission, life and destiny of Jesus of Nazareth. Thus faith reclaims the sphere of world and history as the proper domain of its witness to the transformation of all things.

The plausibility of this reconstruction of faith as faithfulness depends on how it actually enables us to make sense of the basic claims of faith; hence this reflection on the Apostles' Creed. Before actually undertaking this interpretation of the Creed, a few words about the character of this work of interpretation will help to orient the reader to this perspective.

THE INTERPRETATION OF THE CREED

When we approach the Creed with the understanding of faith as loyalty or allegiance we are in a position to understand the various clauses of the Creed in a new way. Instead of enumerating propositions for our assent, these clauses indicate the identity of the one to whom we pledge our loyalty. The clauses serve to clarify the identity of the God to whom we are committed.

In his discussion of eating foods sacrificed to idols Paul writes:

> Indeed, even though there may be so-called gods in heaven or on earth—as in fact there are many gods and many lords—yet for us there is one God, the Father, from whom are all things and for whom we exist, and one Lord, Jesus Christ, through whom are all things and through whom we exist. (1 Corinthians 8:5-6)

The designation of God as Father here indicates which God it is to whom we owe our loyalty, just as the designation of Jesus as Christ indicates which of many possible objects of loyalty (lords) is the one to whom we pledge our lives and our deaths.

Seen in this way the clauses of the Creed do not represent odd propositions to which we must somehow assent, but specify who will receive our loyalty. The God to whom we pledge ourselves is not just any divine being, but rather the one who has adopted us and so is a father to us. Similarly when we say of Jesus that he rose on the third day, we are saying which Jesus it is to whom we are loyal: the one of whom this is attested in the Gospels.

Each of these clauses then serves to further specify the identity of the one to whom we pledge ourselves.

21

Even if we accept this view of the meaning of the clauses of the creed we may be perplexed about how we are to understand the "identity descriptions" that they suggest.

But the earliest commentaries on the Creed illustrate that these clauses are to be understood in relation to the biblical story and especially to the New Testament witness to Jesus as the Christ. The clauses do not stand on their own but are to be regarded as a summary of the biblical witness to the identity of God as Father, Son, and Holy Spirit.[15]

This will mean that in our own attempt to understand and interpret the clauses of the Creed we will do well to seek clarification by way of an exploration of the witness of the gospel. In this way we will avoid proposing a different god from that which is the object of both Creed and Bible.

This means that our method here will be exegetical rather than speculative. When we seek to clarify for example, the loyalty to God the Father Almighty we will not derive the content of almighty from a philosophical or phenomenological analysis of power or omnipotence, but from the way in which the "almightiness" of God is spoken of in Scripture and especially in the New Testament. This procedure resolves a number of traditional difficulties in this and in other doctrines.

Similarly, in clarifying phrases like "ascended into heaven" our emphasis will not be on trying to maintain the literal truth of the proposition that Jesus somehow levitated into the sky, but rather in establishing what it means to be loyal to the one who is identified in this way and thus what this manner of identifying Jesus suggests in the biblical witness.

An exegetical clarification of these clauses of the Creed will also have to illustrate why the one described in this way deserves our unfailing loyalty. On what basis and for what reason are we to be loyal to this god rather than to some other? That this is the appropriate question is already expressed by the formulation of the first commandment: "I am the LORD your God, who brought you out of the land of Egypt, out of the house of slavery; you shall have no other gods before me" (Exodus 20:2). The identity of God is specified in terms of what God has done to warrant our loyalty and allegiance. Above all the God to whom we are loyal is the one who has delivered us. It is the liberating identity of God, then, that stands at the heart of the meaning of the clauses of the Creed as a vow of loyalty.

What is at stake when we speak of God as Father is not some general principle of fatherhood or of origin, but the activity of the one who adopts us and so liberates us from fear and abandonment. What is at stake in the "virgin birth" is not arcane gynecology, but the divine solidarity with the humble and the humiliated, and so on.

An exegetical interpretation of the Creed is also an evangelical interpretation of the Creed, for what is at stake is the identification of the one who liberates us—the one whose word and deed is above all "good news." Thus we are concerned not so much with the logic of explanation as with the logic of deliverance; not with the god who as "supreme being" explains the world, but with the God who as Father and Son and Holy Spirit transforms the world, setting it and us free from the bondage of sin and death, and from the powers of division and domination.

In the Creed we are concerned above all with commitment and loyalty and allegiance. This entails that an adequate interpretation of the clauses of the Creed will have to draw attention at every point to what it means to be loyal to the one whom we name here. No interpretation of the Creed can be adequate that separates theology from ethics, believing from doing, faith from works. For it is the nature of faith as faithfulness that no such separation is even conceivable. How can I be loyal to my friend or my spouse without this loyalty being demonstrated concretely in my actual life in the world? So it is with the one whom we identify in the Creed as the object of our ultimate loyalty. The meaning of this loyalty for our life in the world cannot be left unspecified without rendering empty the vow of loyalty that we make in the affirmation of the Creed. Thus, for example, loyalty to the one identified as the creator of the earth can only entail a commitment to the earth for God's sake and so to the welfare of all creatures great and small. Loyalty to the one who descended to the dead entails that we do not give up on those who seem to have no future. Loyalty to the one who suffered under Pontius Pilate means that we do not turn our backs on those who are the victims of institutional violence, and so on.

An interpretation of the clauses of the Creed that begins with the recognition of the Creed as a vow of loyalty then will seek to clarify the meaning of these clauses on the basis of the biblical witness to the liberating activity of God. In this way it will be established how, from this standpoint at least, this God is worthy of our loyalty and what it means to be loyal to this God.

This way of approaching the Creed already helps to resolve some of the difficulties that have so often accompanied an attempt to interpret the Creed. For example, it is often remarked that, regarded as a summary of doctrine, the Creed is an astonishingly one-sided view of Christian doctrine. There is nothing said here about justification and sanctification, for instance. But if we recall that the Creed is concerned above all with the identity of the one to whom we are to be loyal, then this concentration on the action of God rather than on our own existence in faith becomes intelligible. It then becomes evident that by clarifying the identity of the one to whom we are loyal our life in faith is also clarified, precisely as loyalty to this God rather than to another.

Similarly, it explains why we say "I believe" rather than "we believe" in the Creed. For what is at stake here is not the doctrine of the church but the vow of loyalty that no one can make for another. Here it is my life that is pledged. No one can do this for me and I cannot do it for another. In the end it is I who will be faithful or faithless, loyal or treacherous, confessor or apostate.

At the same time this vow of loyalty is not something that occurs in solitude and inwardness, but rather in the company of those who are similarly pledged and so who will encourage me to be faithful to the vows I have made. Just as wedding vows or baptismal vows are made in public before witnesses who also pledge to support these vows, it is so in the vow that is the Creed.

The Creed has its place in the worship of the community of faith. It stands as a response to the proclamation of the gospel which has announced and applied the liberating word of God. In response to this "good news" the hearer publicly announces her or his intention to be loyal to the one whose word of promise and blessing has been proclaimed. In so doing the hearer reclaims her or his baptismal vow as a pledge of allegiance to the God whose character is recalled in the words of the Creed. It is this understanding of the Creed as a vow made in response to the proclamation of God's grace that will inform our discussion of the meaning of the Apostles' Creed.

ARTICLE ONE

The Father Almighty, Creator of Heaven and Earth

A t least since the time of Augustine it has been customary to concentrate attention on the doctrine of creation when considering the "first article of the creed."[1] Thus the fundamental point of this article is taken to be the relation of God to the world in terms of creation and providence. The article then serves as the basis of a general or "natural" theology independent of the specifically Christian witness to that which occurs in Jesus. But I believe this is a fundamental error.

We cannot know what it means to speak of God as creator unless we first know *who* we are calling creator of heaven and earth. In the Creed, as in the Lord's Prayer, we first name God as "Father." Accordingly, our first task is to understand what we mean by speaking of God as Father. Only then will we be able to say what it means to speak of this Father as the creator of heaven and earth. In this way it will be possible to prevent the substitution of speculative doctrines for evangelical ones. Moreover, in this way the character of the Christian doctrine of creation can be decisively clarified.

In the course of the discussion of the first article of the Creed, it will be necessary to attend to a number of issues that, while not specifically mentioned in the Creed, have nevertheless come to be associated with it and which may be explained on the basis of the perspective on the Creed which is offered here. These issues are dealt with as separate sections following the discussion of each of the three basic features of the article, "Father," "Almighty," and "Creator of Heaven and Earth."

CHAPTER TWO

FATHER

W hat does it mean to speak of God as Father? By what right and on what basis do we do this? It should be noted that Christians are not the only ones who do this, although Christians have certainly made the most rigorous, extensive, and definitive use of this way of speaking of God.

For the faith of Judaism it was appropriate for an individual to speak of God as Father (Jeremiah 3:4). This usage, though rare, appears also in the intertestamental or "apocryphal" writings. In Sirach (Ecclesiasticus) God is addressed as "O Lord, Father and ruler of my life" (23:1) and as "O Lord, Father and God of my life" (23:4). In the Wisdom of Solomon, written near the time of the birth of Jesus, the righteous one is described as follows: "He calls the last end of the righteous happy, and boasts that God is his father" (Wisdom 2:16). The passage continues in a way that parallels the Gospel accounts of the passion of Jesus (Wisdom 2:17ff). The same text addresses God as Father in such a way as to emphasize God's providential care (Wisdom 14:3).

But it is not only in these testimonies to the faith of Israel that we find God spoken of as Father. For Homer, Zeus could be spoken of as the father of humanity. Since Homer was required reading for the educated youths of the Hellenistic world, this usage would have been familiar at least to some early gentile Christians.

But perhaps the most astonishing antecedent to Christian use of the name "Father" to designate God are two references in Plato's Timaeus which have clearly influenced subsequent Christian doctrine.

> Now that which is created must, as we affirm of necessity be created by a cause.
> But the Father and maker of all the universe is past finding out, and even if we
> found him, to tell of him to all men would be impossible. (Timaeus 28c.)

> When the Father and creator saw the creature which he had made moving and living, the created image of the eternal gods, he rejoiced . . . . (Timaeus 37c)

The apparent parallel between Plato's suggestive remarks here and the use of the name "Father" in Christian discourse has led many to emphasize the platonic view of father as principle of origin, and so to conclude that Father should be understood as a metaphor for creator.

Now theology as the reflection on the language of faith does not reject these ways of speaking of God as Father, as though it were necessary to reject the wisdom of others in order to maintain one's own. But neither can theology find its basis or norm in these ways of speaking of God as Father. Our basis and norm must always be the gospel concerning Jesus Christ. It is from this perspective that it is possible to appreciate and, where this seems to be indicated, appropriate these apparently parallel assertions.[2]

Accordingly we must ask ourselves why the name "Father" was appropriated by Christian faith, and why this way of speaking became so extensive among Christians as to attain the privileged status which it so clearly has in the Creeds.

As little as we can find the basis, content, and norm for the Christian conception of God as Father in the antecedent texts of Israel or the Hellenistic world, even less should we attempt to discover the meaning of this idea in our own conceptions of fatherhood. We must beware of making God into the indulgent father of our dreams or the distant and alien father of our fears. When we make God the projection of our wishes or of our fears, we never encounter God in these images, only our own unconscious. Our initial concern then is not with what ideas we may conjure up concerning father or parent but with the confession of faith in and loyalty to God as Father. We must take as our guide the memory and experience of the early communities of faith from whose testimony the confession of faith is derived.

THE FATHER OF THE SON

For Christians to speak of God as Father is to recall the one who gave this name its decisive significance: Jesus of Nazareth. Thus at the beginning of the Creed we are clearly anticipating the christological reflections proper to the "second article." We would not speak of God as Father apart from the one whom we speak of as the Son.[3] We are not then in the sphere of general speculation on the nature of an unknown god, but in the sphere of what might be termed the history of salvation. God is

Father not because of creation and providence, but because of the demonstration of God in the action and message of the Son. We will return to this theme in greater detail later (in considering the phrase "Son of God"). We mention it here only to make clear that with talk of God as Father we are not concerned with cosmology or with a theology of nature and history in general, but with soteriology, the history of deliverance.[4] If the confession of faith in God as Father is to be a Christian confession, it must take its bearings directly from the way in which this God as Father is manifested in Jesus and in the proclamation concerning Jesus. God is *the* Father or even *our* Father only in so far as God is the Father of Jesus. Our method must be rigorously determined then by the saying attributed by both Matthew and Luke to Jesus:

> All things have been delivered to me by my Father; and no one knows who the Son is except the Father, or who the Father is except the Son and any one to whom the Son chooses to reveal him (Luke 10:22; Matthew 11:27).

This saying is repeated and expanded by John (John 3:35, 13:3, 10:15, 17:25) in such a way that the whole of John's Gospel may be regarded as, in a certain sense, a commentary on this saying.

If we compare this saying to the first quotation cited above from Plato's Timaeus we can see that Plato's "questions" receive a surprising response. First, the saying of Plato and that attributed to Jesus are in agreement at a decisive point: an accurate knowledge of the Father is impossible on the basis of a general or speculative reflection on the "way things are." Both rule out natural theology. But while Plato asserts that the Father "is past finding out," the Gospels reply: no, the Father is not mysterious or hidden, but manifest in the Son. Plato asserts that it would be impossible to tell of the Father "to all men," to which the reply of the dominical saying is: no, he is announced to all by means of the proclamation concerning the Son. Plato declared it to be impossible to find the Father. Faith announces that the Father has found us. Plato thought it would be impossible to tell of the Father to all. But that impossibility is our task, through the good news concerning God's Son. This is certainly an audacious counterpart to Plato's circumspection. We will have to see to what extent it is justified.

ABBA/PATER/FATHER

Since the question of Jesus' relation to God is more appropriately deferred to a consideration of the second article of the Creed, we will leave that aside for the moment in order to deal here with the basic content of this first article—the relation of Christians to the God who is for us, as well as for Jesus (for us because of Jesus), Father. Here then we ask, why did the early Christians call God "Father" and what did they mean by it?

When we ask the question in this way we are immediately driven to the text of Paul's letters, the earliest documents produced from within the Christian community. It is in these letters that we encounter the decisive appearances of the title or name Abba/Pater (Father), together with the explanation which is decisive for faith and theology. (See Galatians 4:6; Romans 8:15ff—the only other occurrence is in the later Gospel of Mark 14:36.)

We will begin with the earliest first:

> So with us; when we were children, we were slaves to the elemental spirits of the universe. But when the time had fully come, God sent forth his Son, born of woman, born under the law, to redeem those who were under the law, so that we might receive adoption as sons. And because you are sons, God has sent the Spirit of his Son into our hearts, crying, "Abba! [Pater!] Father!" So through God you are no longer a slave but a son, and if a son then an heir. (Galatians 4:3-7)

Paul is describing the response of faith to the hearing of the proclamation of the gospel. This is a spirited response in that it is itself the gift of God's Spirit. Paul's argument seems to depend on the fact that the Galatians really did respond to the gospel with the acclamation of God as Abba Pater (Father).

This acclamation is one which acclaims God as Father in both Aramaic and Greek. That is, whether in the language of Judaism (abba) or in the language of paganism (pater), both Jew and Gentile respond to the proclamation of God as Father. God is not the father of one people, but of both peoples. Thus the immediate background of the present text is Paul's assertion that "in Christ Jesus you are all sons of God. . . . There is neither Jew nor Greek . . . " (Galatians 3:26, 28).

The acclamation of God as Abba or Pater, and so as Father, envisions the overcoming of the distinction between those who were sons (the Jews) and those who were not (the pagans). I have left the terms in Aramaic and Greek, so that the sense of uniting two distinct peoples in acclamation of God as Father may be seen more readily. The point of the dual acclamation is not that Jesus called God "abba" while we call God "Father" (as is often suggested), but rather that two distinct peoples, Jews and Gentiles, are joined in spite of all cultural and religious differences (represented by two distinct languages) in the acclamation of God as Father.[5]

Paul interprets this acclamation as evidence that God has adopted and

30

liberated us. God is precisely Abba/Pater/Father because God has adopted us and has rescued us from bondage.

First God has adopted us.[6] Paul is quite aware that Israel could be understood as the son of God and that God could be understood as the Father of Israel (2 Cor. 6:18). But Paul's argument is that God is not only the God of Israel but of gentile Christians as well. "Adoption" here means that God reaches out to those who had no claim upon God and adopts them, making them God's own. The theme then is of the astonishing grace of God which reaches out to accept responsibility for those who were previously outside the scope of the divine promise, outside the "inheritance." We who did not know God; we who were not included in the covenant with Israel, we who were even the enemies of God have been adopted by God, taken into the divine household and given the right to inherit that which is God's own. That we respond to this announcement with astonished joy, "Abba/Pater/Father!" is proof that we have heard and understood these incredibly good tidings. Our acclamation of God as Abba/Pater/Father demonstrates that God has indeed adopted us and claimed us.[7]

And this is liberation. For we were, as Paul says, formerly in bondage to the structures and powers of the world. But by God's decisive action on our behalf we have been rescued from this bondage, anxiety, fear, and servitude. Thus we are no longer "a slave but a son, and if a son then an heir." The image that Paul is using is quite dramatic. It is as if we were formerly owned and ruled by powers, worldly structures, and forces against which we were utterly powerless. We were in fact resigned to our condition, we knew our place. Perhaps we had even come to terms with our masters. But then we were snatched out of this place of servitude against all expectation. It is in this sense that the act of God is one of liberation. It rescues us from the house of bondage as the divine act did for the Hebrew slaves of old. The result of this "raid" on the slave quarters of our worldly masters does not merely imply that whereas before we had an evil or despotic master, and now we have a more beneficent one. The change in our condition is far more radical. Now we are no longer slaves at all, but are elevated to the position of sons and heirs. What is indicated here is a radical and total reversal of our condition. Adoption is not only liberation, but also what we may call "dignification." That is, it results in conferring dignity and responsibility upon those who were formerly considered worthless and useless.

In this connection we may also see that it is both appropriate and necessary to modify Paul's "sons" with the addition of "daughters." What Paul has in mind by "sons" is precisely this elevation to dignity and responsibility, and so this identification as heirs." In his own time and culture the most striking way to express this is to speak of sons. And it is a complete misunderstanding to translate this as "children" since that would eliminate the force of this dignification, this making responsible and naming as an heir. It is obvious that Paul meant to include both male and female in this being liberated, adopted, exalted. Indeed in this way the transformation of the status of the female Christian was in some ways even more dramatic. For she becomes the equal of a son rather than being relegated to the traditional place of the daughter. If we keep in mind the significance of being invested with dignity and responsibility through adoption, then it is appropriate to say that God has made us "sons and daughters" and so heirs.

To speak of God as Father then is to speak precisely of this reversal in our condition. It is to recall the liberating and adopting action of God that makes us heirs of the divine rule.[8]

To recognize this God as Father then is to reject all the forms of bondage and servitude in which human beings are held by the forces and structures of the world in which we live. Paul cautions us against the unthinkable possibility that we will actually sell ourselves back into bondage after having been liberated. This alluring bondage can take on many forms. Paul is especially concerned with what we may call the religious temptation: obedience to the religious customs of observing times and seasons. In every age and culture there are new forms of this bondage: political, economic, religious, psychological. The announcement of the gospel is that God rescues us from this bondage and adopts us for God's own, to be heirs of the divine. And to rely on and be loyal to the God who in this way is Father is to turn away from all these forms of servitude, however tempting they may be. In this sense all theology that is a reflection on and speech about this God is a theology of liberation. This is true whether we consider the forgiveness of sins, the liberation from anxiety and fear, the overcoming of the power of death, or the breaking of the forces which enslave people to political oppression or economic dependence. All are manifestations of liberation from the forces and structures of the world.

But this freedom is not simply a new bondage to our own whims and wishes. By this liberation we are summoned into an unheard of dignity and responsibility: that of sons/daughters and heirs of the divine. To speak of God as Father is to accept the responsibilities of being an heir—to do what God does in the world. This is the meaning that John gives to the claim that God is Father—that we are to be, as Jesus was, absorbed in the action of God which reaches out to those who are in bondage, to those who were strangers, to those who have no claim upon us and to love them as we love ourselves, still more to love them as God has loved us. (See reflections on "Son" below.)

Paul further stresses this connection of the name Father to adoption and liberation in the letter to the Romans, where it again occupies a place of great importance.

> For you did not receive the spirit of slavery to fall back into fear, but you have received the spirit of sonship. When we cry, "Abba! Father!" it is the Spirit himself bearing witness with our spirit that we are children of God, and if children, then heirs, heirs of God and fellow heirs with Christ, provided we suffer with him in order that we may also be glorified with him. (Romans 8:15-17)

Again we see the way in which the notion of God as Father is connected immediately to that of adoption and thence to liberation, and how this entails a renunciation of the temptation to fall back into slavery and all that accompanies this slavery.

When we recite the Creed together we recall together the astonishing power of God's love, against which all the forces and structures of the earth are powerless.

THE MERCIFUL FATHER

We should not leave this discussion of the identity of God as Father without pointing to the way in which this designation of God is developed in the "Jesus tradition" of the Synoptic Gospels. In the synoptics it is Matthew above all, who makes use of the name Father for God, usually "heavenly Father" or "Father in heaven." This way of indicating God is generally connected with mercy, compassion, and goodness. Thus, Father is not used to portray God as source or origin, as in Plato nor to emphasize legal demand or emotional distance as in much modern psychoanalytic theory. Instead it is the father who gives good things to his children who is emphasized (Matthew 7:11; Luke 11:13). It is as "Father" that God is said to give good things to both the just and the unjust (Matthew 5:45) and it is the Father who is said to "forgive" (Matthew 6:14).

The emphasis on Father in the Gospels, especially Matthew, is also tied to the notion of imitation. In Ephesians 5:1, the author calls his readers to be "imitators of God, as beloved children," and this is regularly signalled by the use of the name Father for God in the synoptics. Thus we are told to love our enemies, following the example of the God who gives good things to the just and the unjust. We are called to be "perfect, as your heavenly Father is perfect" (Matthew 5:48). Similarly the disciples are taught to forgive others as the heavenly Father forgives (Matthew 6:14).

It is evident in the Gospels that the name of God as Father emphasizes the divine compassion, just as in Paul the acclamation of God as Abba/Pater is a response to the divine grace of adoption. But the synoptics also establish that loyalty to the God who is Father means that we become imitators of this God, loving as this God loves, forgiving as the Father forgives, and so on. The use of this term for God involves us in an imitation of the liberating, adopting, and dignifying practice of God.[9]

FATHER AND MOTHER

In the theology of the last few decades, especially in North America, there has been a growing protest against the use of masculine language in reference to God. It is said that this language operates in such a way as to deprive women of their true dignity as the image and likeness of God. It does this by reinforcing stereotypes concerning the primacy of the male and of male power and virtue. These theologians propose that we abandon speaking of God as Father; or, if that is impossible, that we supplement this language with talk of God as Mother.

As a Christian theologian reflecting on the Creed, I am obliged to attempt to interpret the language of faith. And since this language has talk of God as Father in a prominent position, I am obliged to attempt to understand and interpret this language. Thus I have elected here not to dispense with talk of God as Father.

But I am also persuaded that precisely because of the theological meaning of this term in a trinitarian and evangelical understanding of God, that it is all the more important to pay attention to the protests made against the use of this term in the name of human liberation and dignity. For if the term "Father" in relation to God entails human liberation and dignity, then the protest against "Father" in the name of this same liberation and dignity must be considered with full seriousness.

I believe that faith has complete freedom in the way in which it "images" God, as long as it is clear that what we mean by God is what Jesus meant in calling God "Father." There is nothing inherently appropriate about masculine language about God. All language has a metaphorical character and this is particularly true of language used to refer to the divine. We speak of God as rock and spring, as lion and dove and eagle, as sword and shield, as fire and rain. In all of this, faith seeks to express important aspects of God's relation to us, of God's action on our behalf. And this action of God is of such importance to us that we make use of all the resources of our language to give it voice.

In the Creed we speak of God as Father. We do this not because God is "male," for God is neither male nor female any more than God is literally a rock or mountain, a bear or lion or dove. God exceeds our language; yet the coming of God to us provokes our speaking about God in such a way that the speaking may also become a "word of God" through which God draws near to us and addresses us.

But this freedom and responsibility regarding language about God means that there can be no rejection in principle of feminine language about the divine.[10] Indeed, when we open our eyes to the traditions of faith contained in the Old and New Testaments we may be astonished at the number of feminine images that we encounter there; images that point to feminine aspects not only of what we call the first, but also the second and third persons of the Trinity. God can be spoken of as a mother bear (Hos. 13:8), as a mother eagle (Deut. 32:11-12), as a woman in labor (Isa. 42:14; 66:10-13), as a nursing mother (Isaiah 49:15), as the female head of a household (Psalm 123:2; Luke 15:8-10), as a woman baking bread (Matthew 13:33). Jesus can speak of himself as a woman giving birth (John 16:21; 17:1) and as a mother hen gathering her brood (Matt. 23:37; Luke 13:34). Paul too can speak of himself as a mother (Gal. 4:19) who is giving birth. In each case they are imitating the divine action. Moreover, several of the Hebrew terms that signify the drawing near of God are grammatically feminine: *torah* (law), *hokmah* (wisdom), *kol* (voice), *ruah* (spirit), *raham* (compassion).[11]

Clearly then there is ample precedent for the use of feminine names and imagery for God. This is especially appropriate for speaking of the divine solicitude for those who are the objects of divine love. Some will no doubt be more impressed by the relative paucity of these images than by their presence in biblical texts.[12] But a moment's reflection will suggest why Israelite religion was so reticent in its use of this imagery. The worship of the goddess was apparently a widespread characteristic of Near Eastern religion in the agrarian societies with economically dependent but politically controlling urban centers. These religions were celebrations of the seasonal cycle which sustained the agrarian base of these metropolitan centers. Thus these religious traditions represented the stabilization of the social order oriented toward the privilege of urban elites. The social order was perceived as the mirror of the permanence of the seasonal cycle upon which the life of the urban empire ultimately depended.

In contrast, the rejection of a feminine deity coincided with a rejection both of the cultic and the social order of these cultures. The aim of this rejection was freedom and justice. The prophetic denunciation of urban corruption, of the worship of the goddess, and of the oppression of the poor was woven together into a consistent call for justice and freedom, and for the worship of the God whose will was not the stabilization of imperial order, but the liberation of the oppressed poor.

Yet today the image of the warrior God who leads the guerillas in their opposition to unjust, corrupt, and decadent structures has receded from our memory. And with it too has gone the "Father" whose adoption of us entails the abrogation of these same structures of division and domination. In its place the Father has become the distant "sky-god" of original creation or the inner principle of fugitive piety. In either case this "Father" has often become the principle of oppression who legitimates the status quo, who becomes the name of an authority which imposes and sanctifies the given order.

It is in this context that the protest against the "paternal" god arises through which feminist theologians (not only women) seek to counter the authoritarian and masculine images of God with talk of the motherhood of God and the feminine character of the divine. This protest is of unquestionable theological validity. Similarly, the protest against the god of the social order of repression corresponds to the intent of the protest against Palestinian religion on the part of the patriarchal and prophetic traditions.

This is especially clear in the traditions concerning Jesus that illuminate the way in which the gospel entails the abrogation of all structures of domination. For Jesus, the character of "leadership" is that of humble service, not domination. And this leadership is explicitly contrasted with the ways of the gentile society in which greatness and domination are parallel. It is sharply expressed in the sayings about the new family in which there are no fathers, a position which is ultimately defined in the saying from Matthew that there can be no "lords," no "masters," and no "fathers" among the followers of Jesus. (See discussion of "lord" below for an analysis of the relevant texts.)

The feminist protest against all patriarchal structures then is one that has ample foundation in the biblical witness.[13] It is true that the biblical witness expressed this same protest in terms of the use of the name "Father." Once we understand that this term had a liberating intent, then it becomes possible to discover terminology which fulfills this intention, even if the terminology appears to be directly opposed to the earlier one. In this case, for example, there may be ways in which feminine language about God is the only way to express the liberative intention of earlier talk of God as Father.

When in the Creed we say "I believe in God the Father," we speak not of the one who safeguards the privilege of the strong, but of the one who rescues us from bondage and clothes those who are weak and scorned with an astonishing dignity and responsibility. When we speak of God as Father we speak as well of a Father who is strikingly "maternal," for we speak of one who draws near, who suffers for our birth, who nourishes us and prepares us for adulthood.

Each theologian must choose a way of speaking about God which seems best to convey the gracious and searching love made manifest in Jesus, aware of both the dangers and the possibilities which that language sets before us. Many will decide to continue to speak of God as Father because of the role of this term in Bible and Creed. But this must also mean contesting the expropriation of this terminology by the ideologies of repression, and insisting that it belongs to the perspective of liberation—especially the liberation of women from their condition of dehumanization. Above all, we must realize that "Father" when used of God signifies not the divine authority, still less the divinization of authoritarianism, but the gracious nearness and fierce protection of the One who comes to liberate and to summon into new dignity.

CHRISTIANITY AND JUDAISM

When it becomes clear that the designation of God as Father refers to the gracious adoption and so to liberation and elevation to dignity and responsibility as disclosed in the work and person of Jesus of Nazareth, then the question naturally arises concerning the relationship of Christianity to the elect people of God, that is, to Judaism. If Israel was elected by God, how is it possible for (gentile) Christians also to be elected? And if Christians are elected and adopted, does this then entail God's rejection of the Old Israel?[14]

This question has become especially acute in the aftermath of the Holocaust in which six million Jews were massacred under the National Socialist regime in Europe. This genocide occurred within Christendom. The executioners had no sense of coming into fundamental opposition to Christianity. Indeed the history of the West has been a history of antagonism to Judaism; an antagonism legitimated by Christian claims to be the new and the true Israel and its designation of the Jews as the killers of the Christ. This profound anti-semitism has pervaded and perverted Christianity. But the Holocaust, with its attendant revulsion and horror, has awakened in Christianity the determination to reconsider its own loyalty to Jesus, a Jew among Jews, and to confess its own complicity in this horrible act. No theology can be credible today which does not address this question.

When we raise this question in a serious way as theologians, we discover that the basis of our own election as Christians is the election of Israel. Apart from this election, Christianity would be wholly inconceivable. The election of Israel by God is irrevocable (Romans 11:29), still less is it revoked in the election of Jesus the Jew as the Christ, or in the extension through him of this election to those who were "far off." Israel is the chosen people of God par excellence. If this claim and favor now extends throughout the globe to include persons of every nation, culture, tribe, or language, then it is only on account of Israel that it does so.[15]

To wish to abolish Judaism, then, is to destroy the very root of Christian faith. As Paul makes abundantly clear in Romans 9–11, we are grafted onto the root of Israel. Apart from this root we have no existence.

The continued existence of the people of Israel testifies to the faithfulness of God. To resent this existence, to oppose it, is to refuse the divine election which by divine mercy is extended to include us. Opposition to the life of Judaism is opposition to God. For it is the determination to stand on our own, to possess our own foundation and origin. This we cannot do, for our existence is founded solely on the divine compassion to which Israel testifies by its memory and hope. Paul holds out the hope that in the end the newer and the older people of God will be reconciled in Jesus. This is our hope as well, for we hope for the reconciliation of all things in God through Jesus. But this reconciliation is not and never can be accomplished by force or pressure of any kind. It is accomplished only by and through love.

The shame of Christian history is that we have too often given our allegiance to violence, division, enmity, and domination. In this way we align ourselves with the anti-Christ. That we do this often in the name of Christ only makes the more horrifying our defection, our apostasy. For we thus become that which we falsely accuse the Jews: the killers of Christ.

The Holocaust is the ghastly sign etched in our history that we have betrayed Christ. That sign will remain upon our heads like the mark of Cain as long as Christianity endures. Will this sign be for us a mark of repentance and of return to the message of Jesus, or will it be the mark of the beast—the sign that God must reject those who so pervert God's name? This is today an open question, for while we are powerless to revoke God's election of Israel, we are capable of rendering our own election null and void. As branches, we can be taken out, as Paul reminds us (Rom. 11:17-22). The root will in any case remain; new branches can be supplied.

For my part I hope that the Church will not perish, that we will repent and renounce the perversion of faith which results not in reconciliation, but in violence, division, and death. The gospel of the divine love will endure. But whether we will continue to be its bearers depends upon our rejection of all that opposes this gospel within our own hearts and institutions. To be the elect of God is not to receive a status of prestige—as the history of Israel also makes clear. It is to live close to the fire of the divine love, and to be its instruments.

CHAPTER THREE

ALMIGHTY

W hen we affirm our faith using the words of the Apostles' Creed, we say that we believe in, or trust, or confess our loyalty to, the one who is God the Father Almighty. It is therefore important to clarify the significance of this "Almighty" which modifies and specifies the identity of this "Father."

It is above all necessary to recognize that the "Almighty" modifies the "Father."[16] That is, it is the power of that gracious election, adoption, and "dignification" which is spoken of here. This should warn us against importing into this term the philosophical and speculative issues traditionally associated with the discussion of the divine omnipotence. We are not concerned with the abstract power of an anonymous supreme being or of a first or final cause. When the modifier "Almighty" is thoughtlessly and ungrammatically transferred from "Father" to "Maker" (Creator), and a more or less anonymous cause or creator substituted for the one who is here called "Father," then enormous difficulties arise for our understanding of God.[17]

When this happens we become embroiled in such quasi-philosophical conundrums as "could God create a round square?"; "could God make $2 + 2 = 37$?"; "could God choose not to be?" These and similar problems arise from an abstract definition of the divine omnipotence which could at best be the attribute of an abstract divinity—that of an anonymous supreme being or of ultimate causation.[18]

The one who is called Almighty here is by no means an empty abstraction, but rather the one who is acclaimed by faith as abba/pater/father. It is by rigorous attention to this principle that we will be able to clarify the meaning of this "Almighty" which we here confess and affirm.

We may gain some assistance by attending to those biblical contexts within which this term is applied to God. When we turn to the traditions of

Israel and the Church we discover that the power of God is the power which saves, redeems, liberates. Thus the power of Yahweh is demonstrated through the liberation of the Hebrew people from Egyptian slavery and through the bestowal of the land of promise upon the tribes of Israel.

Our word "almighty" is a translation. The Greek term *pantokrator* is one which seldom appears in the New Testament, but which does occur rather often in the Greek version (Septuagint) of the Old Testament, where it is used to translate Yahweh Sabaoth. While this name appears in some eighth-century texts, during the ascendancy of the Assyrian Empire (for example, Amos 5:14; Isaiah 5:7), it is primarily concentrated in those texts written during the rise of the Babylonian Empire (Jeremiah, Haggai, Zechariah). Within this historical context this term appears to have been appropriated from the imperial ideology that was used to legitimate the conquest of surrounding nations carried out first by Assyria and then by Babylon. The power of the empire was symbolized by the divine powers of the stars (the heavenly hosts). Thus the battalions of Babylon were the extension of the astral battalions whose movements regulated the destinies of individuals, nations, and empires. These "heavenly hosts" or battalions then legitimated the economic, political, and military hegemony of the empire. When the prophets use the name Yahweh Sabaoth (Lord of Hosts) to speak of Yahweh, they are claiming that the power and authority of Yahweh is sufficient to liberate the people of Israel from the grasp of that empire: Yahweh rather than Marduk is truly the Lord of Hosts.

Thus, the origin of the attribute of God as "Almighty" indicates that this designates not some abstract power of God, but the power of God to deliver from the (humanly) superior force of earthly empire. It represents the claim that Yahweh will liberate the people from the yoke of oppression.

Now it must also be noted that the earlier eighth-century texts have in view the liberation of the poor from their oppression at the hands of Israel's and Judah's urban ruling class. Thus the Lord of Hosts is not merely Israel's or Judah's champion but the champion of the oppressed as such (Amos 5:14; Isaiah 5:7).

When we ask about this phrase in the New Testament we are driven even more forcefully to the same conclusion. God is spoken of as Almighty only ten times in the New Testament. All but one of these occurrences are found in the Apocalypse of John.

The first occurrence is in the opening creedal formulation of the Apocalypse (1:4-8). The theological perspective of the seer is concentrated in this brief opening salutation. John opens with words which remind us of the characteristic salutation of other New Testament letters, except that in place of "Father" we have "him who is and who was and who is to come" (1:4). This is echoed in the conclusion " 'I am the Alpha and the Omega,' says the Lord God, who is and was and who is to come, the Almighty" (1:8). Between this strange sequence of tenses (present, past, future) we are referred to a brief summary of the action of Christ in the present (the faithful witness) the past, (has freed us) and the future (is coming). Thus the identity of the Almighty is coordinated to that of Jesus Christ in the closest possible way, so that attention is drawn to the eschatological act which completes the liberation already inaugurated in the cross. It is precisely here that God is encountered as the "Almighty."

After a series of admonitions to the seven churches of Asia Minor, we are once again returned to this foundational set of themes in the vision of the throne room of God in which the four living creatures sing:

> Holy, holy, holy, is the Lord God Almighty,
> who was and is and is to come! (4:8)

This is followed by the seven seals opened by the Lamb (5–8:1) and the seven trumpets (8:2–11:14). In the interlude concerning the nature of Christian witness which follows, we again encounter the hymn, this time in the mouth of the twenty-four elders (11:17-18). Here again God is called "Almighty" and again it is clear that this refers precisely to the power of the one who "will destroy the destroyers of the earth." These destroyers of the earth are clearly identified as the mighty nations and empires—an identification which John takes to include the Roman Empire "which is allegorically called Sodom and Egypt, where their Lord was crucified" (11:8). There follow a number of images which make the identity of this empire as "the Beast" unmistakably clear. At the climax of this set of visions we again find a hymn sung by those who had conquered the beast (15:3-4). Here again, as in the song of Moses (Exod. 15:1-18), God is praised as Almighty in the context of deliverance from imperial oppression, a hymn echoed in Rev. 16:5-7. In the same chapter we view the assembly for the final battle of the great day of "God the Almighty" (16:14).

The transition from the theme of battle to that of the wedding feast is also marked by the praise of God as the triumphant liberator (vv. 1-2) whose reign is inaugurated in the joy of the wedding feast (19:6-8). The identity of the one who presides over the joy of the feast as the one who destroys the forces of oppression is emphasized again in 19:11-16. And the vision of the heavenly city is the context for the final designation of God as Almighty: "And I saw no temple in the city, for its temple is the Lord God the Almighty and the Lamb" (21:22).

This rapid survey of the use of "Almighty" in the Apocalypse of John indicates several important aspects of the use and the meaning of this term.

1. All of these uses of the term Almighty refer not to a mythological time of origin which recedes into the past but to an impending future. That God is Almighty refers above all to the one "who is to come," and whose coming is associated with the actions of judgment, of the wedding banquet, and of the establishment of the New Jerusalem. That God is called Almighty is basically an eschatological ascription. God's power is spoken of in the future tense. What is in view here is not creation, but liberation. (As we shall see it is possible to speak also of creation only on the basis of this same liberating activity.) God is Almighty not on account of what lies in the past, but on account of what lies in the future.

2. This future is essentially the time of the overthrow of the domination of those forces which "destroy the earth." It is essential that we keep clear the dimensions of the judgment upon which John rivets his readers' attention. It is by no means a judgment which is essentially personal, individual, interior, or "spiritual." Rather it is a historical judgment in which God finally triumphs over the public, political, and historical forces which destroy the earth. In the first century these forces were represented by Rome just as before they could be represented by the Selucid Empire in the time of the writing of Daniel, or by Babylon in the sixth century, or by "Sodom and Gomorrah" in the patriarchal traditions. For us this imperial power has many representatives. We live in a world in which many forces, political and economic, have the power to destroy the earth; a world in which the forces of militarism and imperialism, the exploitation of the poor and the humiliation of humanity exhibit stupefying power and boundless arrogance. When we affirm our faith in the Father who is Almighty we stake our lives on the victory of the one who will destroy the destroyers of the earth and thus on the future of liberation and life and love over all forces of oppression and enmity and death.

When we speak in the second article of the Creed of the judgment we will recall that the aim of this victory for which we hope and to which we pledge our loyalty is not destruction but salvation, for it is the judgment executed by the Lamb slain from the foundations of the earth whose lordship is manifested in the new heaven and the new earth—the New Jerusalem.

3. We should also notice that the majority of the passages within which we encounter this identification of God as Almighty have the form of a hymn of praise. When we speak of the Father as Almighty we are using the language of doxology, of praise and thanksgiving. As we have seen, the name of Father has the same form or origin in the glad acclamation of

God as Abba! Pater! This is not the language of description but of ascription, not the language of abstraction but of concrete address.[19]

The praise and thanksgiving of the community of faith is the articulation, the coming to speech of the divine victory. When we speak our joy and gratitude we participate already in the anthem which is the form of apocalyptic existence. The song of praise speaks "as if" the victory is already accomplished and speaks of this accomplishment precisely as joy—for all the earth.

There is one New Testament passage outside of the Apocalypse in which God is spoken of as Almighty. We find it in 2 Corinthians 6:18: "I will be a father to you, and you shall be my sons and daughters, says the Lord Almighty." Here Paul adapts the words by which God adopts David (2 Samuel 7:14) in order to refer to the adoption of all by the divine love and mercy. Here again when we speak of God as Almighty we are referring to the power of that liberating, claiming, and dignifying love made manifest in Jesus of Nazareth. Thus when we speak of the power of God, we are not speaking of the abstract or generalized capacities of an anonymous supreme being or of a first or final cause but of the one who liberates, adopts, and confers upon us the dignity of being the daughters and sons of God.

When we speak of the power of God then we are speaking of that power manifest in Jesus. And this means, as Paul insists, that it is the power defined by the cross. Certainly, for those accustomed either to an abstract power (the Greeks) or to a military image of power (the Jews) this is an astonishing transformation of the talk of power in general and of divine power in particular.

> For Jews demand signs and Greeks seek wisdom, but we preach Christ crucified, a stumbling block to Jews and folly to Gentiles, but to those who are called, both Jews and Greeks, Christ the power of God and the wisdom of God. For the foolishness of God is wiser than [humans], and the weakness of God is stronger than [humans]. (1 Corinthians 1:22-25)

The power of God is demonstrated in the cross of Jesus. Here we do not discover the power of a divine emperor, the unlimited efficacy of a first cause, the implacable might of an iron necessity. Instead we encounter the weakness of a love which loves without limit, without reservation, without condition or qualification.[20] It is to the power of this weakness, and so to the victory of the one the seer calls the Lamb slain from the foundation of the world that we commit ourselves in this Creed and for which we pledge our lives and our deaths.

When Paul returns to the identity of God as the Father in the acclamation of God as Abba-Pater in Romans 8:15-17, he concludes his meditation on the adopting grace of God with these familiar words:

> For I am sure that neither death, nor life, nor angels, nor principalities, nor things present, nor things to come, nor powers, nor height, nor depth, nor anything else in all creation, will be able to separate us from the love of God in Christ Jesus our Lord. (Romans 8:38-39)

When we repeat the words of the Creed: "I believe in God the Father Almighty . . . " we speak of the astonishing power of that divine love against which the forces of death and darkness, of division and domination, shatter and break.

PROVIDENCE AND POWER

Our reflections on the biblical foundation for the reliance upon and loyalty to the One we call Father Almighty undoubtedly opens up a host of questions concerning our traditional ways of speaking of the power of God. It is in this context particularly that we often encounter talk of the providential power of God. Unfortunately the absence of clarity concerning the character of this providence and so of the divine power occasions a great many problems for the church, especially in the area of pastoral care.

Many people inside and outside the church give this doctrine of providence a place of independent significance in order to speak of God as the mysterious cause of both the good and the evil that befall us in the course of our lives. Indeed there are many people who find talk of God as either creator or savior more or less unintelligible, yet have an idea of God and of faith determined entirely by a view of the providence of God. A few illustrations may be helpful to show what we are concerned with here.

There is an automobile accident. The mother and her children are slaughtered amidst the twisted steel and shattered glass. The father and husband is "consoled" by some who think of themselves as Christians saying: "It was the will of God." What sort of being is here named as God?

Two friends go off to war in the service of their country. The life of one is cut short in the fullness of youthful vigor by a bayonet. The other returns home. Perhaps a third friend says: "God saved your life." And the one who perished—what of his life? What sort of god is being spoken of here?

The hopes and plans of a woman nearing the end of her child-bearing years are pinned to the impending birth of her first child. Yet in the process of birth, the infant dies. The pastor consoles her unthinkingly: "It was the will of God." How will it be possible to trust such a god again?

It is clear that the god spoken of in these examples plays an important role in the churches which call themselves Christian. But what possible relation can this god have to the one whose identity is manifest in the life and death of Jesus of Nazareth? Only one of complete opposition.

We need to recognize that virtually all religious traditions employ some such idea of the power of a god or the gods. When misfortune comes it is taken to be a sign of the ire of the gods or the ancestors whose wrath must then be placated with sacrifices and ablutions. But when things go well it is taken as a sign of the favor of the gods. These ideas seem widespread even where belief in a god or the gods has faded into belief in fortune or luck. These abide like the grin of the famous Cheshire cat long after the substance of belief in God has faded. Thus superstitious and magical practices are employed to evade bad luck and ensure good luck. And some see the re-emergence of these practices in the modern guise of neurosis and of psychotic symptoms.

Unfortunately many persons who are or have become Christian have not left behind these ideas and practices of magic and superstition. Quite often indeed "God" is another name for luck or fortune. All too often what separates Christian forms of superstition from other forms is merely the idea that those who are good or pious will have better luck than those who are not. This of course leads directly to the problem of the bad luck of those who are pious or even upstandingly moral—a problem given serious reflection in the book of Job. Here we encounter what is called a crisis of faith. There are always those who live well yet who also encounter "bad luck." From this they may either conclude that there is no "god" (no protection from bad luck for the good people) or that god is wholly arbitrary. But this conclusion is not born of faith, however much disguised with pious platitudes. It is superstition. For it can have nothing to do with the one we encounter in the life and death of Jesus of Nazareth.

Here, as in theology generally, it is essential to ask ourselves *of which* god are we speaking? On which god do we rely? To which god are we committed? Without this rigorous clarification, faith becomes superstition and even idolatry. Certainly when we believe in an anonymous god, a supreme being, this faith may quickly become a belief in an anonymous force such as luck or fortune. Thus it is crucial to ask which is the God in whom we believe. The answer of faith as expressed in the Creed is that we believe only in the God who is called Father. We rely on no other force or power in the world. Certainly there are other forces and powers: the power of death, the power of sin, the power of division and domination, the power of avarice and violence, even the power of luck or fortune. But by no means do we rely on or even acknowledge these powers. Our loyalty is reserved for the one who is Father Almighty, whose power is revealed in the weakness of the cross.

When we turn away from pagan and superstitious, or abstract and speculative notions of providence and turn instead to the testimony of faith to discover the true content of the doctrine of providence, we discover that the biblical ground of this doctrine is found in the story of Genesis 22:1-19, the account of Abraham's sacrifice of Isaac.[21] We encounter the word itself in verse 14: "And Abraham called the name of that place The LORD will provide; as it is said to this day, 'On the mount of the LORD it shall be provided.' " Although a complete exegesis of this text cannot be presented in this context, we can and must note that the providence mentioned is that of salvation. God provided a substitute for the life of Isaac—a ram. In the New Testament another substitution is spoken of, that of the Lamb of God: "Behold, the Lamb of God, who takes away the sin of the world!" (John 1:29).

Here and only here do we encounter the authentic meaning of providence. God has provided a redeemer. There is no other providence alongside of or still less, in competition with this one. There is no other god, perhaps a hidden or mysterious god—alongside the God who is revealed in this way—in the act of salvation.

Thus it is possible to understand divine providence only on the basis of the divine love and mercy made manifest through Jesus of Nazareth. Only by focusing our attention rigorously at this point and on this basis can we avoid the misunderstandings of this doctrine which lead to so many difficulties for the life of faith.

From this point of view it is possible to understand many of the texts which bear upon the doctrine of providence. One of these is found in Luke 13:1-5, in which Jesus is asked concerning the massacre of Galileans in an uprising against Rome, and the death of those who were crushed by the fall of the tower of Siloam. There are two principles here that are quite clear. It is not possible to speak of these and similar catastrophes as the punishment of God for sin. But the occurrence of such events should be an occasion to recall that there is an even more calamitous destruction which lies on the horizon: the destruction of all that stands opposed to the love of God: the destruction of the destroyers of the earth (Rev. 11:18). Thus these calamitous events do not come from the hand of God, but it is possible to appropriate such events in order to remind ourselves that the world stands under divine judgment.

In Matthew's Gospel we encounter several texts that have been applied to the doctrine of providence. One of these is Matthew 5:45 (". . . so that you may be sons of your Father who is in heaven; for he makes his sun to rise on the evil and on the good, and sends rain on the just and on the unjust." The context of this passage clearly indicates that the Father is a God who sends only that which is good, and sends it to every person, whether just or unjust (Matt. 5:38-48). Therefore it is necessary to imitate the "providence of God" in such a way as to love (provide good for) both enemies and friends. The conclusion therefore is: "You therefore, must be perfect, as your heavenly Father is perfect" (Matthew 5:48). The perfection of God (and so of the one who is loyal to this God) is the perfection of love. All of this is as far as possible from any belief in blind fortune.

There remain those who say when something evil occurs that it is a temptation or a test sent from God. While some possibility of affirming this is supplied by the frame of the Book of Job, it is impossible from the standpoint of the New Testament. In James 1:13, 14 we read:

> Let no one say when he is [tested], "I am [tested] by God"; for God cannot be [tested] with evil and he himself [tests] no one; but each person is [tested] when he is lured and enticed by his own desire.

That God does not test or tempt the believer is the basis of the prayer "And lead us not into temptation [testing], but deliver us from evil" (Matthew 6:13). In this as in other petitions of the Lord's Prayer we are assured that God grants what we ask. Thus it is not possible to have this confidence and still to suppose that God sends evil as a temptation or a test.[22]

There are many passages of the New Testament that seem to bear upon this theme of providence. But these examples clarify the importance of understanding this theme from the standpoint of the gospel. Providence is not an independent theme that can be developed apart from this basis in the confidence in the one we call God the Father Almighty.

Thus it is possible to indicate some of the basic principles which must govern the development of a doctrine of providence within the framework of an evangelical faith.

1. When we speak of providence we are not speaking, and must not speak of some god other than the one who liberates and adopts, the one who is Father Almighty.

2. This God is the source of that which is good, and is never to be spoken of as the source of that which is evil. God sends that which is good, above all the one whom we name "son" who is the fulfillment of the promise of God.

3. When we have confidence in this God it is possible to have a new attitude toward the occurrence of the good and the evil in our experience. When we encounter good we have gratitude because we recall that God is the source of all that is good. And the occurrence of that which is good may serve to strengthen our confidence that the good will of God will be consummated in the accomplishment of the divine reign. All that is good

is a sign for faith of that which is the will of God. When we encounter evil we encounter that which is opposed to and opposed by the will of God. Weakness, sickness, oppression and injustice, sin and death—these things bear witness to the necessity of the transformation of all things which God has promised (see the story of the man blind from birth in John 9 and the reply of Jesus, John 9:3). Thus in the presence of evil we pray with even greater urgency for the coming of the reign of God and so oppose ourselves to the structures of evil.

Moreover we know that the power of God is made manifest in the cross of Jesus, and that this power is sufficient to transform even death itself into a sign of life, indeed into the source of life. Thus even in our own suffering we have confidence in the gracious will of God, which cannot finally be conquered, and so are able to give thanks in all things. We do not give thanks *for* all things, but *in* all things (1 Thessalonians 5:18).[23] For in all things God can give the capacity to triumph over evil as God triumphed in the cross and resurrection of Jesus.

In all this we reject the belief in fortune or in a God who is arbitrary or capricious. We rely upon and so are loyal to the God who desires only the salvation of the world, the one who is therefore called the "Father Almighty."

DIVINE SOVEREIGNTY AND HUMAN FREEDOM

An abstract understanding of the divine power not only distorts the understanding of providence but also that of the relationship between divine sovereignty and human freedom. The question is frequently posed on the basis of an abstract conception of the divine sovereignty entailing an absolute or unlimited control of events. To this then corresponds an equally abstract conception of human freedom as an unlimited capacity for choice. Defined in this way divine sovereignty and human freedom are incompatible. If God is indeed sovereign then there can be no freedom of the human will (Luther). But an Arminian insistence on human freedom and responsibility seems to make humanity responsible for its own salvation, and so to render the divine initiative of grace unintelligible.

In the context of this brief discussion of the Creed, and especially of the term Almighty, it is not possible to do more than offer a few remarks aimed at clarifying this issue for faith.

In the course of our reflection on the meaning of "Father Almighty" we have seen that the divine power and sovereignty is the capacity to overcome the servitude of the creature to the dominion of bondage and distortion. The sovereignty of God must then be conceived of in this soteriological sense and not in terms of abstract or speculative categories. What is at stake is the capacity of God to liberate the creature from evil and so to bring the creature into the sphere of genuine freedom and responsibility corresponding to the status of the adopted heirs of God.

Now the sovereignty of God is a contested sovereignty. For we see in the world around us evidence of other powers; powers of division and domination and death. Yet even where the dominion of these "principalities and powers" seems most secure—in the humiliation and execution of Jesus—it is possible to see the sovereignty of the divine love. Of course it is something that is only glimpsed here. Its full manifestation awaits the transformation of all things for which faith waits on the basis of its loyalty to the one revealed in Jesus. In that sense the sovereignty of God is not a datum so much as it is a hope; not a "given" but a longed-for reality which is, therefore, eschatological in character. This sovereignty will also be our theme when we speak of the one who is "seated at the right hand . . . who will come to judge the quick and the dead."

In light of this, what of human freedom? As long as we are under the dominion of the principalities and powers we have no freedom; that is, we are under the yoke of oppression. The coming of God as Father to liberate and adopt is that which bestows, or begins to bestow, freedom upon us. In that sense then we may and must say that in the adhering to the one who comes in this way we discover true freedom. For apart from this action and intervention there is bondage—slavery to the internal and external dominion of death.

And what then of the freedom to reject this gift of freedom, this activity of liberation? Clearly the refusal is not a capacity but a weakness, not liberty but the sign of bondage, a bondage so internalized as to make us in love with our chains.

The sovereignty of God is manifest precisely in our freedom. These two, divine sovereignty and human freedom, belong together; in no sense are they opposing forces. The greater the sovereignty of God, the greater our freedom from bondage; the greater our freedom from bondage, the more clearly manifest is the sovereignty of God who wills this freedom, this liberation.

The converse is also true. For if we fall back into bondage or refuse to accept the liberation from bondage then the more obscure, hidden, contested is the divine sovereignty.

We may desire or fear freedom. In fact we do both. But God comes to us to allay our fear and to increase our desire, to strengthen our resolve and our hope. Precisely as God empowers us to desire freedom do we also gain the capacity to resist the temptation of bondage.

Once we have set up the problem in this way we may ask about human responsibility for "bondage." We discover our responsibility; precisely as we are set free. What we discover is that we have been seduced by our fear and anxiety to pay homage to what are otherwise the "weak and beggarly" (Galatians 4:8) structures of the world of darkness and death. Once these powers have been exposed we find ourselves in a new situation, that of resistance to their alluring and seductive solicitations and of defiant struggle against their dominion in our hearts and in our world.

It is in this resistance and struggle that human freedom is seen, a freedom which mirrors the divine sovereignty. Of course this struggle is not one which claims uncontested victory. The final overcoming of the principalities and powers is a matter of hope, is eschatological. But already in the dawning freedom of the human set free by the "Father Almighty" creation begins to glimpse its own liberation, the universal end of bondage (Romans 8:19-22).

Thus the divine sovereignty, properly understood, does nothing to diminish human freedom and responsibility. The experience of freedom and responsibility is itself the warrant for the assertion of divine sovereignty over the powers that enslave us and the world.

CHAPTER FOUR

CREATOR

I t is important that even here where we appear to enter the sphere of the contemplation of nature, we do not forsake the evangelical and soteriological perspective which is of utmost importance for a Christian confession of faith. We are not confessing the order and regularity of nature, nor its dependence upon a first or final cause. There is no way that I can rely upon, still less swear my loyalty to, such an ultimate cause. Instead I rely upon and commit myself to the creator of heaven and earth. This reliance upon and allegiance to God as the creator of heaven and earth follows directly from a reliance upon the Father Almighty who delivers and adopts, who liberates and confers dignity and responsibility.

That we remain within the sphere of redemption and not of physics or philosophy is made clear from the origin of the phrase which appears in the Creed. In the Apostles' Creed we have "creator of heaven and earth." In the Nicene Creed we have "creator of heaven and earth and all things visible and invisible." This confession of faith derives from Colossians 1:16: "For in him all things were created, in heaven and on earth, visible and invisible." The striking thing to notice here is that in this early Christian hymn quoted by the author of Colossians, we are speaking of Christ. It is the "beloved son" who is described (in terms formerly applied by Judaism to wisdom and by the Stoics to the logos) as the one "in whom all things were created."

This is not merely a christological assertion but a soteriological one as well. That is, the emphasis in Colossians falls on the act of salvation in terms that remind us of what we have already discovered from Paul concerning adoption and liberation. This is clear if we consider the grounding of this hymn in the assertions of Colossians 1:12-13:

> Giving thanks to the Father, who has qualified us to share in the inheritance of the saints in light. He has delivered us from the dominion of darkness and transferred us to the kingdom of his beloved Son.

It is clear that the act of liberation is the indispensable background for the confession of faith in the one who created heaven and earth.

In addition to deliverance from domination in order to share in the rule or reign of the beloved Son, we discover the motif of adoption spoken of as that which has "qualified us to share in the inheritance. . . ." Thus a new status is conferred in which we, who were the slaves of another, are now the inheritors of the divine love.

We are transferred from the dominion of the powers to the reign of the Son of love. God has prepared us, or capacitated us, for inheriting that which belongs to God. Thus we have been given a new condition, for we have been transferred from slavery to the inheritance of divine love. We receive a radical and total transformation of our condition. From bondage (liberation) to the inheritance of sonship (adoption). This transformation from darkness to light, from bondage to liberty, from oppression to dignity is so total and radical as to require speaking of a new creation (2 Corinthians 5:17; Galatians 6:15).

Now the creation hymn is introduced precisely at this point to clarify the meaning of this deliverance and adoption. In the hymn it is asserted that this transfer and qualification, this deliverance and adoption, this liberation and dignification is one which occurs by right. The one who delivers us from the structures and forces of the world is one who created both us and the world. Yet in the meantime this world and its structures have turned against us and against God. They have thus become "dominions and authorities." Often indeed they legitimate themselves and their rule by appeal to God as their origin. The argument of Colossians is that God is indeed the origin of the world, but not in such a way as to authorize and legitimate the status quo. Rather, the status quo is revealed by the cross of Jesus as illegitimate, as rebellion and disorder (2:15). God makes a public example of these principalities by bringing them to expose their opposition to God in the public execution of God's Son at the hands of the religious and secular authorities.

Yet the rebellion of the principalities and powers is not understood in such a way as to give it a provisional legitimacy as simply standing over against God in terms of dualism. The language of dualism is employed here (1:13), yet it is overcome by the assertion that nothing whatever exists independently of God in Christ. The world, visible and invisible, earthly and heavenly, all that is, exists or has reality only in Christ. Christ is no interloper who comes into an alien world and snatches a group of followers from the world while leaving it otherwise unchanged. Something similar is said in the prologue to the Gospel of John:

> In the beginning was the Word, and the Word was with God, and the Word was God. He was in the beginning with God; all things were made through him, and without him was not anything made that was made.

He was in the world, and the world was made through him, yet the world knew him not (John 1:1-3, 10).

The world is the world of the one who comes. When the world does not receive him, it still remains his. Perhaps the "powers" want to say: "God has power in the 'heavens' but we have power on earth. When you are in the heavens you may worship God (or in the private and unworldly place where you commune with the heavens) but here on earth it is necessary to obey us." But God does not accept this division. God is the creator both of heaven and of earth, and in coming in the person of the Word made flesh, God reclaims the earth as well. Thus all ultimate dualism is completely excluded.

It is not God in Christ who is the interloper here. The world is God's world. It exists only through the divine love made manifest in Christ. All that enslaves, dominates, and destroys is nevertheless merely creature—creature run amok perhaps, but creature nonetheless. It is not divine, it does not have ultimate ontological status. It defaces and defames God's creation but it is not of ultimate power. Redemption exposes this rebellion and reclaims the world as God's world.

To flee the world, to abandon it to its own devices, to withdraw from it into a "spiritual" sphere, is to fail to acknowledge the rightness of God's action of redemption. The "rightness" of God's action is the right of the Creator—of the one to whom all things owe loyalty. We testify to our faith in the rightness of God's saving action not by withdrawing from the world but by claiming the world in all its dimensions as the appropriate sphere of the divine love. It exists by and from this love and is summoned into conformity to this love. Christian faith is a worldly faith because it is a faith in the one who created heaven and earth and so rightly, justly, and appropriately intervenes to save and to reconcile.

Since this intervention is the intervention of the Creator, its scope is by no means restricted to its effects on the lives of a few individuals or even the larger community of those individuals. On the contrary, this intervention also inaugurates the work of the new creation. Thus the action of God in Christ has in view the reconciliation of all things, whether on earth or in heaven. The scope of the divine act of deliverance is the universe itself. The universe is intended to become the harmony of all things. This aim or goal is expressed in Philippians: "that at the name of Jesus every knee should bow, in heaven and on earth and under the earth, and every tongue confess that Jesus Christ is Lord, to the glory of God the Father" (2:10-11). This same theme is also expressed in 1 Corinthians in the discussion of the final transformation of reality:

> Then comes the end, when he delivers the kingdom to God the Father after destroying every rule and every authority and power. For he must reign until he has put all his enemies under his feet. The last enemy to be destroyed is death. . . .
>
> When all things are subjected to him, then the Son himself will also be subjected to him who put all things under him, that God may be everything to every one [all in all] (15:24-28).

The aim or goal of the action of God in Christ is that all powers of division and domination, of separation and subjugation, be overcome in such a way that even the separation between God and world may be overcome. In this way God becomes all in all. The theme of creation then is fundamentally eschatological and soteriological in character. The creation which is the principle object of faith is the new creation (Galatians 6:15) and in relying upon and being faithful to this creative act of God, the new creation becomes a reality in the believer (2 Corinthians 5:17). Thus the life of faith anticipates the new heaven and earth (2 Peter 3:13; Isaiah 65:17, 66:22).

Because of this soteriological and eschatological orientation, the name "Creator of Heaven and Earth" directs us not toward a primordial past but toward the ultimate future which has already been inaugurated in the life and death and destiny of Jesus.[24] To rely on the "Creator of heaven and earth" is to rely on the one who will "do a new thing" (Isaiah 43:18, 19). Our attention is focused not backward on some earlier age of perfection, but forward to the reconciliation of all things through that love made manifest in the cross and resurrection of Jesus.

It is in this light that we may understand the importance for Christian faith of acknowledging and making its own the faith of Israel in the one who created heaven and earth. The poem of Genesis 1-2:4 is the testimony of faith to the one who made heaven and earth. For our purposes here it must suffice to note only a few of the most important features of this confession.

1. The work of God in creation is understood as itself an act of salvation or deliverance. The separation of night from day (1:4) and the separation of the waters and of the waters from land (1:6, 9) all indicate the sovereignty of God over the forces of chaos represented by night and water. In order to understand this creation poem it is important to recall that it was written during the Babylonian captivity. In this era the urgent question was whether God had the capacity to restore Israel. The prophets, especially Ezekiel, gave an affirmative reply. This creation poem clarifies the basis of that confidence. The hope of liberation is based on trust in the one who is Creator. Thus the doctrine of the poem has the

same form and intention as the creation faith we have found in the New Testament.

2. That the world is created means that no power other than God has legitimate authority over the earthling. Thus even the stars, the sun, and the moon receive their power from God, and are granted no dominion over us. Every attempt to make the forces of nature or of the heavenly bodies into determiners of human destiny is interdicted. All of this is only creature, like ourselves, not "divine." Whatever force or power that diminishes the dignity of humanity is in rebellion against the Creator.

3. The affirmation that God is Creator is at the same time an affirmation of the dignity and liberty of humanity. The forces of nature are not the image of God, nor are the stars (as perhaps Plato supposed in the Timaeus). The only image of God in all the created world is humanity, male and female (Genesis 1:27). At the same time this ascription of the divine image and likeness to the human being is also the ascription of responsibility. The human is to be the reflection and representative of God on earth. And to this responsibility belongs a severe restriction. It is not just any god who is to be represented by the human but precisely the God who creates and protects the earth. In this way the theme of liberation and adoption is anticipated in the creation poem.

4. That which exists is pronounced to be good. The world, heaven and earth, is not the sphere of evil matter as the Manichaeans would have it. The world, teeming with abundance and diversity, is good. It is good because it is the work of divine grace and freedom. God rejoices in this world: "And God saw that it was good" (verses 10, 12, 18, 21, 25, 31). Six times God saw that it was good! Here we hear of the joy of God in the world. The world is good because it is the creature of the grace and freedom, the love and joy of God. Often religion, even Christianity, has forgotten the joy of God in the creation. All too often we hear that the world is evil, is contaminated, is dangerous for faith. But however severely we must expose the actual bondage of the earth to darkness and death, the creation poem reminds us that the world in its origin, its foundation, is the world that God has declared to be "very good."

5. The aim of all creation is the sabbath rest of the divine joy. This sabbath rest of God is understood both by Judaism and by Christianity as the image of the final goal of history.[25] The sabbath laws originally had this intention, to anticipate the freedom and joy of all creation in the joy of the Creator. Thus fields were not to be tilled, for the earth itself was to participate in the joy of the end of time. Animals, too, were to be permitted their share in this rest and joy. The sabbath is also the jubilee which is the subject of hope. Thus when Jesus announces his message it is to announce the coming of the sabbath of sabbaths, the year of "the Lord's favor" (Isaiah 61:2; Luke 4:19). It is this healing of the earth, this

transformation of the earth into the sphere of joy, peace, and rest which is anticipated in the sabbath rest and is effected in the reconciliation of "all things" in Christ.

Of these themes the one which calls for special emphasis is that of the goodness of the world. To speak of God as creator of heaven and earth is to bring oneself into opposition to all who find the world to be inherently evil, fundamentally devoid of value and importance. There is a profound religious and philosophical tendency to see the world in just this way—as fundamentally alien. Salvation in this view consists in escape from the world. But with this article of the Creed it becomes clear that the world as such is claimed by God, that the world is the sphere and object of the divine love. It is this which is safeguarded by the assertion that God is the "Creator of heaven and earth." This theme is used not only in the Old Testament but also in the New to combat all those religious and philosophical tendencies that encourage a withdrawal from the world. In Colossians the theme of the creation of heaven and earth through the Son is used to oppose the introduction of asceticism into the Christian community. Colossians 2:16-23 opposes religious legalism and rigorism whether based on philosophy or a return to pharasaic law. This is opposed on the basis of Christ's having vanquished the powers of the world, including the law. In 1 Timothy 4:1-5 a similar argument is made on the basis of creation more directly. All of this reflects the freedom of Jesus who came not as an ascetic but as one who ate and drank (Matthew 11:19) and so celebrated the inbreaking of the "acceptable year of the Lord" (Luke 4:19).

What do we learn from a consideration of the assertion of God as Creator of heaven and earth?

We learn first that the "doctrine of creation" is a doctrine concerning God—it further clarifies for us the identity of the God in whom we have confidence and to whom we are loyal. We have confidence in the God who is gracious Father, the one who rescues us from slavery and adopts us to be God's heirs. Thus we do not have confidence in an anonymous supreme being, but in the Father of Jesus whose fundamental nature is love, whose goal is the transformation of all things. And we learn that we may have confidence in this gracious love, for it is the power from which and for which all things exist.

To rely on this God then is to refuse the temptation to flee the world or to resign ourselves to "the way things are." The world appears to be ruled by forces of domination and division, but these forces are being brought into submission to the power of love against which they have rebelled. We can neither accept their present dominion (for it is rebellion against God) nor simply escape from them, leaving the rest of the world to their merciless dominion. Our existence as an existence in loyalty to the

Creator of heaven and earth must be a sign in the world of the overcoming of these powers of division and domination.

This is perhaps especially significant today as we become more and more aware of the way in which our actions and our carelessness threaten to permanently disfigure the very earth made by the one we acclaim as our loving Father. Loyalty to the "Maker of heaven and earth" must clearly entail a renunciation of the ways in which we are engaged in "unmaking" the earth. The destruction of its plant and animal species, the pollution of land and water and air, the turning of the garden into desert and waste, all can only be seen as rebellion against rather than loyalty to the one we call Father, who is also "Maker of heaven and earth."

In view of the world as creation, we may deal with the things of the earth as the good gifts of God. We may and must renounce every form of dualism which would cause us to flee the earth in asceticism or rigorism. The earth is created to be the sphere of joy and reconciliation. Thus we are invited to see in food and drink, in love and laughter, that which is the good gift of the one Jesus called Father.

Christian existence in view of the creation, then, is characterized by both resistance and celebration. It is resistance to all that dominates, enslaves, and divides. And it is celebration of the earth which is the good creature of God. Both celebration and resistance testify to the one God whom we name as "Father Almighty, Maker of Heaven and Earth."

FAITH AND SCIENCE

In the last century a great deal was made of the apparent contradiction between faith and science. This contradiction seemed most acute at the point of an understanding of Genesis 1 and 2, the creation accounts. If Genesis is regarded as giving us information regarding the beginning of the world (and how there came to be human beings on this planet), then the perspective of the sciences seems to provide a striking contrast. Not seven days but millions of years, not a direct creation of Adam and Eve but a process of evolutionary development, not a single pair of ancestors but a whole species of ancestors. In the light of modern scientific theory can we still honestly confess that God is the Creator of heaven and earth? If we continue to insist on this confession does it then require of us that we renounce the "discoveries" or the theories of modern science? Certainly a number of people have been attracted to one or another of these positions.

A third position is represented by those who claim that faith and science cannot possibly come into conflict since science concerns the world of nature, while faith is concerned with the historical character of human beings. This view is unpersuasive if only because there are also human sciences which deal with the most interior and intimate features of human motivation and decision (including the decision of faith). Here then, the debate about physics, geology, and biology is renounced only to find similar issues arising in relation to history, sociology, and psychology. Science seeks to understand the whole of reality. Nor can faith withdraw from one or another sphere to content itself with some remaining sphere of "mystery," for mystery in this sense turns out to be a shrinking domain. Faith can no more leave the world of nature to the natural sciences than it can leave the human world to the human sciences.

Does this mean that we are thrown back to the alternative of faith *or* science? I think not. First of all faith and science have a shared set of commitments. Both are opposed to the sacralizing of the world, that is, both oppose superstition. The confession that the world was *created* entails that the world is not divine, that, for example, the stars do not control our destiny. Where the world is thought of as sacred, no science is possible. Moreover, both faith and science are committed to the rationality and so to the intelligibility of the world. When faith confesses that everything that is exists from the Word, it articulates the basis for an inquiry into the intelligibility of the world. Without this confidence in the intelligibility of the world, no science would be possible. Moreover, faith and science are in tacit agreement that the world is intrinsically good, something of real value. Without that conviction the vocation of science as a careful attention to the world would be impossible to sustain.

Now I do not suppose that the only source for all of these convictions is the Judeo-Christian tradition; there is ample ground for these convictions in some aspects of Greek philosophy. The point is not that science requires faith—Christian faith—but that both faith and science share certain commitments.

Science and faith are also agreed with respect to their attitude toward knowledge. Both must regard their own understanding to be provisional, that is, subject to correction. Both accept the limitations of their knowledge while seeking to understand more clearly. Moreover, both are concerned to make themselves intelligible to others. It is of the very nature of Christian faith as a proclamation to the world that it must make itself intelligible and persuasive to others. A good deal of the Reformation was concerned with the recovery of this intelligibility through the elimination of traditions and ecclesiastical authority which restricted or opposed this intelligibility. Similarly, scientific inquiry must proceed by appeal to intelligibility and rationality. Its integrity is threatened where procedures for general verification are restricted (as, for example, in the imposition of "government secrecy" or ideological dogma).

Yet despite these shared values and commitments science and faith do, in fact, come into conflict. This is especially the case when either lose sight of their emancipatory commission. Both science and faith stand in service to humanity, in order to liberate humanity and the earth itself from bondage to powers of destruction and division. When faith seeks to hold the mind and heart captive to a particular world view, science rightly chastens faith by fulfilling its own commission to liberate from illusion and fear. Yet science, too, is capable of forgetting or misunderstanding this commission. When science becomes mere technology in the quest for power it becomes an instrument of domination and division. Nowhere is this more evident than in the use of science to produce instruments of destruction capable of eliminating life from the planet. The development of destructive capacity is but the most horrifying example of the technological threat to destroy the ecology of the earth. At this point faith is obliged, precisely as faith in the Creator of heaven and earth, to protest against this threat and this destruction. For the earth is not to be terrorized by humanity. The earth and humanity have a common origin and a common destiny in the love of God. The destruction of the earth has the same root as the division and domination of its people. The extraction of wealth from the earth also serves the exploitation of people who are made to be the instruments of this exploitation. The development of destructive power only terrorizes the population of the earth and divides that population against itself in the interest of the most powerful. Here then the witness of faith to the God who overcomes division and domination, who loves the world into being, and delights in the earth made by his love is a witness that is necessary for our survival and for the survival of the earth.

Yet this witness does not entail the abolition of science and technology. It recalls these to their true basis and goal. The basis of science is the careful and truthful attention to the world around us and within us. The aim of science is to secure the proper freedom of life from fear and division. It is this basis and goal which faith specifies in its confession of faith in "God the Father Almighty, Maker of Heaven and Earth."

It is the task of faith to articulate this basis and goal in every age and within the linguistic capacities of every world view. Just as faith articulated itself within the linguistic capacities of ninth century B.C.E. Palestine (Genesis 2:4ff.) and sixth century B.C.E. Babylon (Genesis 1) and within those of the first century Hellenistic world (Romans Colossians, John), so also has it sought to express itself in the available terminology of the late Hellenistic world (Basil) and the Aristotelian categories of medieval science (Thomas Aquinas). It must do the same today. Faith does not produce its own scientific categories. It does, however, articulate its ultimate confidence in God within the terms of any world view. This does not mean that it can simply accept any world view of the past or present without question. It was because theology absolutized the science of Aristotle that it resisted the science of Galileo. Wherever science turns humanity or the earth itself into an object of domination and destruction, faith must protest in the name of the Creator. But when in openness to the truth and in hope of emancipation and reconciliation science opens itself to the complexity, the ambiguity, and the reality of the world, then faith must both rejoice and learn.

CONCLUSION: ELECTION

The theme which unites all that we have discussed in this first article of the Creed is that of God's gracious election. It is the divine grace which calls us and the world into being.

Israel testified to the power of God that called it into being through deliverance from Egypt. The word of promise and deliverance gives to those who were no people a new identity and destiny. At the core of Israel's faith is the sense of being summoned into being before God.

Yet this calling could be understood as conferring upon Israel a privilege and a position which it could possess on its own without continual reliance upon the creative word of God. Thus it could turn inward upon itself, its law, its cult, its national identity, its land. And when this occurs the word of God unmakes Israel—and Israel discovers itself without a land, without a national identity, without a temple or a king. But this divine judgment is by no means a rejection of Israel as such. It does represent the ferocity of the divine love that will not permit the attempts of its elect to transform the divine election into an excuse either to forget the poor and the stranger, or to pride itself on its position in the world. In its dereliction and apparent abandonment, the word of God comes to the people in exile to again claim Israel, to give it a law not of stone but of the heart (Jeremiah) to give life to the dry bones of its exile (Ezekiel), to create it anew (Isaiah). It is in this context of renewed expectation that Israel learns to praise God with the hymn of creation (Genesis 1:1–2:4). For the one who called Israel into being and who calls Israel into new being is the one who called the world into being and who promises a new heaven and a new earth. Thus gracious election unites the themes of deliverance and liberation, of adoption and reconciliation, of creation and new creation.

Election basically means that the historical creation and re-creation of Israel is founded in the creative word that summons the world itself into being. Thus from before the foundation of the world God's love intends the deliverance of this people and their fashioning into bearers of the divine name. This theme of predestination may apply to the individual (as in Jeremiah 1:5 or Psalm 139) or to the people of God as a whole (Deuteronomy 7:7-8). But in either case what is at stake is the fidelity and invincibility of the divine love that brings Israel and the world into being.

This theme characterizes the New Testament as well, and receives an astonishing extension. For God has chosen not only the people of a single nation, but peoples of all nations to be the bearers of the divine name and nature, to be the recipients of, and witnesses to, God's unfailing love.

The Reformation rediscovered this theme of election as the key to an understanding of the nature and will and action of God. Yet this rediscovery led to a number of fatal misconceptions. Among these is the notion that God wills the destruction of some and the salvation of others. As Karl Barth has clearly demonstrated, God has only one will and intention. This will is salvation.[26] It is because God wills deliverance and reconciliation that the forces of division, domination, and death are destined for annihilation. Judgment consists simply in this: that we align ourselves with the forces and structures that are passing away and so turn away from the divine generosity and love. Yet our turning away, our resistance to the divine love is continually being overcome by that love itself. We observe in horror the way in which, in both our inner and outer life, we conspire in our own destruction. We hear in joy the ways in which we are being delivered from our own complicity in self-destruction by the love of God which takes our condemnation upon itself. However we may work out the consequences for our lives, we can attribute to God only that gracious election which intends our redemption and that of the world as a whole.

Election, then, is the doctrine which explicates the gracious aim and intention of God initiated in creation, realized in Jesus Christ, consummated in the new heaven and new earth. It is this gracious and invincible intention upon which we rely when we affirm our faith in God the Father Almighty, Maker of heaven and earth.

PART ONE: CHRISTOLOGY

And in Jesus Christ, His Only Son, Our Lord

W e come now to the central article of the Creed, which deals with Jesus of Nazareth who is called by faith the Christ, the Son of God, the Lord. This section of the Creed is central not only because it comes between the beginning and the end, and not only because it is by far the longest and most detailed of the three articles of the Creed, but also and most importantly because it is determinative for the interpretation of that which goes before, concerning the Father, and that which comes after, concerning the Spirit.[1] We have already seen that the first article of the Creed concerning the Father Almighty points us decisively and clearly to a consideration of the significance of Jesus as the Christ. God is confessed as Father on account of the testimony of Jesus as the Son. God is confessed as "Almighty" in as much as the power of God is demonstrated in the "weakness" of the cross. God is confessed as Creator because that which the Father accomplishes in and through Jesus is nothing less than a new creation which aims at a new heaven and a new earth. Thus it is exceedingly important that our reflections on this second and longest and most basic article of the Creed have a clear and precise character.

To this end it will be necessary to become as clear as possible concerning the identity of Jesus Christ, who is the subject of this section of the Creed and so of the Creed as a whole. In Jesus as the Christ and Son of God and Lord we find clearly articulated the identity of God who is Father Almighty, Maker of Heaven and Earth. For the Christian there is no secure knowledge of God apart from a consideration of the preaching and action, the life and death, the fate and destiny of this Jesus.

This section of the Creed begins with the identification of Jesus as Christ, Son of God and Lord. This sets the stage for the narrative-like sequence that follows and which further specifies the identity of the one in whom we believe and to whom we therefore pledge our loyalty. We will deal first with the "titles" by which the object of this loyalty is named. As we shall see, the clarification of these titles also entails the preliminary clarification of our own identity as those who pledge themselves in this way to this Lord.

CHAPTER FIVE

THE CHRIST

I t is always necessary to test our understanding of faith by the question: "Do we really know Jesus?"[2] Thus every generation must return to the figure of Jesus to clarify for itself the authenticity of its understanding, its proclamation, its faith. For all of us confront the temptation to substitute a Jesus of our dreams and speculations for Jesus of Nazareth. But it is only Jesus of Nazareth who awakens faith.

The earliest title given to Jesus was that of the Christ—the anointed one. Both in Hebrew (and Aramaic) and in Greek the title signified the office of kingship. But the original significance of this kingship for the earliest community of faith was that of the eschatological king who would come to inaugurate the reign of God. This inauguration of the reign of God could be understood in a variety of ways, as a survey of apocalyptic literature makes clear.[3] But the theme that united these conceptions was that of liberation, especially liberation from the tyranny and humiliation of foreign rule. To speak of Jesus as the Messiah or Christ is to speak of him as the liberator.

So intimately is this title associated with Jesus that it becomes his proper name already by the time of Paul—that is, within about twenty years of Jesus' death. Thus the most fundamental significance of Jesus' identity is that he is the Messiah, the one who inaugurates the rule of God by overthrowing the barriers to this rule.

At the end of the nineteenth century and the first decades of the twentieth it was customary to separate Jesus from Christ, assigning the first to history and the second to theology. But this division fails on account of the impossibility of separating the man from his mission. We know nothing of him apart from this mission. Even the accounts of his birth are determined by the mission of establishing the reign of God. Thus when we turn to the Gospels to inquire about the identity of Jesus we are confronted with texts supremely indifferent to the questions of biography and history. Their only concern is to place before the reader a narrative concerning the Jesus who is the Christ, the Jesus whose mission it was (and is) to inaugurate the rule of God and so to deliver the earth from tyranny.

But the supposition that Jesus is the Christ, or rather that Jesus and Christ are interchangeable designations of the same reality is by no means simply asserted. Indeed it is quite possible for the authors of these documents to contest strongly certain ways of conceiving of Jesus as the Christ. Hence the strong rebuke delivered by Jesus to Peter's confession in Mark 8:29. Instead of contenting themselves with an assertion of christological office, these narratives seek to demonstrate quite concretely (and over against alternative conceptions of messiahship) what it means to say that Jesus is the Christ. Thus for example when the disciples of John inquire whether Jesus is indeed the awaited one we are told of the reply:

> Go and tell John what you have seen and heard: the blind receive their sight, and lame walk, lepers are cleansed, and the deaf hear, the dead are raised up, the poor have good news preached to them. And blessed is [the one] who takes no offense at me. (Luke 7:22-23)

The clarification of the identity of Jesus is at the same time the clarification of the meaning of the assertion that he is the Christ. In either case we are concerned to understand the meaning of his mission, its characteristic features. By means of this analysis we may see more clearly what it is to be loyal to the one who has this mission, and to carry that mission forward in our own time and place.

Accordingly in what follows I will attempt to sketch some of the characteristic features of the ministry and mission of Jesus as this is portrayed in the Gospels. This procedure is not intended to produce a description of the "historical Jesus" but to present some of the common features of the tradition about Jesus the Messiah as this is expressed in the Gospels, especially the Synoptic Gospels.

1. The Proclamation of Jesus

Mark provides us with the most concise summary of the proclamation of Jesus: "Now after John was arrested, Jesus came into Galilee, preaching the gospel of God, and saying, "The time is fulfilled, and the [reign of God is come]; repent and believe in the gospel" (Mark 1:14-15). The theme which characterizes the proclamation of Jesus, and indeed all that Jesus says and does, is that of the reign of God. Israel longed for the coming of that reign as promised by the later prophets. Jesus announces that the time is now ready and that this reign has come upon the world.

This theme is amplified in a number of parables that begin "the reign of God (or of heaven) is like . . . ." These parables emphasize the coming of the divine rule which overturns the existing order. They underline its importance, as that for which all else may and must be sacrificed (Matthew 13:44-45). Moreover the suddenness and unexpectedness of its coming is emphasized with stories that stress the importance of a constant watchfulness and readiness (Matthew 24:32–25:30).

In many ways this proclamation is similar to that of John the Baptizer and may be regarded as a continuation of that proclamation.[4] Yet there is also an apparent difference, for Jesus generally gives to the notion of the reign of God the content of mercy. Jesus' proclamation is for the most part directed to the poor, the outcast, the despised. To them he announces that the coming of God is good news. Those who have not abided by the religious requirements—prostitutes, publicans, the poor—are confronted with the news that God is coming not to condemn them but to embrace them. Thus the parables of the prodigal son (Luke 15:11-32), the good shepherd (Matthew 18:10-14; Luke 15:3-7), and so on, all point to the astonishing generosity and liberality of God's love for those who have been excluded by the religious authorities of their culture.

2. The Action of Jesus

Jesus not only announces the coming of God's reign, but also demonstrates the meaning of this reign in action, thereby actualizing this reign and rule.

This actualization takes the characteristic form of healing and exorcism. In the first chapter of the Gospel of Mark, the summary of Jesus' proclamation is followed by a whole series of accounts of Jesus' activity (1:21–2:12). In this activity Jesus confronts the worst forms of human distress: the insanity of those possessed by demons, the agony and shame of leprosy and myriad other diseases. And this is but the beginning. What is the meaning of this activity?

All of this is an illustration, a demonstration, of the meaning of God's reign. When God's reign is actualized, disease of mind and body is banished. The explanation given in Luke's Gospel is decisive: "But if it is by the finger of God that I cast out demons, then the [reign] of God has come upon you" (Luke 11:20). The phrase "the finger of God" signifies the liberating power of God, for it recalls the astonishment of the magicians in the court of Pharaoh when confronted by the signs of Moses (Exodus 8:19). But in Exodus the finger of God afflicts the Egyptians in order to persuade Pharaoh to give freedom to the slaves. In Luke the finger of God causes healing, overthrowing the power of evil, and thus signifies that God is coming to free God's people.

The accounts of Jesus' healings and exorcisms are not then to be read as random accounts of Jesus' power. They are a demonstration of the arrival of God's reign. And they teach us that this reign is not merely a "spiritual" rule that deals only with our "souls," but that the reign of God means health and healing for our bodies as well. How could it be otherwise since the one whose reign comes is the "Maker of Heaven and Earth"?

3. The Friendship of Jesus

The proclamation and action of Jesus call to his side a roving band of followers and friends. And what an astonishing company it is! It included guerrilla fighters (Simon the Zealot, Luke 6:15) together with tax collectors (Matthew 10:3). The guerrillas fought in the mountains to expel the Romans, the tax collectors collaborated with Roman rule. What could bring these adversaries together in friendship and fellowship with one another? The company also included ignorant laborers and a number of women. It was unheard of for women to travel about in this way. Some of them had apparently been prostitutes, others, like Mary Magdalene, may have been healed of disease or demon possession (Luke 8:2), at least one was the woman of an official of Herod's court (Luke 8:3).

Women and men, freedom fighters and collaborators, none apparently very pious, many of them were notorious sinners. Yet it was this group that heralded the coming of the reign of God. From the hundreds of thousands who followed, some were chosen to represent the twelve tribes of a reconstituted Israel—to be a sign that God's reign would reconstitute God's people (Mark 3:13ff. and parallels). Seventy were sent out to announce the reign of God throughout Palestine and in this way represented the seventy elders to whom Moses had imparted his spirit (Luke 10:1 ff.; Numbers 11:16 ff.). These people who followed Jesus were empowered to act as he acted: to announce the reign of God, to heal and to cast out demons. Here is no passive congregation; these are agents of the reign of God.

This companionship is itself a demonstration of the reign of God that abolishes those divisions to which the world is subjected: the division between men and women, the division between the pious and the impious. It was an extension of this fellowship that overcame the religious separation between Jew and Gentile, the cultural separation between Greek and barbarian, the class separation between master and slave (Galatians 3:28; Colossians 3:11). The existence of such a community is the sign that God has broken through the barriers that divide us from one another and so from God as well.

4. The Joy (Life-Style) of Jesus

Others before Jesus, especially John the Baptizer, had announced the coming of God's reign. But they had understood this advent primarily in terms of repentance and purification. The Essenes had withdrawn from the world into a holy community that stressed purification. John emphasized repentance and had himself lived as a solitary hermit.

Jesus is presented as having a strikingly contrasting life-style. Over and again in the Gospels we encounter him drinking and feasting, not only with his disciples, but with sinners and even with Pharisees. Among his favorite images for the reign of God was that of the wedding feast. Many of his teachings have the form of a kind of "party etiquette": whom to invite, what to wear, where to sit and so on. It is this dimension of his life which John expresses in the story of Jesus at the wedding feast in Cana of Galilee (John 2:1-11). According to John, Jesus' first "sign" was that of changing bath water into hundreds of gallons of wine so that the party could continue.

This behavior scandalized the serious and religious people of Israel. How could this indulgence in wine and food possibly be a sign of the coming of the reign of God? They dismissed Jesus as a drunk and a glutton (Matthew 11:19).

Yet the life-style of Jesus demonstrates that the reign of God is truly good news. The coming of God means that there is something worth celebrating and it evokes a party in which there is plenty to eat and drink and the celebration lasts all night.

5. Jesus and the Law

The religious authorities of Jesus' day were scandalized by his behavior. They were horrified by his companions. They were suspicious of his healings and exorcisms. But nothing so outraged them as his apparent disregard for the religious law.

This disregard for the laws, especially of purity or holiness, took many forms. When Jesus healed a leper he actually touched him (Mark 1:41) thus making himself unclean, that is, unfit to worship God, let alone represent God. The same is true of his healing of the woman with a discharge of blood. By coming into contact with her he made himself religiously impure (Mark 5:27). Moreover, Jesus and his disciples did not observe the washings prescribed for the purpose of making one pure from the contaminations of everyday life (Mark 7:1ff.). Perhaps these laws seem odd to us today. But they were ways in which Israel demonstrated its belonging to God, the Holy One. Still, Jesus had no such scruples.

This disregard for the law came to a crisis at the point of the observance of sabbath law. This was at heart of the identity of the people of God. Yet Jesus healed on the sabbath (Mark 1:21ff.; 3:1-5) and his disciples plucked grain on the sabbath as they walked through the fields (Mark 2:23ff.). This disregard for the holiest of days and most rigorous of religious laws is remembered in the Gospels as the provocation that inspired the plot to destroy Jesus (Matthew 12:1-4; Mark 2:23; Mark 3:6; Luke 13:10; 14:1; John 5:16).

This disregard for the law was understood as an assault on the holiness of God. That one should act in this way in the name of God could only be outrageous for those who, through careful observance of every religious duty, attempted to pay appropriate honor to the Holy One of Israel. But this observance also served to disqualify the majority from participation in the blessing of God, branding them "sinners." This charge lay most heavily upon the poor.

Those who regarded the holiness of God did so in such a way as to impose heavy burdens on the poor (Matthew 23:2-4). For this Jesus condemned the theologians (scribes) and the zealous laity (Pharisees). The poor heard him gladly because he set a higher value on the widow's mite than the elaborate tithes of the rich (Mark 12:41-44), more value on sinner's simple desire for mercy than on the impressive "righteousness" of the religious (Luke 18:10-14).

6. The Command of Jesus

In many respects those who heard Jesus learned of the lifting of a heavy burden (Matthew 11:28-30): the multitude of religious laws which were a burden even to those who could bear them and which had the effect of excluding the poor from the reign of God.

Yet Jesus was no anarchist or antinomian. Rather, he went to the heart of the meaning of the law and insisted on the law in this sense with a breathtaking radicality. The law of God could be summarized as the law of love (Mark 12:29-31). Yet this was by no means sentimentalized. Rather, it meant a total commitment to the good of the neighbor. The rich were to sell all that they had and give to the poor (Mark 10:17-21). The love of the neighbor was to include the love of the enemy as well (Matthew 5:43-48). It must be so strong as to go the second mile, turn the other cheek, give cloak and coat as well (Matthew 5:38-42).

In the perspective of this absolute love even anger could be seen to be as serious as murder (Matthew 5:21-24) and the mere desire to use another person for one's own sexual gratification was already adultery (Matthew 5:27-28). So severe was this love that it could take the form of renouncing one's own family for the sake of befriending the friendless and giving testimony to the reign of God (Matthew 10:37-39).

This severe command to love could be made the test of one's relation to God. Settling a dispute with one's neighbor was more important than worship (Matthew 5:23) and failing to forgive the offender meant excluding oneself from the divine mercy (Matthew 6:14-15; 18:35). The final judgment would depend not on one's religious attitudes or theological opinions but on whether one had given a cup of water to the thirsty, clothed the naked, or visited the sick and imprisoned (Matthew 25:31-46).

The command to love is all. There is nothing else. But this means a complete commitment to the outcast, the enemy, the estranged, the poor. Why this command to love? It is the command of the reign of God which, in its coming, abolishes the separation between friend and enemy, between privileged and excluded. To live in anticipation of the reign of God is to live in the light of the divine love which transforms the world, which gives all for the sake of that transformation.

7. The Authority of Jesus

In all of these characteristics of Jesus' ministry there is to be seen an astonishing freedom, sovereignty, and authority. There were those who maintained that the law and the prophets were the unchangeable word of God. Yet Jesus manifested complete freedom with respect to the received form of this law, rejecting everything that prevented a total and radical commitment to the welfare of the other. Those who heard him were astonished at his authority, his sovereignty over the Scriptures and traditions of faith (Matthew 7:28-29).

This same sovereignty was demonstrated in the activity of forgiving sin. The power of guilt and impurity is regarded by all religious traditions as breakable or removable only by God, whose mercy is invoked by innumerable forms of sacrifice and purification. Israel had its own system of these propitiations by which it invoked the divine forgiveness. But Jesus does away with all of this by a simple word: "your sins are forgiven" (Mark 2:5). This word of deliverance could only be regarded as blasphemy by those who maintained that only God (with the help of the sacrificial system) could forgive sin. Yet Jesus exercises this authority as one who stands in the place of God. Even worse: he seems to authorize this same authority for "human beings" (sons of men) generally (Matthew 9:8).

We see this same authority in the word that abolishes sickness and possession, in Jesus' authority over the demonic powers which enslave the minds and bodies of humanity (Mark 1:27-28). It is only an extension of this same authority that is expressed in the raising of Jairus' daughter (Mark 5:41), or Lazarus from the dead (John 11:38-44). In the life and action of Jesus we see demonstrated an astonishing authority over the law, sin, and death.

The effect of this authority is not that others should be flabbergasted at his sovereignty, and do him homage. Rather, the authority of Jesus is contagious. In all of this Jesus claims no special authority for himself. Instead he authorizes his disciples to exercise the same authority and freedom. Those who hear him are commissioned to exercise the same authority over demons and disease (Mark 3:13-15). They are made "lords of the sabbath" the determiners of what is and is not appropriate to do on the day of God (Mark 2:23ff.). They are commissioned to forgive sins as well (Matthew 16:19). The sovereignty of Jesus is a shared sovereignty; the sovereignty of the image and likeness of God that is conferred upon all who share in this identity.

Perhaps no single word of Jesus has been so directly associated with this sovereignty as the word which he uses for God and commands us to use: "Father." This is not Jesus' private word for God, connoting a relationship which he and he alone may have with the divine. Rather, it is one we are both permitted and commanded to use as well. With this name we express the drawing near of God, of God's reign, of God's love. This drawing near of God is the meaning of Jesus' initial proclamation: "The time is fulfilled, and the [reign] of God is at hand; repent, and believe in the gospel" (Mark 1:15). It is the proclamation of the acceptable year of the Lord (Luke 4:19).

These characteristics of Jesus' mission and ministry indicate that he is the promised and expected one, the one who comes to inaugurate the liberation of Israel and the direct rule of God (Matthew 11:2-6; Luke 7:18-23). These characteristics still require clarification and correction from the standpoint of Jesus' destiny. But together they suggest what was initially meant by acclaiming him as the Christ.

CHRISTIANITY AND JUDAISM (AGAIN)

The identity of Jesus exhibited in the Gospels is at the same time the identity of the one who is expected. The contention between Christianity and Judaism includes the question whether the one we encounter here is the one in whom the promises of God acquire their object and so their clarification and ratification.

Judaism must continue to reject this announcement until such time as it is decisively clarified. The community of Jesus has yet to demonstrate its claim that the divine future promised by the prophets is indeed shaped like Jesus. If we who are his followers fail to exhibit this shape, how shall we expect those who are entrusted with this promise as "light to the nations" to be able to accept this announcement? For the rejection of the Christian message is in a certain sense the sign of Israel's stubborn faithfulness. Of course this faithfulness is ambiguous, as the prophets of Israel maintained from the beginning. The stubbornness in faithfulness and in faithlessness is a characteristic of God's people whether Christians or Jews. After all, the words of the New Testament are themselves generated in an attempt to contest the faithlessness, the betrayal of the gospel by those who claimed to be followers of Jesus as the Christ. So for example when Paul attacks the "judaizers" in Galatians this cannot indicate that Judaism is in the wrong, while Christianity is in the right. On the contrary, what is in view is the faithlessness of Christians who seek to impose, through the law, a form of security upon the risk of faith.

These two forms of faith are not simply alternatives. Christianity is always second while Israel is always first. Nor can Christianity claim to be the last for it too has a "younger brother" in the form of Islam whose emergence is a perduring sign not only of our own failure to demonstrate clearly and persuasively the way of Jesus, but also the sign of the veracity of Paul's warning that the Christian branches can be cut off and new branches grafted onto the root of patriarchal promise and prophetic word (Romans 11:21).

John the Baptizer's question, whether Jesus is the one in whom the hopes generated by divine promise find their fulfillment, is answered in the messianic mission and life-style of Jesus. It remains to be seen whether the community derivative from Jesus can give a similarly persuasive testimony by its mission and form of life.

The claim that Jesus is the Messiah, the Christ, must be demonstrated in the loyalty, the faithfulness of those who make this claim and who cast their lot with him. The weakness and ambiguity of our faithfulness not only serves to legitimate the refusal of Judaism to be persuaded of this claim, but also to provoke the emergence of Islam and its supplanting of Christianity in the lands of its first expansion and success.

Christianity takes its name from the claim that Jesus is the Christ. But we have seen that this claim cannot be a speculative one, a mythological one, or even a merely historical one. It is a question of mission. To claim that Jesus is the Christ is to identify oneself with his mission to announce and enact the inbreaking of the divine reign. Where the claim is separated from faithfulness it becomes empty. Here, as elsewhere, it is not a matter of paying Jesus metaphysical, mythological, or soteriological compliments, but of following him, of commitment to his mission in the world.

CHAPTER SIX

THE SON

To speak of Jesus as the "Son of God" is to speak of Jesus as being completely transparent to the God whom he called "Father." As we have seen, Jesus' words and deeds, his manner of life and teaching, all point to the coming of God in person to liberate and transform the world. It is this transparency to God, to God as the loving Father, that makes Jesus the "Son of God."

1. THE SON OF THE FATHER

Nowhere in the New Testament do we hear more of the sonship of Jesus in relation to the Father than in the Gospel of John. Here the emphasis falls upon the complete transparency of Jesus' word and deed to the God he called Father. The Gospel makes this clear in several ways.

First, what Jesus does is what God does: "The Son can do nothing of his own accord, but only what he sees the Father doing" (John 5:19). "For the works which the Father has granted me to accomplish, these very works which I am doing, bear me witness that the Father has sent me" (5:36). "If I am not doing the works of my Father, then do not believe me" (10:37).

And what is it that Jesus is doing? He is breaking the sabbath law in order to heal and he is forgiving sins (John 5:1-14; 9:1-41). In this action which overcomes the oppressive power of law, of disease, of guilt, Jesus is acting as God acts. It is in this way that he is the Son of the Father.

Second, what Jesus says is what the Father says: "My teaching is not mine, but his who sent me" (7:16). "What I say, therefore, I say as the Father has bidden me" (12:50). "I do nothing on my own authority but speak thus as the Father taught me" (8:28). And what is it that Jesus is saying? That God wills wholeness and healing.

The Gospel of John prepares us in these ways to understand the transparency of Jesus' life and teaching to the rule of God in terms of the relationship of father and son. Thus John records Jesus saying: "I and the Father are one" (10:30) and, "He who has seen me has seen the Father" (14:9). In this way the central section of John's Gospel may be understood as an expansion and explanation of the saying found in Matthew and Luke: "All things have been delivered to me by my Father; and no one knows who the Son is except the Father, or who the Father is except the Son and any one to whom the Son chooses to reveal him." (Luke 10:22; Matthew 11:27). This saying, and its elaboration in the Gospel of John, illustrates that what is at stake in the word and deed of Jesus is nothing less than the identity of God.

When the church in its Creed identifies Jesus as the Son of God it seeks to establish that it relies on no other God than the God whose identity, intention, and deed is made manifest in Jesus of Nazareth. That is why we had to say at the very outset that to speak of God as Father is to speak already of Jesus, for it is in and through Jesus that we are able to speak of God as Father.

2. THE SON AND THE SONS

But to speak in this way of the identity of God is to speak of our own identity as well. The unity of the Son with the Father is by no means a static and self-enclosed identity. It does not ascribe to Jesus a metaphysical identity which is somehow only to be admired, wondered at, or blindly accepted. For this unity of the Father and the Son reaches out to include us as well.

This expansion of the unity of the Father and the Son is one of the primary themes of the "farewell discourse" of John 13–17. Three passages in particular make this theme clear:

> In that day you will know that I am in my Father, and you in me, and I in you (14:20).

> As the Father has loved me, so have I loved you; abide in my love. If you keep my commandments, you will abide in my love, just as I have kept my Father's commandments and abide in his love (15:9-10).

> I do not pray for these only, but also for those who are to believe in me through their word, that they may all be one; even as thou, Father, art in me, and I in thee, that they also may be in us (17:20-21).

These passages already reveal that the unity of the Father and the Son is expanded to include the disciples. Thus, following the resurrection, Jesus can say, "I am ascending to my Father and your Father, to my God and your God" (20:17), and so can tell the disciples, "As the Father sent me, even so I send you" (20:21).

This remarkable group of passages (I have only cited some of the most important) demonstrates that just as the unity of Father and Son is a unity in action, so also the unity of the believer with the Father and the Son is also a unity in action. The disciple also has God for a Father and this means, as it did for Jesus, to love as God loves (John 3:16). Here again the commandment is reduced to its essential form: to love. And the meaning of love is defined by reference to Jesus' own action. Thus we are sent into the world, just as Jesus was, to engage in the work of love and forgiveness (20:22).

Thus our unity with Father and Son is not spoken of as a "status" but as a commission for mission. It is only insofar as we, like Jesus, do as the Father does that we participate in this unity. But as we take on this mission of love and forgiveness, our life and action is permeated by the presence of this unity of Father and Son. We will return to this theme again when we speak of the Holy Spirit, for it is by the Holy Spirit that we are empowered for this task and responsibility.

Let us now summarize the way we have been led by this brief reflection on the Gospel of John.

1. To speak of Jesus as the Son is to speak of him as one whose word and deed is transparent to the word and deed of God.

2. To speak of God as Father is to speak of God as one who wills and does nothing other than what Jesus wills and does.

3. This unity of Father and Son is a unity of word and deed.

4. As such this unity is not primarily a status but a mission. The mission is simply that of love (John 3:16).

5. As a unity of love this unity is by no means a self-enclosed "metaphysical principle" but is a dynamic "unification" which reaches out to the world and to us.

6. That this unity of Father and Son is a unity of love means that we too are included in this unity insofar as we accept the reality and the mission of this love.

7. In this way the Father becomes our Father and Jesus as the Son is no longer our master but our friend (15:14-15).

The unity of the Son with the Father then is the basis for our existence as characterized by freedom (8:36), truth (8:32), life (11:26), joy (15:11), and love (15:12). It is because there is no division, no separation between the Father and the Son, that our freedom is true freedom, that our lives are based on truth rather than illusion and are abundant rather than partial or fragmentary, and are characterized by joy without anxiety, and a love that loves to the end.

3. THE LANGUAGE OF PHILOSOPHY

Accordingly, the Gospel of John testifies that the unity of Father and Son is a unity which is by no means partial or provisional but which extends backward to creation (John 1:1-18) and forward to final consummation (6:35). What this means is that neither in the beginning (creation) nor in the end (resurrection) is God in any way different from that which is discernible in the remembered word and deed of Jesus.

This testimony of faith is articulated in terms of the image of the "Word." This image became decisive for faith because it clarified the identity of Jesus in terms intelligible both for Jewish wisdom and for Hellenistic, especially Stoic and Platonistic, philosophy. Both of these traditions could understand, in terms of their own perspective, the opening verses of the Gospel of John:

> In the beginning was the Word, and the Word was with God, and the Word was God. He was in the beginning with God; all things were made through him, and without him was not anything made that was made. (1:1-3)

Upon this much both Jewish and Greek philosophers could agree. This they already knew or suspected. But the Gospel of John turns this philosophical understanding into a properly theological and evangelical one when it declares:

> And the Word became flesh and dwelt among us, full of grace and truth; we have beheld his glory, glory as of the only Son from the Father. And from his fullness have we all received, grace upon grace. For the law was given through Moses; grace and truth came through Jesus Christ. No one has ever seen God; the only Son, who is in the bosom of the Father, he has made him known. (1:14, 16-18)

In this way the Gospel of John appropriates for faith the vocabulary of philosophical reflection. But in so doing the language of philosophy undergoes a profound transformation. It becomes clear that to speak of creation itself is to speak of that grace and truth which is manifest in Jesus of Nazareth. Thus the world is the sphere and object of the divine love (3:16) and however much the world of humanity may reject this love, its true foundation and meaning, it cannot extinguish that light by which it was made (1:4-5; 10-13). Thus the existence of the community of love bears witness in history to the true foundation and destiny of the world.

The secret of the universe, its origin and end, is manifest not in the laws of nature but in the life of love. As a consequence, that which prefers darkness and illusion to light and truth, that which prefers domination and dependence to responsible freedom, that which prefers division and enmity to love, has chosen death rather than life, for it opposes its own foundation in the love of God.

We can see then that the insistence upon the identity of Jesus as the Son of the Father is no idle metaphysical or cosmological speculation. It is the witness of faith that however much division, darkness, domination, and death appear to rule the earth and our life, they are, nevertheless, a lie. The real structure and essence of reality is the freedom, love, and joy made manifest in the word and action of Jesus and in the community of freedom, love, and joy that is constituted in his name.

4. ONLY SON?

In the Apostles' Creed we say that we believe in Jesus who is the *only* Son. What is the meaning of this "only" which we here affirm? We have seen that the acclamation of Jesus as Son by no means entails that Jesus is the only Son in the sense of separating him from those who are called and commissioned by him to carry on his ministry and mission. It is not only in relation to the Gospel of John that we can see this; it is at the heart of Paul's notion of God as Father: that we are adopted as sons.

What then are we to make of this "only"? I think this "only" serves two related purposes. In the first place it indicates that Jesus is the son in a unique way. This uniqueness is precisely the way in which his sonship is not exclusive, but inclusive. The uniqueness of Jesus' sonship is that it is "contagious," that it extends outward to include and to establish others within the sphere of this identity. Thus when "sonship" is interpreted in such a way as to drive a wedge between Jesus and his followers in the name of a high Christology, then the distinctive feature of Jesus' sonship is abandoned. Only that sonship is the sonship of Jesus which overcomes the temptations of an exclusive identity (Philippians 2:6-8).

To this positive inclusiveness corresponds a negation as well. It is the negation of all who claim sonship in a different way. In the time of the origin of the gospel there were others who were said to be sons of God. Conquerors like Alexander or the most powerful emperors could be called "son of God." But this sonship is clearly of a different order than that which is encountered in Jesus. For in Jesus the sonship is not the legitimation of domination and conquest, but is expressed in a love which seeks nothing for itself but rather gives itself.

In this connection it is important to recall that in the Gospel of Mark the acclamation of Jesus as the Son of God depends on his death on the cross. It is precisely in his utter loss of self, in his abandonment and humiliation—and not in his victory and self-assurance—that he is recognized by the centurion as the Son of God (Mark 15:34; see below, "was crucified").

All attempts to claim divinity on some other basis than that of self-giving love are interdicted by the Creed. The historical context of the emergence of the Creed confirmed the denial that the Caesars, the world rulers, were sons of God. Their sonship was excluded in affirming that of the one who was their victim.

The assertion that Jesus is the only son then should not be taken as a metaphysical claim but as a moral claim:[5] only this sonship is real. This is a sonship that denies itself so as to include others rather than exclude them. Thus it is also a mistake to understand this only as a polemic against other religions. It asserts that the only sonship is the sonship we encounter in Jesus. But this sonship is unique precisely because it does not exclude others but includes them.[6]

Above all, to say that this is the true sonship is to say that it is the sonship which constitutes and serves as the basis and pattern for our own.

CHAPTER SEVEN

THE LORD

I t is this Jesus that we acclaim as Lord. Among the earliest confessions of the community may have been the bare assertion: "Jesus is Lord" (1 Corinthians 12:3), or "Jesus Christ is Lord" (Philippians 2:11). But what is the meaning of calling someone "Lord"? Some may recall that the term is simply one of respect, equivalent to "sir." Others emphasize that it was the common translation of the divine name YHWH for the Greek version of the Hebrew Scriptures. Still others emphasize that it was a title for the emperor in the cult of emperor worship, or the title used in mystery religions for the dying and rising god. All of these and more were possible in the first century. Often the meaning in a particular place must simply be guessed at depending on the context and on the apparent cultural associations of writers and readers.

But the basic and unifying theme of these various possibilities seems to be that to name someone as Lord is to affirm one's loyalty to the one so named. Lordship and loyalty are correlative concepts. The implied loyalty may be rigidified into an acknowledgment of the claim of obedience (as in masters and slaves) or may become simply a token of polite deference (as in "sir"). But what is fundamentally at stake is the implicit acceptance of fealty or loyalty, an adherence to the direction, the leadership, the claim of the other.

The translation of God's name as "Lord" expressed Israel's commitment to remain loyal to, to adhere to, the one who had brought them out of bondage in Egypt. Negatively this means to refuse this loyalty to the "other gods" who sought to give Israel a more secure place in the family of nations. "Lord" is not simply another term for divinity or god. It expresses the affirmation of a loyalty which is born of liberating action and which persists in the face of counter-claims for the loyalty of the people.

Now when lordship is separated from this context of liberation and loyalty, it becomes simply a way of acknowledging one's location within the social pyramid of power and privilege. When viewed in this light, the claim that Jesus is Lord must appear to be bitterly ironic. For Jesus refuses to claim for himself any position of privilege. Indeed he seems to go out of his way to renounce any such claim. When the young ruler comes to him to inquire concerning eternal life, bowing before Jesus and calling him "good master," Jesus seems to refuse this kind of homage, answering that "God alone is good" (Mark 10:18; Luke 18:19). Only God is the proper object of human homage. And this renunciation of homage is carried forward with special consistency in the Gospel of Mark where Jesus regularly responds to acclamations of his special status with commands for silence.

Nor does this appear to be in the least whimsical. Rather it seems to accord with a specific policy, a determined critique of the ideology of lordship. Jesus insists that "the son of man came not to be served but to serve" (Mark 10:45). He does not come to receive homage, but to engage in concrete service to the fellow human.

Nowhere is this more graphically illustrated than in the Gospel of John, where there is the greatest emphasis on the exalted identity of Jesus. For it is precisely here that we encounter the story of Jesus humbling himself before the disciples, stripping himself naked as a slave, and performing the most menial service of washing the feet of the dinner guests (John 13:1-11).

What would it mean to call him Lord? Certainly it would be absurd to suppose that the one who behaves in this way wishes to make any claim concerning a privileged position in the pyramid of power and prestige. If we have these sorts of views in mind when we call Jesus the Lord then our acclamation self-destructs on the word and example of this servant, the one who chooses the form of a slave.

This renunciation goes even further. For Jesus makes absolutely clear that his own renunciation of privilege is to be the pattern for the attitude and action of his understudies or disciples as well.

In the Gospels of Mark and Luke (Mark 9:33-37; Luke 9:46-48), Jesus becomes aware that the disciples were disputing among themselves about who would be "the greatest in the [reign] of God." In Matthew, the disciples actually bring the question to Jesus directly (Matthew 18:1-5). The reported responses of Jesus are as follows:

If any one would be first, he must be last of all and servant of all. (Mark 9:35)

Truly, I say to you, unless you turn and become like children, you will never enter the [reign] of heaven. Whoever humbles himself like this child, he is the greatest in the [reign] of heaven. (Matthew 18:4-5)

> Whoever receives this child in my name receives me, and whoever receives me receives him who sent me; for he who is least among you all is the one who is great. (Luke 9:48)

The replies of Jesus are related in that they point to a reversal in worldly estimation. Whether expressed in the reversal of first and last, in the figure of one who is servant of all, or in the figure of the humble child, the word of Jesus seeks to turn all worldly notions of prestige and privilege upside down.

The same theme occurs in a subsequent episode concerning the "sons of Zebedee." In the Gospel of Mark it is James and John who raise the issue, claiming the privilege to be seated at the right and left of Jesus in his reign (Mark 10:35ff.). In the Gospel of Matthew it is their mother who claims this privilege for them (Matthew 20:20ff.). In the Gospel of Luke no individuals are singled out, rather we have again an anonymous dispute among the disciples (Luke 22:24ff.). The replies in Matthew and Mark are similar, with Luke providing significant variation:

> Whoever would be great among you must be your servant, and whoever would be first among you must be your slave. (Matthew 20:26-27; see Mark 10:43-44; see also Matthew 23:11-12)

> Let the greatest among you become as the youngest, and the leader as one who serves. For which is the greater, one who sits at table, or one who serves? Is it not the one who sits at table? But I am among you as one who serves. (Luke 22:26-27)

Again we have a number of figures that represent the transvaluation of values, the reversal of roles, that corresponds to the reign of God. The servant, the slave, the youngest, the waiter: these are the "greatest" in the reign of God.

And this is not only descriptive but also prescriptive. This is the way the disciples are to behave, this is the greatness they are to emulate: that of the younger rather than the elder, that of the slave rather than the master, that of the least of all. And in this way, precisely in this way, they emulate the example of the one they call "Lord."

With characteristic force the Gospel of John makes this the point of Jesus' washing of the disciples' feet. Jesus himself connects this with the affirmation of his lordship (13:13) and confirms that what he has done is to be an example for them (13:15).

This means that the very principle of lordship as ordinarily construed is abolished within the community of Jesus. It is abolished because Jesus himself renounces this form of lordship. And those who are his understudies must continue this "leveling," this undermining of all forms of worldly privilege and prestige.

That the community of Jesus is one in which all roles of privilege and authority are abolished is expressed in a saying that we find in Matthew in the context of Jesus' critique of the Pharisees:

> But you are not to be called rabbi, for you have one teacher, and you are all brethren. And call no [one] your father on earth, for you have one Father, who is in heaven. Neither be called masters, for you have one master, the Christ. (Matthew 23:8-10)

We have already seen that calling God "Father" means that all patriarchal structures are abolished. But here this is amplified. That Jesus is teacher means that no one can assume the status of teacher. That he is leader means that no one can claim the rank of leadership. The ascription of lordship to Jesus is authentic only insofar as it entails the abolition of all structures of lordship within the community of Jesus. For only so is it possible to emulate the one who has chosen to be servant of all.

A moment's reflection will verify how far the Christian community has been from actually carrying forward the implication of Jesus' lordship. We instead emulate the hierarchical structures of the world, seeking to gain honor. We seek not to serve but to be served. And we have an ongoing lust for titles of honor: father, professor, leader, greatest. Things have changed somewhat from the days of the Middle Ages when Christianity mirrored the hierarchical structures of imperial and feudal society. But is this change the result of closer adherence to the meaning of Jesus' lordship? Or is it instead due to the attempt to conform still to the changing mores of social and institutional structure?

It is in any case clear that the Gospels seek to present a fundamental contrast between the way of Jesus and the way of the world. The point of Jesus' renunciation of privilege for himself and his followers is this contrast with, and critique of, all existing forms of privilege and prestige. The saying just quoted from Matthew undermines the prestige structures of Judaism. And the Gospels report that Jesus' example and instruction to his followers also entails an explicit critique of the gentile structures as well. Thus Jesus sets up an opposition between his community and the community of nations:

> You know that the rulers of the Gentiles [nations] lord it over them, and their great men exercise authority over them. It shall not be so among you (Matthew 20:25-26; see also Mark 10:42-43; Luke 22:25-26).

The abolition of structures of lordship within the community stands in permanent contrast to the way of the world. The inversion of these structures within the community of faith corresponds to the subversion of these structures in the world.

Perhaps the most striking example of such subversion is to be found in the Apocalypse of John where the ideology of emperor worship is expropriated to apply to the "Lamb slain from the foundations of the earth." For here it is the one who was the victim of imperial policy who is acclaimed in the words of the standard adulation of the imperial court: Lord of Lords, King of Kings.

> These are of one mind and give over their power and authority to the beast; they will make war on the Lamb, and the Lamb will conquer them, for he is Lord of lords and King of kings. . . . (Revelation 17:13-14, see also 19:16)

To acclaim Jesus in this way as the Lord is to defy all forms of earthly lordship. It is to subvert the systems of domination. That is, after all, why the early Christians were recognized as a threat to the order of the empire. Their refusal to acknowledge the claims of the imperial ideology go much deeper than a refusal to worship as divine one who is "only a mortal." Rather, the antipathy between the followers of Jesus and all forms of lordship structures, all systems of privilege and prestige, is fundamental and permanent.

To acclaim Jesus as Lord then is to affirm and declare one's loyalty to the one who abolishes all earthly forms of domination and hegemony. It is to follow him in renouncing these structures and in choosing the way of service as the only path to distinction.[7]

Unfortunately the affirmation of the lordship of Jesus has always been subject to fatal distortion. Already in the Gospels we are warned that the claim that Jesus is Lord must not be turned into a way to avoid his call and command. In Matthew we are warned that "not every one who says to me, 'Lord, Lord,' shall enter [into the reign of God], but [the one] who does the will of my Father who is in heaven" (Matthew 7:21). And in Luke, Jesus asks: "Why do you call me 'Lord, Lord,' and not do what I tell you?" (Luke 6:46, author paraphrase).

The affirmation that Jesus is Lord all too readily becomes a way of betraying the claim of Jesus to our loyalty. It becomes a way of sanctifying and perpetrating the structures of privilege and domination which Jesus abolishes, for himself, for the community, for the earth.

But the authentic meaning of the affirmation of faith in Jesus as the Lord is that we pledge ourselves in loyalty to the one who abolishes these structures, that we defy all such structures in the name of the one who is alone worthy of dominion; the one who has renounced it completely.

Paul reminds the Philippians that they are to emulate the one whom they call Lord:

Have this mind among yourselves, which you have in Christ Jesus, who, though he was in the form of God, did not count equality with God a thing to be grasped, but emptied himself, taking the form of a [slave] . . . . Therefore God has highly exalted him and bestowed on him the name which is above every name, that at the name of Jesus every knee should bow, in heaven and on earth and under the earth, and every tongue confess that Jesus Christ is Lord, to the glory of God the Father. (Philippians 2:5-7, 9-11)

The assertion that Jesus Christ is Lord is nothing less than the claim that all forms of human authority are abolished in him (every knee should bow).[8] It is as well the claim that the community is to emulate his example in choosing the form of a servant (or slave) instead of domination. It is in thus subverting the principle of lordship and in renouncing its allures for oneself that Jesus Christ is truly named as Lord.

CONCLUSION

The Apostles' Creed proposes three titles that attest to the identity of the Jesus to whom we pledge our loyalty: Christ, Son, Lord. The theological and ecclesiastical tradition that employs these titles, however, has often interpreted them in ways that run counter to the meaning that they are given in the New Testament itself. They are often taken to designate a kind of separate status for Jesus which divides him from the follower and makes confession an acknowledgment of this status rather than loyalty to the one acclaimed as Christ, Son, and Lord. In our discussion of each of these titles we have seen that the main New Testament texts do not employ these titles in such a way as to drive a wedge between Jesus and the follower, but rather to designate a form of life and mission which is the pattern for the follower. Thus the identification of Jesus as the Christ points to Jesus' mission and ministry, a mission and ministry which the follower is charged to continue. Faith in Jesus as the Christ that does not take on this messianic mission can only be a betrayal of him no matter how cloaked in words of praise for him. This is also true of the identification of Jesus as the Son. Although the Gospel of John emphasizes the unity of Father and Son, it also insists on the participation of the follower in this unity, through the imitation of the practice of the Son. Finally, the acclamation of Jesus as Lord is faithful to the meaning of lordship in the New Testament only insofar as it entails the ongoing renunciation of the prestige and power of earthly lordship within the community of Jesus.

In important respects the Christology of the Bible and the Creeds is an "anti-Christology." That is, it entails the reversal of the dominant theological interpretations of messianic or divine identity. Although it is sometimes noticed that Jesus reverses the features of messianic expectation in contemporary Judaism, the irony of the assertion that he is the Christ is immediately forgotten. This is also true of the assertion that the servant of all is the lord, or that the victim is the son.

A biblical reading of the Creed will not let us forget the irony that is necessarily involved in acclaiming Jesus as Christ, Son, and Lord. And the interpretation of these titles within the context of the Creed will necessarily focus on them not as designations of Jesus' privileged identity, but as attestations of loyalty to his mission, his practice, his way.

PART TWO: DANGEROUS MEMORY

Conceived, Born, Suffered, Crucified, Dead and Buried

While the second article of the Creed begins with a recital of the titles by which Jesus is known in the community of faith it continues with a series of verbal clauses that designate the activity of God in Jesus which clarify further what it means to affirm our loyalty to him. This is in fact a double series of clauses. The first which ends with "dead and buried" places us before the "dangerous memory" of faith regarding the life and death of this Jesus.[1] The second series indicates how this dangerous memory bridges from the past to the future so as to become the interpretive framework for the life of faith in the present. Thus it is characteristic of this sequence that "dead and buried" stands not at the end but at the center of the series as a whole.

While crucifixion and resurrection are the pivotal themes of Christian proclamation and so must receive the greater stress in our interpretation of the Creed, it is still true that other dimensions of the gospel related to these basic themes are important and must be attended to in the discussion of the Creed. We begin then with the dangerous memory that is concerned with the beginning and the end of Jesus' mission.

With this set of verbs (conceived, born, suffered, crucified, dead and buried) we recall the fate of the Jesus whom we have acclaimed as the Lord. In many ways it is the narrative history of every person; all are conceived and born, all suffer and die. Yet this common plot line of life is historically modified by reference to Mary and Pilate and by the decisive reference to the manner of origin (Holy Spirit) and end (crucified).

It is characteristic of the creedal formulation that the reference here is to the beginning and end of the life of Jesus. There is nothing here of the typical features of his ministry and mission, the healing and exorcizing, the teaching and preaching, the companionship and celebrative form of life. All this is already presupposed in the reference to Jesus who was the Christ, as we have seen. Now the focus shifts to beginning and end and so to what it means to be loyal to the one whose beginning and end is here described in this strange way.

CHAPTER EIGHT

CONCEIVED AND BORN

The language of incarnation which characterizes the prologue to John's Gospel (as well as Colossians, and to a lesser extent Ephesians) is the key to an appropriation by faith of the philosophical conceptuality of Word and of Creation, as well as for an understanding of the meaning of Jesus as the Son. The vocabulary to which we now turn is quite different. It is the language of legend, known to us from stories about significant figures of history (Alexander the Great, to take an example well known to the first century). Yet this language, too, is appropriated by faith to give testimony to the meaning and reality of Jesus of Nazareth.

There are many who prefer the philosophical vocabulary of John to the vocabulary of legend to which we now turn. They regard the prologue to the Gospels of Matthew and Luke as crude and superstitious in comparison to the lofty and sophisticated heights attained by John. Yet that preference may very well conceal a misunderstanding of John—a refusal to see that John transforms philosophical discourse into the discourse of faith. It is not the philosophical vocabulary but its appropriation for faith which is the point of the prologue.

The same principle holds true for the language of legend to which we now turn in the Gospels of Matthew and Luke. There are those who prefer these stories to the philosophical poem of John, who feel most at home with tales of wonder and miracle and only shudder at the cold heights of the philosophic logos. Yet here, too, a profound misunderstanding lies in wait for the unwary. Luke and Matthew are as little concerned with legend for its own sake as John is interested in an autonomous philosophical discourse.

In truth we are not dealing with philosophy as such in John or with legend as such in Matthew and Luke. Rather, we are confronted with the testimony of faith to the gospel, a testimony that has nothing to do with the idle curiosity and credulity of legend or with the speculation and sophistication of philosophy, but is concerned solely with the expression (by any means available) of the good news of God's coming to the world to deliver and to transform.

In this appropriation of the discourses of legend and of philosophy, faith makes use of the Pauline principle of becoming "all things to all" (1 Corinthians 10:33) in order that by whatever means some may be persuaded of the truth that most intimately concerns them and the world of which they are a part. If this means communicating the gospel in terms of speculative logos in order to reach those who are already persuaded of this logos, so be it. If this means using the vocabulary of legend to capture the attention of the superstitious or adventurous, so be it. In either case, one is operating as "a liar but truthful" (2 Corinthians 6:8). One is using the given language in order to express that which transcends that language. Faith has no "natural" language. It is in any discourse like the son of man, with no place to lie his head (Matthew 8:20). This is true because of the way in which the message of faith exceeds given discourses, and in being thus articulated, actually subverts them and at the same time gives them fresh power and creativity.

It is this "evangelical" principle which must be the basis of our understanding of these phrases "conceived by the Holy Spirit and born of the virgin Mary." Just as it is true at every step of the way in our interpretation of the Creed so also here we must beware of importing content into these phrases from our own speculations and whims, instead of governing our reflections by the witness of faith.

CONCEIVED BY THE HOLY SPIRIT

What does it mean for faith to confess that Jesus was conceived by the Holy Spirit, to confess that it relies upon and is loyal to the Jesus whom it designates in this way?[2] It is first necessary to clarify at once that we do not say that we believe in, or rely upon, either this conception or the "virgin birth." Instead we say that we believe in or rely on or will be faithful to Jesus Christ the Son of God. It is by way of saying which Jesus it is upon whom we rely that we speak of this origin. The miracle in which we believe is the miracle of Jesus, his message and action, his mission and ministry. Our faith is not a believing "that" but a believing "in" and so a relying upon and faithfulness to this Jesus.

The Conception of Jesus

Yet it is precisely in testimony to this Jesus that two of the authors of the New Testament speak of Jesus as conceived by the Holy Spirit and born of the virgin Mary. The order of the Creed itself confirms that we do not confess Jesus as the Son of God *because* of the manner of Jesus' birth. Certainly the Gospel of John, which is primarily concerned with the identity of Jesus as the Son of God, makes no mention whatever of the manner of his birth. It is because Jesus is the Son of God, that is, wholly transparent to God, that we also may speak in this way of Jesus' birth.

What does conceived by the Holy Spirit mean for the New Testament witnesses themselves? They were aware, of course, that this manner of speaking had been employed before them to describe the origin of heroes and kings.[3] The mysterious or astonishing birth of the hero functioned to foreshadow their astonishing exploits or legitimated their claim to absolute obedience. Do we find something similar in the accounts of Jesus' birth, or is something else at stake?

In the Gospel of Luke we begin not with the astonishing birth of Jesus, but with that of John the Baptizer. As in the Gospel of Mark, the first figure is that of the mysterious prophet who preceded Jesus in announcing the coming of the divine rule. Throughout Luke's "prologue" the birth of John and that of Jesus are tied together (as, later, is their mission and their death). In the case of John we are told of the miraculous conception in a barren womb reminiscent of the birth of Isaac to Abraham and Sarah as recounted in Genesis (18:10). In the case of Jesus, the maiden Mary conceives a son. In both cases the news of conception is brought by an angel or messenger of God; in both cases the impending birth is taken as a sign of the advent of the divine rule.

It is in fact this coming of the divine reign that is at the heart of the story of this double conception and birth, these two mothers, these two astonishing figures of John and Jesus. The meaning of this double event is the coming of the reign of God. Thus the long-awaited future in which God would deliver God's people begins to take place in the unexpected pregnancies of these two kinswomen. The interpretation of this event in terms of messianic expectation is provided by the text itself through the language of the angelic announcement:

> And he will turn many of the sons of Israel to the Lord their God, and he will go before him in the spirit and power of Elijah, to turn the hearts of the fathers to the children, and the disobedient to the wisdom of the just, to make ready for the Lord a people prepared. (Luke 1:16-17)

And with respect to Jesus:

> He will be great, and will be called the Son of the Most High; and the Lord God will give to him the throne of his father David, and he will reign over the house of Jacob for ever; and of his [reign] there will be no end. (Luke 1:32-33)

It is remarkable that in both cases the birth of the child is interpreted by the messenger in terms of conventional Jewish apocalyptic expectation. This expectation will be revised, criticized, and corrected at several points in Luke's narrative (4:24-27; Acts 1:6-8). But at this point the births of John and Jesus are interpreted as the inauguration of the restoration of Israel itself. This interpretation is echoed by Mary (1:46-55) and by Zechariah (1:68-79).

The consequence is that these births are understood to be important not for their own sakes, but for the sake of that which they anticipate—namely, that God will deliver God's people. This is precisely the same point made in Matthew's Gospel by the name which Joseph gives to Mary's child: "Jesus, for he will save his people from their sins" (Matthew 1:21, 25).

Born from Above

The idea of being conceived by the Holy Spirit receives a new and far-reaching interpretation in the Gospel of John. John's interpretation makes explicit that which is implicit in Luke, namely that the reality created by the Spirit is faith and that this faith is itself the sign of the coming of God. This interpretation is conveyed in the discussion that Jesus has with Nicodemus in John 3:1-21. The critical passage is verses 5-8:

> Jesus answered, "Truly, truly, I say to you, unless one is born of water and the Spirit, he cannot enter the kingdom [reign] of God. That which is born of the flesh is flesh, and that which is born of the Spirit is spirit. Do not marvel that I said to you, 'You must be born [from above].' The wind [spirit] blows where it wills, and you hear the sound of it, but you do not know whence it comes or whither it goes; so it is with every one who is born of the Spirit."

What this passage asserts is that *all* must be born of the Spirit and that whoever is born in this way is a mystery or miracle. Furthermore this discussion confirms that what is at stake in this birth is faith in Jesus as the crucified (vv. 14-15). If we accept John's understanding then, "conceived by the Holy Spirit" is a phrase that applies to all who rely upon Jesus.[4]

Once again the true miracle here is the miracle that we may and do rely upon God and that we are permitted, called, and empowered to do this on account of Jesus who is the crucified. Thus the "miracle" is the rule of God (it is in connection with this interpretation that John makes one of the two references in this Gospel to the notion of the reign of God [3:5]). That reign is already present in the person of Jesus and the continuing sign of that reign is the mysterious reality of the believer as one who is born from above. Thus as signs which already anticipate that reign, both Jesus and the believer may be spoken of as having the Spirit as the agent of their birth. With Jesus this is true (in Matthew and Luke) from the very beginning, since his entire life is this sign of God's reign and is the basis for our glad acceptance of the gospel, and so of our spiritual origin, our being also born of the Spirit.

Both for Jesus and for us this "spirited" birth entails a commission. We have already seen this in connection with Jesus' conception in the Gospel of Luke (1:32-33) and Matthew (1:21). That this is true for us as well is illustrated by John 20:21-23:

> Jesus said to them again, "Peace be with you. As the Father has sent me, even so I send you." And when he had said this, he breathed on them, and said to them, "Receive the Holy Spirit. If you forgive the sins of any, they are forgiven; if you retain the sins of any, they are retained."

According to John, the disciples of Jesus first receive the Spirit here and this reception of the Spirit is understood as their commissioning as well, in this case having to do with the forgiveness of sins. Thus the notion of spiritual birth refers not to a status but to a task, a commission, both for Jesus and for us.

This is also the theme of the baptism narratives, which, unlike the birth narratives, are common to all four Gospels. In his baptism Jesus becomes the first to be baptized "by water and the spirit."[5] He not only enters into the Jordan, but also receives the Spirit coming to him as a dove (Matthew 3:16; Mark 1:10; Luke 3:22; John 1:32). And this baptism by the Spirit is also understood as an adoption and commissioning. He is adopted and commissioned to be the Son, to represent the reign of God (Matthew 3:17; Mark 1:11; Luke 3:23; John 1:34). This is a commission that will subsequently be entrusted to the follower as well, as we have seen in our discussion of the meaning of "sonship" above.

Although the clause "conceived by the Holy Spirit" has often been interpreted in light of christological dogma as referring to the divinity of Jesus as the Son of God, this must be regarded as an error. On the terms even of conventional Christology Jesus is not regarded as Son of the Spirit but as Son of the Father. Moreover the divinity of the Son cannot be regarded as originating with conception. Thus it is best to abandon the attempt to link conceived by the Holy Spirit directly with the divinity of Jesus and instead focus, as all the relevant New Testament texts do, on mission as the meaning of this conception. Accordingly we will return to the notion of conception by the Spirit when we consider the meaning of faith in the Holy Spirit.

BORN OF THE VIRGIN MARY

In speaking of the origin of Jesus, the Creed mentions a double beginning or source; on the one hand the Spirit, on the other, Mary.

The theme of Mary has always been an important and controversial one in the life of the Church. It is not possible to enter into a discussion of the controversial questions either in the New Testament context (Mark 3:31 following and parallels) or in the patristic (*theotokos*) disputes, or in the controversy between Protestants and Catholics relative to the proper respect for and/or adoration of the virgin, or in the disputes between fundamentalists and liberals concerning what may best be termed the gynecology of the text. Instead we will concentrate our attention in the direction indicated by the Creed and by the narratives of Matthew and Luke (the only places in the New Testament where this is made a subject for reflection).

a) Son of Mary. We begin by noticing that which is most obvious and therefore most often overlooked, namely, that from a social and historical point of view Jesus must be regarded as "illegitimate."[6] This point of view becomes the explicit theme of reflection in the Gospel of Matthew, where Matthew reports that Joseph, upon discovering that Mary was pregnant, resolved to divorce her quietly—or rather to terminate their engagement (1:19). This means that Mary's pregnancy could be regarded, and actually was regarded, as a cause for shame. In the culture of that time had Joseph actually divorced her, Mary would most likely have had to undertake the vocation of prostitution to support herself and her child. It is significant in this regard that Jesus had particular compassion for prostitutes who were generally the victims both of men's lust and of society's contempt and social hypocrisy.

The "illegitimacy" of Jesus' origin precisely corresponds to our own situation. For as Gentiles who originally had no place in God's covenant or promise we have been adopted and so made legitimate by God's own act. The gospel of divine grace by which we live has already been foreshadowed in the apparent illegitimacy of Jesus. Both Jesus and his followers are from a human standpoint "outside the law" and thus in this technical sense "illegitimate." But for Jesus, as well as for us, God's sovereign grace is made manifest in such a way as to be good news for all those who are excluded or marginalized by the legal structures of privilege and respectability. For Jesus comes to save not the righteous, the "legitimate," but the "sinners," the "illegitimate," whom the righteous condemn and exclude (Matthew 9:13; Mark 2:17; Luke 5:32).

b) Mary as the Prototype of Faith and the Church. She is, according to Luke's Gospel, the first to believe and trust the good news concerning Jesus: "Let it be to me according to your word" (Luke 1:38). This is not only the expression of her own faith, but also opens the way for the one who gives birth to faith in all of us. Moreover, the role of Mary in these narratives is depicted as remembering and reflecting upon the events that inaugurate the gospel (Luke 2:19, 51). This corresponds to the task of the inner life of the Church, which is precisely to keep the memory of these events fresh and to reflect upon their meaning. In our worship and in our study we imitate Mary in precisely this respect.

It is in this light as well that we can understand Jesus' saying that "whoever does the will of God is my brother, and sister, and mother" (Mark 3:35, Matthew 12:50). There is much that is astonishing and controversial about this passage, but for our purposes it is enough to notice that those who do the will of God may be called the mothers of Jesus. Church tradition has formalized the role of Mary as the mother of Jesus by calling her "the mother of God" (*theotokos*).[7] But this saying of Jesus indicates that *all* who do the will of God may be termed his mothers. We have already seen that this will is concentrated in the command to love. It is also expressed in the Great Commission (Matthew 28:19-20). Those who are commissioned to awaken and nurture faith are, properly speaking, the mothers of Jesus. While this commission applies to all Christians, in the historical Church it is the particular responsibility of pastors and preachers. We are forbidden to call anyone father (although we break this rule both in our families and even in our churches). If we were to take the words of Jesus in the literal sense we would call all those who awaken and nurture faith not fathers but mothers. Certainly we must accept that we are charged with this maternal task and responsibility for the community of faith.

In this connection it must be regarded as a subversion of the gospel when it is said that women may not be pastors. That this is said by the very branch of Christendom which traditionally places so much stress on the role and person of Mary, is testimony to the obstinacy that characterizes the would-be followers of Jesus.

c) The Humanity of Jesus. That we confess our faith in the Jesus who was born of the virgin Mary further emphasizes the earthly and worldly character both of Jesus and of his disciples.[8] In the early Church there were many who came to be so impressed by the ascription of divinity to

Jesus as Son of God that they were led to deny his earthly and human reality. They were led to do so on the basis of a severe renunciation of earth and body (and, not incidentally, of women). These Gnostics, as some of them were called, claimed to have secret knowledge of a higher reality and supposed that on account of that knowledge they would escape the confines of body and earth to live forever in a heavenly realm. The Church found in Gnosticism its greatest temptation and its greatest foe. This was especially true since the Gnostics claimed to be Christians of a superior sort, to know the hidden truth of Christianity. The battle against Gnosticism was fought on many fronts. We have already encountered the phrase "Maker of Heaven and Earth" which was used as a powerful weapon against the Manichean form of the Gnostic heresy. The phrase "born of the virgin Mary" has played a similar role in the struggle against "docetic" denials of the true and full humanity of Jesus.[9]

The Docetists denied the full humanity of Jesus, and thus the fact that Mary was his mother, because they knew that any serious recognition of the humanity of Jesus would involve faith in the sphere of the earthly and bodily—the very sphere from which they wished to escape by means of a completely "spiritual" interpretation of faith. In asserting "born of the virgin Mary," faith rejects this understanding of Jesus and of faith in his name. We rely not upon some ethereal being but upon the one "who was born of the virgin Mary."

d) The Christmas Hope. Thus faith is directed resolutely to the earthly and bodily reality of our world and life. We hope not for escape from this reality but for its real and public, its radical and total transformation. Few words of the Bible express this hope more vigorously than the words of Mary herself in the Magnificat (which echoes the prayer of Hannah in 1 Samuel 2:1-10 on the occasion of the astonishing birth of Samuel):

> He has shown strength with his arm, he has scattered the proud in the imagination of their hearts, he has put down the mighty from their thrones, and exalted those of low degree; he has filled the hungry with good things, and the rich he has sent empty away. (Luke 1:51-53)

This is the central meaning of Advent and Christmas. Here we celebrate not the tinsel and satisfaction of the rich and powerful, given public display in store windows and television advertisements, but the fulfillment of the hope of the poor and oppressed who long for justice and dignity. Only those who share this longing can receive the message of Christmas with joy; for it is to these, like the shepherds who are poor and outcast and treated with contempt, that the divine messengers bring tidings of great joy. It is precisely to them and for them that this child is born, whose birthplace is a filthy stable, whose destiny is the place where they execute criminals and revolutionaries.

And it is precisely these "little ones" at the margin of society who have always heard this message most gladly and who hear it most gladly today. All too often the Church has allied itself with the rich and the powerful, and turned the good news into bad news for the poor. Yet in all its long history of forgetfulness and even apostasy, the Church has, like Mary, kept alive the memory of this glad tidings. This survival of the dangerous memory of Christmas in spite of forgetfulness and apostasy is an important part of the meaning of Christmas.

And today, as on that holy night, as the planet spins beneath the stars, a great sigh of longing arises from the burdened hearts and bodies of millions upon millions of "these little ones." To them we are entrusted with the message, "unto you a child is born . . . a savior." To all who will become, or who already are, like these little ones, there is the beginning of joy in the world. Even for those of us who by the world's standards are rich and powerful there can come this joy if only we enter into the longing of those who hunger and thirst for the divine justice.

But for those who do not share their longing and their joy, there is another name in the Creed and in the story of Jesus: the name of Pontius Pilate.

CHAPTER NINE

SUFFERED UNDER
PONTIUS PILATE

Three people are mentioned in the Creed: Jesus, Mary, and Pilate. Both Mary and Pilate testify in very different ways to the identity of Jesus. The story concerning Mary and the story concerning Pilate stand at the beginning and at the end of Jesus' life. The one his mother, the other his executioner; a memory of honor for the peasant woman whose pregnancy seemed from a human point of view a cause of shame, and of shame for the proud ruler whose position as agent of the world's most powerful empire seemed so honorable. Already with the mention of these names it is clear that the poor have been exalted and the proud brought low (Luke 1:52).

What do we learn from the astonishing figure of Pontius Pilate, whose name is repeated whenever Christians joyously and defiantly affirm their faith using the words of the Creed? With the name of Mary we hear of the hope of advent and the joy of Christmas. With Pontius Pilate we hear of those who share neither this hope nor this joy, and so we enter into the mourning of Lent.

1. This name reminds us first of all that with Jesus of Nazareth we are concerned with a particular man who lived at a particular moment in human history.[10] This time is marked by the names of its rulers: Caesar Augustus, the shining sun of the Roman Empire, honored as a god, Quirinius, governor of Syria, Herod the Great and Herod Antipas, kings in Galilee and Judea—and Pontius Pilate. All of these play their part in the drama which unfolds here and to which faith turns to discover its origin and foundation.

It finds this origin, not in myth and legend, but in the sphere of human history, the sphere of war and conquest, of intrigue and dominion, of power politics and imperial force. It is this world that is designated by the name "Pontius Pilate." We then remember that the sphere of faith and the sphere of political history intersect one another.

This, of course, is already true for the faith of Israel, which finds its bearings in this sphere. Neither Israel nor the Church can escape history, for it is in history that God acts to deliver the chosen people from slavery in Egypt, to grant them the conquest of the land of the Canaanites, to raise up great kings like David and Solomon, to send prophets to meddle in affairs of state, to subject Israel to conquest at the hands of Assyria and Babylon, to deliver the people from exile by the generosity of the Persian emperor. From beginning to end, the faith of Israel is faith in the God who is at work in the world of political history.

That our faith is not a faith in a different God is remembered here in the Creed, as it was also in the Gospels, with the name of Pontius Pilate. Thus we are reminded that Christianity is not a religion of the timeless eternal but of timely history. In this it is distinguished from many of the religions of the world that care nothing for history, but rather seek in myth and cult and philosophy an escape from the sphere of political history and so from the suffering which is encountered in this sphere.

2. To be reminded of Jesus in time and history is to be reminded that he "suffered," for history is the sphere of actual human misery, of oppression and conflict, of hunger and death. Into this world—a world that is also ours—Jesus came, and in this world he suffered, as those who come into this world always do.

By entering history (and precisely this history, the history of domination and division) God the Son in the life of Jesus of Nazareth accepts the lot of humanity, actually casting God's lot with us and accepting human suffering as the divine destiny as well. For long ages the voice of suffering humanity has been raised to the heavens: "Why do the just suffer?" "How long, O Lord?" How could God in God's power and goodness permit this long and anguished cry which rises from our planet with every breath of a wounded creation, a disgraced creature, a shackled humanity? And the answer of faith is that God is not out there beyond the starry sky, unaware of and untouched by the wailing of an abandoned child. God is in the very midst of suffering, not as its cause but as its victim! And the voice that protests against this suffering is God's own voice. Behold then, God: dishonored, shamed, whipped, spat upon, tortured, bloody, scorned, abandoned, dying. Behold the human! Behold our God!

It is thus an astonishing phrase that we encounter in the Creed that we use to affirm our loyalty to this God, "Suffered under Pontius Pilate." To the abandoned child wailing in the city street, the mother weeping over her stillborn infant, the man moaning in the torture cell, the parent with no food or medicine to give a dying child, the Indian hunted down by the rancher's dogs, the one betrayed by a friend—to all the wounded and suffering, despised and dishonored, the gospel points to Jesus and says, "Behold your suffering, behold your God!"

Perhaps we do not want a God like this. Perhaps we prefer to dream of a god beyond our suffering, an unmoved mover, or a first or final cause. Philosophy and myth will be happy to provide us with any number of other gods, more imperial, more omnipotent, more heroic, more impassive. We sometimes prefer to dream of the divine hero, who at the last minute takes out his sword and fights his way out of the torture chamber. If so, Hollywood or the other dream factories of our civilization will happily provide us with such heroes. Both in ancient and modern times we long for a different god, a different lord, a different exemplar of our humanity. But in the Creed and in the Gospels, God gives a different answer, follows a different path—a path into the heart of human suffering, away from the dreams and into the tortured flesh of our reality. As long as we keep our gaze fixed here we shall not be led to exchange dreams for reality. We cannot close our eyes to the reality of suffering, for it is the reality chosen by the one we name Lord and Christ. And the path he walks here is the one he bids us to follow.

For all who know the reality of human suffering, for all who cannot escape that reality, for those for whom no dreams can assuage the pain of life, the message that God walked and still walks this path is the occasion of wonder:

> Who has believed what we have heard? And to whom has the arm of the Lord been revealed?
>
> He was despised and rejected by [all]; a man of sorrows, and acquainted with grief; and as one from whom [all] hide their faces he was despised, and we esteemed him not. (Isaiah 53:1, 3)

The affirmation of faith in the Jesus who suffered distinguishes Christian faith from those religions that seek either to deny or to escape from suffering, and so to deny the importance of, or to escape from, the realm of history and the world. In the Creed we affirm that we commit ourselves not to the divinity of our dreams of escape or success, but to the one who suffers and who actually did suffer under Pontius Pilate.

3. Yet it is not just any form of suffering and death of which we speak here. The religious imagination has long given itself over to embellishment upon the theme of suffering, of the man of sorrows acquainted with grief. Yet this rich, if often maudlin, vein of religious poetry must not be permitted to distract us from the essential feature of Jesus' suffering; that it is suffering "under Pontius Pilate." There is nothing here in the Creed to warrant psychologizing or poeticizing Jesus' suffering. It is quite clear what sort of suffering is meant—the suffering made evident in the

Gospels themselves: betrayal, interrogation, condemnation, derision, torture, execution. The Gospels leave us no alternative but to speak of the suffering of the political prisoner.

The degree to which this is strange or foreign to us is the measure of how far we are from a simple and obedient attention to the plainest assertions of Bible and Creed. We don't want to speak of governors and soldiers, of the political and military sphere. We would often prefer to speak of a suffering that is thoroughly "religious" or "spiritual" rather than political. But should we do so we would cut ourselves off from any relation to the suffering which is here indicated in the Creed and remembered by the Gospels. When we speak of Jesus who suffered under Pontius Pilate and was crucified, this sphere of political confrontation is at the center of attention.[11]

When we affirm our faith, we say that we rely upon and are loyal to this Jesus whose life and death have this definite relation to Pontius Pilate and thus to this sphere of political history. The relation of Jesus (and thus of God) to this sphere is expressed in a single word: suffered. That is, it is a relation of opposition and contradiction. The way of Jesus is the way of the cross, and thus the way of opposition between the reign of God and the reign of Caesar; the contradiction between the way of love for the oppressed and the way of the power of domination and division. That God is committed to the poor and oppressed we know quite clearly from the words of the law and the prophets. But here we encounter something even more astonishing: those who exercise worldly power are revealed publicly as the torturers of God.

And this is at the same time good news for everyone who lives under the power of these earthly authorities. The gospel says that these powers are not sanctioned or legitimated by God, they are not eternal, they do not express the will of God. Rather, they are opposed by God, opposed with life and blood by means of Jesus, God's Son. Thus it is possible to have hope. And with hope comes as well the possibility of protesting against the dominion of these powers.

Whenever we affirm our faith, we affirm that we rely upon the same Jesus whose life and death stands in this peculiar relationship to Pontius Pilate, a relationship of confrontation, contradiction, and thus of suffering.

4. The suffering of which we speak here is not a sort of blind fate that accidentally or even inevitably overtakes Jesus. Jesus is not merely the victim of historical forces. Rather, the Gospels make clear that he chooses this path, that he deliberately sets out on the way that leads to Pontius Pilate, to suffering and to death. The narrators of the Gospels portray Jesus as one who deliberately chooses the path to Jerusalem, knowing

full well that this path must lead to confrontation and conflict, to rejection and condemnation, to suffering and death (Mark 8:31; 9:31; 10:33-34). Indeed, the hymn that Paul quotes in his letter to the Christians of Philippi even speaks of the incarnation as the deliberate choice of this path, when it refers to Christ Jesus.

> Who, though he was in the form of God, did not count equality with God a thing to be grasped, but emptied himself, taking the form of a [slave], being born in the likeness of [humanity]. And being found in human form he humbled himself and became obedient unto death, even death on a cross. (Philippians 2:6-8)

Thus the entire career of Jesus from his birth (and indeed from the divine decision that is the ground of his existence) is the way that leads to this suffering and death. Wherever we place the beginning of Jesus, whether in his inaugural sermon (Luke 4) or his baptism, or his birth, or in the inner election and decision of the Godhead, that beginning points deliberately to this end.

The actual ministry in Jerusalem is one of calculated defiance of the authorities. His ride upon the gates of the city hailed as a king, his blockade of the Temple are actions calculated to outrage those who are the guardians of both City and Temple. This defiance continues in Jesus' confrontational tactics in dialogue with the various representatives of the Jerusalem power structure. In these disputes he manages to systematically alienate the scribes, priests, and elders (Mark 11:27ff.), the Herodians and Pharisees (12:13ff.) and the Sadducees (Mark 12:18ff.). His behavior at the trials continues this pattern, for he does not rebut any of the charges brought against him, however outrageous they may have been. And when the testimony given against him seems inadequate to convict him, Jesus speaks in such a way as to convict himself (Mark 14:62; 15:2).

Jesus is no passive victim of history, but has chosen the path which leads to Pontius Pilate and so to suffering and death. In his passion, Jesus is not "passive" but acts to provoke the hostility of the structures that guard the status quo.

5. In the Creed we do not simply say that we believe that Jesus suffered under Pontius Pilate, but that we are loyal to the Jesus who suffered in this way. This means that we affirm our own commitment to take upon ourselves the contradiction between the reign of God and the reign of worldly power. We affirm our willingness to accept the cost of this contradiction and to bring it out into the open. The turn of Jesus to Jerusalem marks also the training of the disciples to take up this same path: to go knowingly toward their own time of persecution and martyrdom, to accept as well the burden of the cross.

Thus, in his "apocalyptic discourse" Jesus can warn his followers that they, too, will be delivered over to judges, to councils, and to kings (Mark 13:9). And in thus being delivered over they will become the instruments of the proclamation of the good news concerning the reign of God "to all nations" (Mark 13:10-11).

There can be no following of Jesus which does not accept the appropriateness of witness which is also martyrdom.[12]

That is why the Creed is the Creed. It is a pledge of resistance, to the death, against all the powers that destroy God's creature, against all that opposes the reign of justice and generosity and joy. It is no harmless moment, but a point of utter defiance of these powers when we confess, "I believe . . . in Jesus . . . who suffered under Pontius Pilate."

EXCURSUS: FAITH AND POLITICS

We must be careful here not to demonize either the Roman Empire in general, or Pontius Pilate in particular. It is quite clear that the Roman Empire represented perhaps the most enlightened form of government that had yet been seen in the world. The development of Roman law and the genius of the empire for military, economic, and political organization, together with the policy of toleration for religious and cultural differences which it inherited from Alexander the Great, have made a permanent mark upon human history. The commitment of the empire to legal justice is given tribute in Romans 13:1-8.

Moreover, the narratives of the evangelists demonstrate that Pontius Pilate was not to be regarded as a bloodthirsty tyrant, but rather as an administrator sensitive to the currents of opinion and passion that characterized the people it was his duty to govern.[13]

This relatively benign picture of Rome and of Pilate could produce a view of Jesus and of Christianity allied with the civilizing forces represented by Rome and by Pilate. The effect, however, is precisely the opposite. For what becomes evident in this perspective is that there is a fundamental conflict between Jesus and even the most enlightened forms of earthly rule. For it is, after all, Pilate and not some blood-drenched maniac who orders the execution of Jesus. And it is precisely this enlightened form of government that discovers in Jesus and his movement a threat equivalent to that of terrorism and slave revolt.

Is this opposition merely a case of tragic misunderstanding? Or is it the inevitable consequence of forces which, however "humanitarian" they may seem, are nevertheless irrevocably and inexorably opposed? The historical events and the Gospel narratives leave us in no possible doubt in which direction our interpretation must go. Jesus and Pilate are not and can never become allies.

Precisely here we must confront the radicality of Jesus' claim, his message, and his way. The radicality of this way strips away the mask of just and enlightened government to reveal the secret and hidden reality of domination and division.[14] For no matter what benefits are conferred by this government (and they are no doubt both real and impressive) we must nevertheless not forget the insistence of earthly rule that it preserve itself, preserve its own power and privilege. Indeed, it cannot cease to do this without ceasing to be government. Yet the path chosen by Jesus is a path that entails the abolition of power, authority, and privilege in favor of the path of friendship, service, and self-giving love.

We must be clear that to say that even the most enlightened government is at root in opposition to the gospel does not entail that it makes no difference what form the opposition takes—that we are condemned in this matter to the night in which all cats are equally gray.

There is a very notable difference between the attitude taken by the New Testament to the person of Pilate and to the empire in its most virulent opposition, as in the Apocalypse of John. The differences are respected, nuances preserved, distinctions made. We must also remark upon the restraint with which the fundamental opposition becomes visible in the Gospels. We do encounter revolutionary invective in the Apocalypse of John. But this is missing from the Gospels and from other New Testament writings. The radicality of the perspective of the Gospels is measured not in terms of rhetoric, but in terms of actual martyrdom. But both the Gospels and the Apocalypse maintain that the empire is in conflict with the reign of God. Nothing is more difficult to sustain than a radical critique of the principle of earthly rule, on the one hand, and an appropriate recognition of the differences in which this rule manifests itself on the other. But this is what these texts require of us.

CHAPTER TEN

WAS CRUCIFIED

With this clause of the Creed we enter into the very center of Christian faith.[15] When we speak of the cross we are not speaking of one event in the career of Jesus, alongside of which we may place others (for example his parables or his healings). Nor are we speaking of one doctrine among others. There can be no Christian theology which is not at every point a theology of the cross. There can be no faith which is not a reliance upon and loyalty to the crucified. There can be no following of Jesus which is not a taking up of this same cross. This is the meaning of Paul's reminder to the Corinthians: "For I decided to know nothing among you except Jesus Christ and him crucified" (1 Corinthians 2:2).

Nor is this Paul's view alone. The four Gospels all point in the same direction. Each of these texts is constructed in such a way that the crucifixion of Jesus shapes and determines the narrative as a whole. Each punctuates the ministry of Jesus with anticipations of the cross as the fitting destiny of the one who undertakes the mission of announcing and actualizing the reign of God. And each gives more careful attention to the story of Jesus' death (the Passion narrative) than to other events. It is as if already for the second and third generation of Christians it had become urgent to make clear that interpretations of faith that forgot the centrality of the cross were fundamental distortions of the gospel.

It must be admitted that this decisive principle is regularly ignored and even repressed from consciousness altogether in much contemporary Christianity. In the life of the Church the meditation on the cross is often relegated to Holy Week. Consequently, the majority of Christians pass directly from Palm Sunday, with its celebration of Jesus' "triumphal entry into Jerusalem" to Easter and its celebration of the resurrection of Jesus. This move from victory to victory without passing through the contradiction of the cross produces the anti-gospel of success and "positive-thinking." In that respect, the situation of the earliest Church and our own are alike. For both appear to be characterized by the temptation to forget the centrality of the cross. To the Church, both then and now, the writings of the New Testament are addressed—to remind us that there is no Christianity without the cross.

Distortion occurs not only in the life of the Church, but also in its theology when doctrines are developed in independence from one another, with the doctrine of "atonement" simply standing alongside other doctrines like creation, providence, and so on. The result of such theological isolation is catastrophic. Thus a doctrine of creation and providence separated from the cross becomes the theory of an anonymous divine being, a first cause, an unmoved mover. A doctrine of regeneration and sanctification removed from the cross degenerates into individualism and moralism.

Ironically, the isolation and marginalization of the cross is sometimes provoked by the very ways in which the cross has been interpreted in the community of faith. A subjective "imitation of the cross" all too often becomes a morbid fascination with death and suffering. An "objective" theory of the cross often entails views of a god who must be placated with human sacrifice, a god quite different from the "Father" of Jesus, the God who is love. The danger that we encounter here is an interpretation of the cross that is isolated from the "good news of great joy" which is the true horizon of meaning for the cross. A cross that leaves us preoccupied with sin, that focuses our attention in a masochistic, sentimental, or maudlin way on suffering, a cross that transforms God from loving Father into bloodthirsty judge cannot possibly be the cross of Jesus.

Thus, a forgetfulness of the cross and a one-sided preoccupation with the cross actually belong together and provoke one another. Neither can withstand the test of being truly an "evangelical" understanding of the cross of Jesus.

There is also the problem of the intelligibility of the ways in which the cross has been traditionally understood. In the course of the history of the Church, we encounter a variety of ways to clarify the centrality and the meaning of the cross. Each one of these theories explains how the cross of Jesus leads to our salvation, our liberation, our transformation. For example, we encounter the language of sacrifice which serves to express the meaning of the cross in terms familiar to those who understood Jewish or pagan sacrificial practices. We also find the use of the language of rescue and redemption that was familiar to those who had experience with the laws regarding slavery and prisoners of war in the Roman

Empire. We have the language of the law court with its declaration of guilt or innocence. We have the use of economic language with its emphasis on the notion of debt. In the Middle Ages, the use of the feudal categories of honor served Anselm and others to illustrate for their time the centrality of the cross.

Despite this variety of ways of articulating and interpreting the meaning of the cross, they are largely unintelligible for modern people. For example, we no longer live in a world in which cultic sacrifice is taken for granted and widely understood and practiced. And this fact is not due to the ravages of secularization, but to the success of Christianity in abolishing these practices. As a result of this success, talk of Jesus' death on the cross as a "sacrifice for sin" no longer connects with our everyday social experience, as it did for those who lived in the Hellenistic world and were familiar with Jewish and pagan sacrificial systems. Consequently, the use of the language of sacrifice no longer clarifies, but obscures the meaning of the cross. A reflection on the cross that is designed to be generally intelligible cannot rely on language games and world views that no longer function in our culture.

In articulating the meaning of the cross we are confronted then with three interrelated issues: Can the cross be generally intelligible? Can it be heard as good news? Can it be perceived as central to the life of faith?

In order to make the message of the cross generally intelligible we cannot rely on the language of the tradition. Instead, we must attempt to see the cross as a historical event related to the mission and ministry of Jesus.

With respect to understanding the cross as good news a somewhat different issue arises. While intelligibility must be universal, the cross is not to be understood as good news for all in the same way. As Paul indicated in his day, the cross was a scandal for the religious and was foolishness for the wise. He insisted that those for whom it was good news were not among the privileged and respectable elements of society, "God chose what is low and despised in the world" (1 Corinthians 1:28). It is above all for these that the cross was good news. And this must be a decisive clue for the interpretation of the good news of the cross for our own time as well.

For whom then is the message concerning the cross to be understood as good news? Obviously not for those who are "at home" in the world as it is, but for those who find themselves socially, religiously, and politically marginalized.

Finally, if the cross is to be understood as central for faith it must be clear how it actually makes a difference in the life of the community of faith and in shaping the character of Christian existence.

Therefore, in attempting to clarify the meaning of the cross for our time it will be necessary to observe three tests of adequacy. The first is that the interpretation of the meaning of the cross must establish that it is precisely the cross of Jesus that is being interpreted. That is, we must attend to the way in which the execution of Jesus is a consequence of his proclamation and practice of the coming reign of God. The cross must be understood in the closest possible relation to the ministry and mission of Jesus as the Christ.

Furthermore it must become evident how the execution of the Jesus acclaimed as Son of God generates a fundamental reversal in the way in which God is understood in relation to the world, a reversal capable of being understood as good news for the marginalized.

Finally it must be clear how the cross of the Jesus affirmed as Lord entails a loyalty to his practice, a practice that produces a fundamentally new form of individual and community life.

In our discussion of the cross we will attend to four basic ways in which the message of the cross is good news for the marginalized: the cross as good news for the oppressed (which follows from our previous discussion of "suffered under Pontius Pilate"); the cross as good news for those whom the religious and respectable classify as sinners; the cross as good news for outsiders (specifically for Gentiles and then for others who are the subject of exclusion from privilege); and finally as good news for those who are estranged from God.

1. THE CROSS AS THE GOSPEL FOR THE OPPRESSED

The message of the cross is, in its most basic and literal sense, a message about the reversal of worldly power. We have already encountered this dimension in our discussion of "suffered under Pontius Pilate." But this most elemental and obvious meaning of the cross is regularly obscured. Often the emphasis is placed on Jesus' condemnation by the religious authorities of Israel. But this emphasis only serves to make the cross as such unintelligible.

It is essential to recall that the punishment for many violations of the commandments of God was stoning. This was the punishment for the violation of the law concerning the sabbath (Numbers 15:32-36) which was certainly one of the "crimes" of Jesus (Mark 3:1-6). This was also the punishment for disobedient sons (compare Luke 7:34, Deuteronomy 21:19-21). In addition, we encounter stoning as the punishment for blasphemy and false prophecy (Exodus 19:13; Leviticus 24:14-23). According to the Gospel of John, some Jews wanted to stone Jesus precisely on account of blasphemy (John 10:30, 31; 11:8). And the response of some of the Sanhedrin to Jesus' condemnation shows that they interpreted his crime as false prophecy (Mark 14:65). In any case, stoning was the punishment that Stephen received (Acts 7:59) and which was also received (though not mortally) by Paul (Acts 14:19; 2 Corinthians 11:25).

But Jesus was not stoned. He was crucified. We don't have stones on our altars, but crosses. We don't say we are saved by "the stone" but by the cross. This distinction is rather obvious, but it is regularly forgotten or ignored by those who seek to avoid the true scandal of the cross.

The cross is the punishment for crimes against the state. The cross has its place in the public sphere, the sphere of politics. Those who seek to interpret the cross exclusively in intimate, personal, and religious terms don't wish to understand the cross, but to evade it. If our faith has no relation to this public and political sphere, then our faith has no relation to the historical cross of Jesus.

The cross was the punishment for rebellion against the authority of the Roman Empire. The accusations against Jesus as reported by Luke are: "We found this man perverting our nation, forbidding us to pay taxes to the emperor, and saying that he himself is the Messiah, a king" (Luke 23:2). The accusation that Jesus claimed to be a king is also found in Mark (15:2-5) and in Matthew (27:11-14). All the Gospels record that this was the charge which was placed on the cross to explain his execution (Matthew 27:37; Mark 15:26; Luke 23:38; John 19:19). This accusation means that Jesus was executed as a rebel against the law and authority of the empire.[16]

Thus the question is: Who really is the Lord of the world? Who truly represents divine authority within the world? The powers of this world declare and claim that they are the "legitimate" and divinely sanctioned authority. From their point of view the verdict against Jesus carries the force of divine rejection of his mission. But the reversal of this verdict by way of the confession that the crucified is the Son of God shows that they are the torturers and executioners rather than the representatives of God. This is the meaning of the passage that we find in the letter to the Colossians: "He disarmed the principalities and powers and made a public example of them, triumphing over them in [the cross]" (Colossians 2:15).

The clearest expression of this meaning of the cross is found in the Apocalypse of John where the Lamb "[that was] slain from the foundations of the [earth]" (13:8 KJV) wages war against and conquers the imperial authorities (17:14).

Thus the message of the cross is always good news for the oppressed, the poor, the marginalized. For Jesus is not only a rebel against the structures of domination, but is also the "Son of God." Therefore, the structures of domination are revealed as in rebellion against God, and God has entered into profound solidarity with the hope and the destiny of the poor, the oppressed, the marginalized of the world.

As we know from Luke's Gospel, the mission of Jesus begins with the citation from Isaiah: "The Spirit of the Lord is upon me, because he has anointed me to preach good news to the poor" (Luke 4:18). Precisely because Jesus is the Messiah of God, he is in person the divine response to the hope of the marginalized "who hunger and thirst for justice." For those who had been led to believe that God was on the side of the powerful and that the oppression of the poor was somehow the will of God, the message of the cross entails an astonishing reversal that can only be good news of great joy for the poor and the oppressed.

Loyalty to the one who stands with the oppressed and those who yearn for justice means that the community of his disciples becomes a community determinedly in solidarity with those who are regarded as dangerous to the state. Jesus had told his disciples that they, too, must take up the cross, and show concretely and dramatically their own willingness to be executed, if they truly hoped to follow him. And he warned them that inevitably they would also be handed over to trial by the political powers. This was made evident in the early years of Christian history, as the followers of Jesus were indeed regularly executed as enemies of the state.[17] And though Christians have subsequently found ways to avoid this solidarity with the oppressed and to make themselves virtually identical with the state, still there are those who have continued this witness to the cross as the determinative form of Christian existence in loyalty to the crucified. Wherever this loyalty to the crucified takes the concrete form of solidarity with the oppressed and unflinching resistance to and defiance of the powers of division and domination, there one encounters the living presence of the crucified as Lord.

THE CROSS AS GOOD NEWS FOR "SINNERS"

Although the cross is in its most literal sense the execution of a political criminal, it is also evident that those who condemned Jesus are characterized not only by political, but also by "religious" power. This religious identity and privilege is bound up in the relation to the law. As we know from that portion of the Bible known to Christians as the Old Testament, the Torah or law is the word and gift of God, the fulfillment of which constitutes the identity of Israel as a people. It is the covenant of God with the people and of the people with God.

But the fiercest opponents of Jesus in his homeland are precisely those who are most careful in their observance of the law, in their guardianship of the religious identity of Israel, and thus of the covenant with God. Jesus is not opposed by the irreligious, the secular, the immoral or amoral but by the upholders of strict morality. The scribes are the interpreters of the law; the Pharisees are the most zealous of all in scrupulous adherence to the law. As we have seen, the ministry of Jesus appears to strike at the very heart of this moral, literal, and religious attitude toward the law. According to the Gospels, the plot to destroy Jesus has a profoundly religious meaning. It is focused on and motivated by Jesus' abolition of the religious law associated with the sabbath (Mark 3:1-6).

But Jesus' condemnation as a "sinner" has an even wider basis in his practice. For Jesus seems to go out of his way to be classified as a "sinner" in terms both of the question of purity and that of morality. The purity code proscribes contact with, for example, lepers, corpses, and menstruating women. Jesus touches each of these, becoming legally impure. From the standpoint of the purity codes, he becomes a sinner. Moreover, the friendship of Jesus pointedly includes those who are excluded on account of the evident sinfulness of their life-style. Thus Jesus is known as a friend of tax collectors and sinners. The condemnation of Jesus as a "sinner" is firmly rooted in the deliberate policy and practice of Jesus himself.

That Jesus is rejected by the guardians of the law means either that the law is vindicated, or that the law itself has come into opposition to God. It is precisely the latter that is the view of Paul, expressed most vigorously in his letter to the Galatians. The gospel concerning the cross then is that the law, with its separation of clean and unclean, godly and ungodly, circumcised and uncircumcised, religious and profane, just and sinner, is overthrown. To uphold this law is to side with the opponents of Jesus and to legitimate their verdict of rejection and execution. But to stand with Jesus, to acclaim the one rejected by the guardians of the law as the Son of God, is to say that salvation comes apart from the law.

The message of the cross then is the message of the grace or favor of God that abolishes the barrier of the law and so abolishes the distinction between the godly and the ungodly. The message of the cross is the message that God's love is directed not only to the righteous but also to the sinner. The parable of the prodigal son already points us in this direction (Luke 15:11-32). This becomes a basic theological principle in the words of Paul:

While we were yet helpless, at the right time Christ died for the ungodly. (Romans 5:6)

> But God shows his love for us in that while we were yet sinners Christ died for us. (5:8)

These assertions are regularly interpreted in terms of ritual sacrifice. But they have a more directly accessible meaning: Jesus is found among the sinners as a matter of deliberate choice. Thus Paul can say of him that "he [became] sin who knew no sin" (2 Corinthians 5:21). And the acclamation of him as Son of God means that those who were once regarded as sinners and so as separated from God, are now told that in fact God is "on their side"; that is, on the side of the condemned rather than that of those who condemn. This is the proclamation of the grace or favor of God toward sinners.

Loyalty to the one who is thus found to be on the side of sinners will mean that his community will not judge one another, but will engage in the relentless and radical practice of mutual forgiveness. This practice of forgiveness is made the mark of Jesus' community by repeated instruction in the Gospel of Matthew. (See commentary on the forgiveness of sins.) And the mutual welcoming of one another by the "weak" (those who adhere scrupulously to the law) and the strong (those who live by grace in freedom) is heavily emphasized by Paul in Romans 14 and 1 Corinthians 8. Wherever the practice of "welcoming" and of forgiveness abolishes the practice of judging and condemning, the message of the cross becomes the agent of fundamental transformation in human relationships.

THE OPENING TO THE GENTILES

We should note that the Gospels often maintain that it was Jesus' intent to restrict himself to the people of Israel (see Matthew 10:5-6; 15:24). This is even true of Acts where the mission to the Gentiles is finally made necessary by the continued resistance of the leaders of the synagogues (compare Acts 1:6 and Acts 28:28).

But Jesus was rejected by the representatives of the national identity of Israel. The consequence of this rejection is that the gospel is proclaimed to those who are "outside" Israel: the Gentiles (nations, pagans). Thus this rejection becomes the basis for the extension of the gospel to the entire world.

In this rigorous historical sense the cross is the event of salvation because precisely on account of the cross (here focusing on Jesus' being rejected by the leaders of Israel's national identity) the gospel of God's love reaches the whole earth. The cross makes Jesus an outsider to Israel.

He is "turned over" to the Gentiles. But this fate is prefigured as well in the practice of Jesus according to the Gospels. He is first acclaimed as "King of the Jews" by Gentile sorcerers (Matthew 2:1-11); and this leads to the first attempt to eliminate him as a threat to the established order (2:16-18). The hostile reaction to Jesus' first sermon as reported by Luke comes not on account of the audacity of his announcement that Isaiah's hope for the Lord's jubilee had been accomplished, but in his reminder to the crowd that the mission of the prophets included not only Israel but the Gentiles as well (Luke 4:24-30). Jesus' association with foreign women (Greek in the case of Mark, Canaanite in Matthew, and Samaritan in John) prefigures the Gentile mission, as does Jesus' assertion that the faith of the (gentile) centurion exceeded that of the people of Israel (Matthew 8:10). Thus Jesus leaves unanswered the charge that he is himself a Samaritan (John 8:48). His mission and ministry is recalled as breaking the barriers between Jew and Gentile. In this way his being "turned over" to the Gentiles and his execution "outside the gates" is the culmination of Jesus' own messianic practice as recalled by the Gospels.

The two great historical events of early Christianity—the execution of Jesus and the spread of the message concerning Jesus to the Gentiles—have an intimate relation and a mutually clarifying significance. This relationship is dramatically expressed in the Gospel of Mark. Immediately after the death of Jesus, "the centurion who was facing him, seeing that he died in this way, said 'surely this was the son of God' " (Mark 15:39, author paraphrase). The faith of the Gentiles becomes possible on account of the cross. The message concerning the love of God that overcomes despair, domination, division, and death is a message that comes to us because Jesus was rejected by the authorities of Israel. Paul further emphasized this rejection by those who are the custodians of an ethnic identity and privilege in his letter to the Romans. The first eleven chapters of this letter seek to clarify the meaning of this rejection and so the relation between the election of Israel and the election of the Gentiles by means of faith in Jesus. In this context Paul maintains that the rejection of Jesus by the responsible leaders of Israel becomes the instrument for the salvation of the nations: "through their trespass salvation has come to the Gentiles . . . their trespass means riches for the world, and . . . their failure means riches for the Gentiles . . . their rejection means the reconciliation of the world" (11:11-12, 15). The cross is the verdict of the custodians of the identity of Israel as the chosen people of God. The revocation of this verdict through the identification of Jesus as Son of God is the revocation of the frontiers of election. By means of the cross,

113

the gospel "crosses" these frontiers to reach the whole earth. And it is precisely because the rejection of Jesus by the Jews has this character of good news that Israel, too, is included in the good news of God's love and mercy: "So they have now been disobedient in order that by the mercy shown to you they also may receive mercy" (11:31). Thus the cross of Jesus that follows from the rejection of Jesus by the guardians of Jewish identity means that the good news of God's love, mercy, and election escapes the boundaries of ethnic identity to become universal.[18] Thus we have this sequence:

1. The Jews are elect of God.
2. They reject Jesus.
3. This rejection is reversed by God (by means of the resurrection).
4. The message of divine adoption by means of grace passes the frontiers or barriers of ethnic identity to become universal.
5. The Jews' rejection of Jesus becomes the instrument for the salvation of all. Thus they will not lose their election but will also receive the grace of God.
6. This leads Paul to speak of the absolute universality of grace: "For God has consigned all to disobedience so that God can have mercy upon all (11:32, author paraphrase).
7. It is this universality of God's triumphant grace manifested and actualized in the cross that elicits from Paul his ecstatic doxology: "O the depth of the riches and wisdom and knowledge of God! How unsearchable are his judgments and how inscrutable his ways! For from him and through him and to him are all things. To him be glory forever. Amen (11:33, 36).

The proclamation of the cross as the event of salvation has a historically intelligible meaning. Jesus announced the love of God. The rejection of this message results in the message becoming universal rather than parochial. Thus the proclamation of the divine love comes to be announced even to us.

To understand the cross as the consequence of Jesus' rejection by the guardians of ethnic identity and privilege leads to the understanding that the cross entails the abolition of every separate and divisive identity. The rejection of Jesus, his suffering and death come at the hands of the guardians of division. When the cross is made the basis of the gospel, the principle of division that negates Jesus is itself negated. The positive meaning of this reversal is reconciliation as the overthrow of the structures of division. It by no means entails a coming to terms with these structures, a "peace at any price" which is so often mistaken for reconciliation. Rather, it is an active and militant overcoming of division, and so of isolated and privileged identities that govern worldly existence. Accordingly:

> There is neither Jew nor Greek, there is neither slave nor free, there is neither male nor female; for you are all one in Christ Jesus. (Galatians 3:28)

> Here there cannot be Greek and Jew, circumcised and uncircumcised, barbarian, Scythian, slave, free man, but Christ is all, and in all. (Colossians 3:11)

The separated and closed identities that characterize our existence as individuals and as groups are overcome in the cross. Thus, national and cultural identity (Greek and Jew, barbarian and Scythian); economic and political identity (slave and free); sexual and personal identity (male and female) are all abolished in favor of the reconciliation of all in Christ, whose cross is the end of all divisions. That the crucified is confessed as Lord of the community entails the abolition of all principles of division within that community.[19]

RECONCILIATION WITH GOD

The overcoming of the power of division which is the meaning of the cross extends to the overcoming of the division between ourselves and God. It is precisely this division and separation that appears most starkly in the cross of Jesus. In the cross we encounter not only Jesus' rejection by Israel and Rome, the powers of division and domination, but we also encounter what appears to be the rejection and abandonment of Jesus by God.

The mission and ministry of Jesus is the announcement and enactment of God's nearness, of God's love, of God's mercy. In word and deed, Jesus announces the coming of God's reign of justice and peace. His abolition of the sabbath laws, his forgiveness of sins and empowerment of others to do the same, his identification of his mission with that of "the Father" are all remembered as bringing him into conflict with those who guard the separation between God and humanity. It is Jesus' vision of the union of God with humanity ("You will see the Son of man seated with God") that brings upon him his final condemnation. The cross as a historical event appears to demonstrate that God is not near but distant, that the message of justice and peace is a utopian illusion.

The gospel of Mark exhibits with terrifying force this contradiction between the message of Jesus and his fate. The contradiction is expressed in the derision of those who stand around the cross:

> And those who passed by derided him, wagging their heads, and saying, "Aha! You who would destroy the temple and build it in three days, save yourself, and come down from the cross!" So also the chief priests mocked him to one another with the scribes, saying, "He saved others; he cannot save himself. Let the Christ, the King of Israel, come down now from the cross, that we may see and believe." (15:29-32)

But these words of derision scarcely compare in force with the words that we hear, not from those who stand beneath the cross, but from the one who hangs there: "My God, my God, why hast thou forsaken me?" (15:34). Earlier in this Gospel we heard a heavenly voice that claims Jesus as son (Mark 1:11; 9:7). But here there is no voice. The sky is dark, the heavens silent, there is only the cry of protest, of abandonment.

When we recall that "sin" is the separation and division between ourselves and God we can understand the saying of Paul that "he who knew no sin, was made sin for us" (2 Corinthians 5:21). That the cross is the center of proclamation can only mean that the cross overcomes the separation between God and ourselves. This is the meaning that Mark's Gospel supplies. It is precisely this death, so like despair, that provokes the centurion's acclamation: "Truly this man was a son of God!" (Mark 15:39). In place of the voice from the heavens we hear the voice of faith.

To acknowledge the crucified as "Son of God" is to affirm the end of every separation between God and humanity. It is precisely this reversal of separation and abandonment that is the meaning of reconciliation with God. If the separation, abandonment, and despair of the cross is not the last word but is instead reversed in such a way that the cross is the "power of salvation," as Paul says, then Jesus and God are present in this event in such a way that we must speak of God the Son and God the Father. Thus the reversal of this abandonment of Jesus is the basis of the Church's affirmation of the doctrine of the triune identity of God in which Father and Son are joined together in the mission of love and mercy that embraces us as well.

Thus the meaning of the cross is not only the reconciliation of Father and Son but our reconciliation to God as well. The well known words of Paul in his letter to the Romans express exactly the consequences of this love made manifest in the cross, a love that overcomes every form of separation between ourselves and God.

What then shall we say to this? If God is for us, who is against us? He who did not spare his own Son but gave him up for us all, will he not also give us all things with him?

Who shall separate us from the love of Christ?

For I am sure that neither death, nor life, or angels, nor principalities, nor things present, nor things to come, nor powers, nor height, nor depth, nor anything else in all creation, will be able to separate us from the love of God in Christ Jesus our Lord. (Romans 8:31-32, 35, 38-39)

CHAPTER ELEVEN

DEAD AND BURIED

The phrase "dead and buried" is proverbial for indicating something that is finished, that is "washed up," that has become irrevocably past and no longer has a future. It indicates a finality, an "over and done with" toward which all life goes and against which all life protests. That is perhaps why most of us cannot grasp emotionally the idea of being ourselves "dead and buried," nor do we find it much easier to accept the finality of this word in the case of loved ones. It goes "against the grain" simply to accept this finality. Yet it is a finality that, protest or no, all life encounters, however it may seek to escape.

These words, applied to one who is said to be the embodiment of human hope—the Christ, the Son of God, the Lord—have a kind of brutal finality. It is as if the last glimmer of hope has now receded forever into this "dead and buried" which is the final "no" to human hope.

With these words the Creed opposes itself to all illusion concerning the desire to escape this fate. Even among the Christian community there were many for whom these words, even more than those concerning the cross, served as a stumbling block. The insistence that Jesus was the "Son of God" seemed to imply the impossibility that this fate would be appropriate to him. The last hope of the Gnostic refusal of the human condition was the denial that the Son of God could be said to be literally "dead and buried." With the resolute finality of this clause the Creed puts an end to any evasion of this fate for the one who represents God in person.[20]

In this way the one who is said to be Son of God enters into full and final solidarity with the creature whose common fate it is to be "dead and buried."[21] Not even the escape of Enoch or of Elijah is to be allowed him. He enters fully and irrevocably and without reserve into our fate.[22]

Yet these are by no means the last words concerning Jesus that we find in this narrative-like section of the Creed. Indeed, they come barely at the halfway point.[23] They are not even the last words concerning the past of Jesus—for they are followed by descended, rose, ascended. This marks the past of Jesus as an open past, one that is open to becoming the present (sits) and the future (will come) of humanity.

The narratives concerning the death of Jesus seek to portray both the unreserved solidarity of Jesus with the fate of "dead and buried" while at the same time indicating that it is precisely this final solidarity that opens the way to a future for all human beings.[24] Here I will indicate briefly three narratives in which this takes place.

First, in the Gospel of Mark we find the following: "And Jesus uttered a loud cry, and breathed his last. And the curtain of the temple was torn in two, from top to bottom" (Mark 15:37-38). The "end" of Jesus is also the end of the curtain, or veil that separates humanity from God. The temple veil protects the hiddenness of God, the holiness of God, from human contact. Thus the veil becomes the very principle of religion itself, with its distinction between the sacred and the profane. It marks the unconditional qualitative distinction between God and humanity. But the death of Jesus rips this veil, shredding it and the fabric of religion that it represents. That the one who represents God shares our fate unreservedly means that the separation between God and humanity is shattered.

Second, while Matthew's Gospel shares with Mark the same starting point,[25] it adds additional striking features.

> And Jesus cried again with a loud voice and yielded up his spirit. And behold, the curtain of the temple was torn in two, from top to bottom; and the earth shook, and the rocks were split; the tombs also were opened, and many bodies of the saints who had fallen asleep were raised, and coming out of the tombs after his resurrection they went into the holy city and appeared to many. (Matthew 27:50-53)

This is one of the oddest tales in the Gospels. It is especially odd since it risks eliminating the significance of Jesus' resurrection by having an apparent multitude of resuscitated corpses going about the city at the same time Jesus is appearing to his disciples (verse 53).

What is the meaning of this strange story? In this narrative Matthew combines two elements of apocalyptic expectation concerning the end of the world: the great earthquake (in connection with the darkening of the sky) and the return of those who had been martyred for their steadfast loyalty to God. We will return to this last when we come to the clause concerning "the resurrection of the dead." Here the critical point seems to be that the becoming "past" of Jesus obliterates the division between past and future. Far from meaning that the very possibility of a future

119

which he represented is now "over and done with," Jesus' death actually triggers the arrival of that future "in advance" or ahead of time.

That Jesus comes to be "dead and buried" means that death and the grave are now themselves broken open.[26] Their power becomes past, and is in a sense now over and done with. That Jesus is dead and buried means that the tables are turned on the last and most dire of the enemies of human hope. This pertains not only to Jesus, but also to us and to all human beings. Thus the saints of whom we read here are certainly not "Christians," but rather are those who have been steadfast in their loyalty to God. The death of Jesus gives them a future, and so robs death and grave of victory (1 Corinthians 15:54-55).[27]

Third, the assertion of Jesus as "dead and buried" has an additional significance. We have already noted that in the Gospel of Mark the death of Jesus elicits the confession of faith from the lips of the centurion who supervises his execution: "Surely this was the Son of God." It is not Jesus' escape from death, but the final entrance into death that evokes this confession of faith. In this way the becoming "past" of Jesus becomes the basis of the future of the proclamation.

This is further underlined when the same centurion who was the executioner of Jesus is summoned before Pilate to testify to the death of Jesus. This testimony foreshadows the spread of Christian witness "to the ends of the earth."

The occasion for the testimony of the centurion is the request of Joseph of Arimathea for the body of Jesus. Earlier in the Gospel of Mark we were told that at the death of John the Baptist his disciples came to claim the body (Mark 6:29). Here, it is one who is a member of the council that condemned Jesus who comes to fulfill the office of discipleship. Those who live in lands ruled by terror know only too well the significance of the act of Joseph. Claiming the body of one who is executed for crimes against the state is a way of identifying oneself as an associate of the subversive. This is all the more true if the one whose body is claimed is not a relative. The burial of Jesus by Joseph of Arimathea is itself a sign that the mission of Jesus, rather than being terminated, now acquires an unexpected future.

That Jesus is "dead and buried" is by no means a redundant addition to "was crucified." For we see here that the one to whom we affirm our loyalty did not shrink from final and unreserved and deliberate solidarity with the fate of humanity, and that this solidarity itself turns the tables on the power of the grave. In this way, the "becoming past" of Jesus is the very beginning of his future, and so of ours as well.

PART THREE:
FROM MEMORY TO HOPE

Descended into Hell,
on the Third Day He Rose from the Dead,
He Ascended into Heaven
He Sits at the Right Hand
He Will Come to Judge

That Jesus is "dead and buried" is by no means the end of the narrative description of his identity. It is not even the end of the narrative of his past. For this is followed by three other events in the past tense. The continuation of the past of Jesus is what makes his past open to become the present (is seated) and the future (will come) of humanity. It is to a clarification of the meaning of this further "past" of Jesus that we now turn.

CHAPTER TWELVE

DESCENDED INTO HELL

F or a period of several centuries, many Protestant versions of the
Creed omitted this clause on the view that it provided a basis for
some doctrines of traditional Christianity (Roman Catholicism)
that it found objectionable. Moreover, it was supposed that this clause
lacked firm biblical support. Finally it had become clear through
historical inquiry that this clause did not appear in some early versions of
the Creed.[1] This negative assessment led to the temporary abandonment
of this clause among many Protestant groups, although some, notably
Anglican and Lutheran bodies, retained it. Even where it was retained,
however, these objections seemed to produce some embarrassment. The
clause seemed to those of a more modernist bent to be heavily influenced
by a mythological conception best reduced (for it certainly could not be
eliminated) in the Creed.

However, in more recent times, there has been a growing concern to
reintroduce the clause. This has to do with a recognition that it does in fact
have some biblical support, that it was treated positively by both Luther
and Calvin, and that it is appropriate to have the Creed represent
Christian unity rather than division. Accordingly, liturgies which
formerly eliminated the clause or reduced it to a footnote now have the
clause (descended to the dead) with a footnote indicating the provincial
tradition of omitting it.

Of course it remains true that this clause bears the impress of a
pre-modern world view. The notion of a descent into the realm of the
dead is a staple of myth and legend, and played a prominent role in the
lore of the Hellenistic world.

However, the mere association of elements of the Creed with a mythic
vocabulary is by no means restricted to this clause of the Creed. The
notion of divine conception of the hero, of virginal birth, and of dying

and rising all have important parallels in the mythology of the Hellenistic world and in mythologies of other cultures as well. This should not be surprising, since myth has generally been the language in terms of which human dilemmas are presented and resolved. The currency of such language in the Hellenistic world, in which early Christianity had to communicate, made it not only inevitable but also desirable that Christian faith express itself in these terms if it were to get its message across.

More to the point, is what the use of this conceptuality enabled the gospel to express, and why this was considered sufficiently important that it came to find a place in the Creed by which the Christian community expressed its unswerving loyalty to Jesus of Nazareth, the Christ, Son of God, Lord. When asked in this way, the question enables us to distinguish several important and related features of the significance of this clause of the Creed.

1. Contemporary versions of this clause exchange "hell" for realm of the dead. Although this may have more to do with an attempt to make the Creed palatable for those to whom language of hell (or even heaven) is alien, it also represents correctly the earlier conception of the clause. The term hell is the translation of "sheol" or "hades," which connoted simply the domain of the dead. In Greek and Hebrew thought the dead, who were buried in the earth, were conceived of as having a shadowy existence whose basic characteristic was a radical diminution of vitality and a disconnection from the realm of the living. This thoroughly reduced life permitted some notion of the apparition of the dead (ghosts), but has little or nothing of the notion of strong influence and activity so often found in African and Asian reverence for and even placation of the ancestors. This latter view was not wholly absent from the Hellenistic world and came to play a significant role in subsequent Christian cults associated with martyrs and their burial places. This martyr cult, in turn, became the mainspring of a cult of the saints[2] which was able to incorporate the most active views of the realm of the dead into popular Christianity in Europe and the Americas.

However, the earliest Christian use of this clause of the Creed built upon the view that the dead were to be understood as continuing a shadowy existence in a kind of underground holding area. The principal feature of their existence was the deprivation of life and reality. The contrast between their status and that of the living corresponded to a strong positive valuation of life in both traditional Hebrew and Greek world views.

On this view then the significance of saying that Jesus descended into the realm of the dead was that the Jesus who was crucified, dead, and buried really and fully partook of the universal human fate of death. This insistence interdicted the possibility of limiting this reality under the influence of Gnostic or Docetic views. The unity of the Christ with this fate of humanity was unrestricted. In this way, Jesus enters into unbroken solidarity with those who have indeed become already past, whose reality has become the shadow of memory, the deprivation of the wholeness of life. Even as Son of God, Jesus is not immune to this fate, but really enters into it—was dead and buried, descended into hades.

2. According to the perspective of Israel, the dead were not only those who had become past without a future (although they may have had a kind of shadowy present) they were also without God. For pre-Hellenistic and traditional Judaism God was primarily a God of the living (see Mark 12:27). This meant that the dead were separated from the activity of God and continued in a shadowy existence characterized by the absence of this relation. Thus, the Psalmist could say that there was no praise of Yahweh in Sheol (Psalm 88:12, see Isaiah 38:18).[3]

In the Christian story this would mean that Jesus' descent into the realm of the dead completes the separation of Jesus from God expressed in the final words from the cross in the Gospels of Matthew and Mark: "My God, my God, why hast thou forsaken me?" (Mark 15:34; Matthew 27:46). The descent of Jesus into the realm of the dead completes this abandonment.[4] But as we have seen, the solidarity of Jesus with the suffering of humanity and with its fate of becoming dead and buried is at the same time the overcoming of this separation. Jesus' identification with humanity means either that he really is abandoned by God, or that God is fully present in this abandonment. If the latter is true, it means that this separation from God is finally and fully overcome, not only for him, but for all.[5]

In order to claim that this fate has been entered and so reversed by the grace of God, one must first insist that Jesus has really entered into this fate, that he has not been spared its full reality, its radical negation. The assertion that he fully shares this fate means that this fate is itself altered, not only for him (he is not merely a hero), but for all (he is the Christ, the Son of God).[6]

3. It is this reversal of the fate of the dead that is expressed in the texts from 1 Peter that serve as the basis of this clause of the Creed.

> For Christ also died for sins once for all, the righteous for the unrighteous, that he might bring us to God, being put to death in the flesh but made alive in the spirit; in which he went and preached to the spirits in prison, who formerly did not obey, when God's patience waited in the days of Noah, during the building of the ark, in which a few, that is, eight persons, were saved through water. (3:18-20)

After an excursus on baptism brought on by the reference to water, Peter returns to the theme of the present age of licentiousness and the judgment that must come to the living and the dead. In this connection the author again mentions the "descent": "But they will give account to him who is ready to judge the living and the dead. For this is why the gospel was preached even to the dead, that though judged in the flesh like men, they might live in the spirit like God" (1 Peter 4:5-6). This passage, although it presents a number of exegetical difficulties, is nevertheless important since it is not only the source of the clause concerning "descent," but also one of the principal texts for the last two clauses of this section of the Creed: "seated at the right hand" and "to judge the living and the dead."

Here it becomes evident that the central meaning of the descent is the announcement or proclamation of the gospel to those who had become past. Those who have become past (and whose present is but the shadowy prolongation of that past) are now suddenly and unexpectedly confronted with a future, and so are awakened into the present as the time of decision and of hope. In this way, the coming "to judge the living and the dead" is already anticipated in the act of bringing the gospel to the dead as well as to the living.

It should be clear that this proclamation to the dead has already been anticipated in the mission and ministry of Jesus. Those who were confronted with the gospel were in a figurative, but dramatic sense "dead," that is, living under the shadow and rule of death. Life in the "flesh" is life lived under the dominion of the fate of death, a fate made evident in the sway of the powers of division and domination, in the life of anxiety and self-preoccupation. The announcement of the good news of the coming reign of God, of the forgiveness of sins and so the liberation from the past, is already the resurrection from the dead (John 5:21, 24).

The image of a descent into the realm of the dead as a proclamation to the dead is but an extension of this image. But this extension produces something new as well. The notion of a descent in order to proclaim to the dead means that those who have become past receive a new future. This is in its own way no more strange and miraculous than that we who are "among the living," but really ruled by death, should also have received this awakening to hope.

In this way the proclamation of the gospel exceeds, or rather ruptures, the barrier of "pastness" which seems to separate those who lived prior to the announcement of the gospel from the possibility of having become awakened by the proclamation of that gospel.

In popular Christianity, when the emphasis is placed on belief in the gospel in a rather straightforward literal way, the question of the "unfairness" of the fate of those who never had a chance in life to respond to this gospel, and so to find the future that it promises, can become acute. If it is necessary in some sense to believe the gospel in order to be saved, then what of those who never had a chance to hear this gospel preached?

The descent into the realm of the dead in order to proclaim the gospel to those who are held captive by death serves to indicate the response of faith to this question. It means that none will be excluded from the possibility of hearing and responding to this good news. In some way, here figured as the "descent into hell," all who have ever lived are included in the possibility of responding to the good news of the forgiveness of sins, to the proclamation of hope, to the announcement of the coming of the divine reign of justice, generosity, and joy. None are excluded.[7]

Exactly how one should conceptualize this is left open.[8] We find in the Creed no speculation, and only the barest allusion to the language of myth and legend. What is important is that none are excluded from the gospel, even though it may not be clear *how* this is so. What is emphasized is that the same gospel we encounter in Jesus of Nazareth is announced, not only to the living, but also to those who are dead. Just as the gospel shatters the bounds of ethnicity to become a gospel to the nations, so also the gospel shatters the barrier of death to be presented to both the "living and the dead."[9]

4. The discussion of this clause of the Creed has so far relied on the understanding that "hell" should be understood as the "realm of the dead." But much theology, not only of the late patristic and medieval period, but also of the Reformation, takes into account the notion of hell as the place or domain of that which is opposed to and by God. Thus a popular Christianity associates hell with the domain of Satan and the rule of the demonic. Although this cannot be said to be the earliest significance of this clause of the Creed, it nonetheless is not an entirely inappropriate association. The Gospels depict the mission of Jesus as an assault on the sphere of demonic power, as evidenced by the characteristic activity of Jesus in casting out demons. When Jesus is accused by his opponents of being in league with Beelzebub he replies that the despoiling of the demons means that the "strong man" is bound (Mark 3:27). That is, his activity of exorcism and healing shows that satanic power has been made captive by the coming of the divine reign.

In the Gospel of Luke, when the disciples return from carrying on Jesus' mission and ministry, Jesus exclaims that he has seen Satan falling out of the sky. The continuation of his ministry by the disciples topples the dominion of all that opposes the divine rule (Luke 10:17-18).

Thus, the notion of the descent into hell, even when furnished with the lurid detail of medieval imagination (still appropriated, for example, by Martin Luther) carries forward this notion of the divine assault upon the domain of the demonic through the announcement and enactment of the reign of God.

In this way the notion of the descent into hell can be a salutary restraint on the kind of religious imagination that preoccupies itself with the power of Satan, the devil, demons, and hell. The good news is that this realm is shattered by the gospel. It can no longer be used as a kind of spiritual terrorism to frighten and to fascinate. It is finally and fully broken by the invasion of the gospel even into this sphere.

The point here is not to attempt to revive the demonic imagination in order to make this clause of the Creed intelligible. As we have seen, the clause is quite intelligible without embellishment. The point is rather that wherever people continue to be frightened or fascinated by the demonic and the satanic (something which occurs in post-modern suburbs as well as in primitive villages), the gospel shatters this power and invades even the darkest pits of human despair to bring the cleansing light of the good news that there is no place, no dominion that can escape the coming of the one who is love and mercy, light and life.

The descent into hell, then, represents on the one hand, the most profound solidarity of Jesus with the fate of human beings who fall under the sway of death, of abandonment, and even of despair; and, on the other hand, the invasion of this realm of death by the gospel of the divine love. While Calvinist dogmatics have traditionally emphasized the solidarity, Lutheran dogmatics have emphasized the liberating invasion of this sphere.[10] But the two belong together and are ultimately unintelligible apart from one another.

CHAPTER THIRTEEN

ROSE FROM THE DEAD

W hen we consider the resurrection of Jesus we must recognize that here, as in virtually every clause of the Creed, we are dealing with metaphor. In this case the metaphor compresses an analogy: death is to sleep what x is to waking up. This is by no means the only metaphor employed to designate the destiny of the crucified, and it is not in any straightforward way fully adequate to designate the reality which is signified. For example, the New Testament also employs the agricultural imagery of seeds and fruit, and of first fruit and harvest. Alongside this the Gospels also make some use of "ghost" language, and Paul (and Acts) makes use of "vision" metaphors. In general, the literal character of these metaphors is denied by the very texts that employ them.

We may be helped to see the non-literal character of the resurrection accounts if we see how these accounts differ from apparently similar accounts of resuscitation in biblical literature. For example, we find the resuscitation of a person by Elijah (1 Kings 17:17-24) and another performed by Elisha (2 Kings 4:18-37). In the Gospels we have the story of the resuscitation of the daughter of Jairus (Mark 5:21-32 and parallels), and in Luke the story of the raising of the youth of Nain (Luke 7:11-17). In John we have the story of the raising of Lazarus (John 11:1-44). In the Acts of the Apostles we have the raising of Tabitha (Dorcas) by Peter (Acts 9:36-43) and the raising of Eutychus by Paul (Acts 20:7-12).

It is important to recognize that we do not proclaim our faith in Lazarus or Tabitha, nor do we announce our commitment to Peter or Paul, Elijah or Elisha. We rely on and are loyal to Jesus of Nazareth. It is clear that the resurrection of Jesus is to be distinguished from these more literal accounts of the resuscitation of a corpse.

On the one hand, in any treatment of the resurrection it is crucial to recognize that this event is not one that can be simply assimilated into language, and certainly not the language of explanation. This recognition is not an apologetic strategy to make the resurrection more palatable to modern as opposed to mythic temperaments. It is instead required by the very texts which bear testimony to the resurrection. The biblical witness is consistently betrayed by those who seek to turn the resurrection into a simple nature miracle or a kind of "brute fact."

On the other hand, there is no straight line between the fact of the cross and the proclamation of faith; it is not enough to point to this proclamation as somehow self-founded or self-authenticating.[11] The proclamation of faith is provoked by that which eludes speech.[12] In order to make this clear it will be necessary to review the resurrection accounts, first of the empty tomb, and then of the appearances, to demonstrate that the texts are unanimous in insisting that the resurrection is not something that can be contained in literal discourse.[13]

1. THE TOMB

The empty tomb tradition is found only in the longer narrative accounts of the mission of Jesus. We have four different accounts of this event, each markedly different from the others. The points of agreement can be quickly summarized. On the morning following the sabbath (or about 40 hours after the death of Jesus), certain persons who had followed Jesus arrive at the tomb where he had been buried only to discover that the tomb is empty. (We have no idea how long it has been empty in the accounts of Mark, Luke, and John.) One of those who discover the tomb is Mary Magdalene. These are the only points of agreement. Beyond this all is contradictory.

1. There is confusion about who discovers the empty tomb. According to Mark, Mary Magdalene is accompanied by Mary, the mother of James, and by Salome. According to Luke, she is accompanied by Mary, the mother of James and by Joanna (not Salome) and perhaps a large group of other women. According to Matthew, we have only Mary Magdalene and "the other Mary" while John has Mary Magdalene subsequently followed by Peter and "the other disciple."

2. There is even more confusion about what is actually seen at the site of the tomb. According to John, it is merely an empty tomb (although Peter and the other disciple later see folded grave cloths—nobody else reports this).

In Mark, the women find a youth inside the tomb "at the right hand" dressed in white. (This appears to be the same youth who ran naked from the garden of Gethsemane when Jesus was arrested.) In Matthew, we do not have a youth in the tomb, but an angel descended from heaven who looks like lightning. He is not inside the tomb but outside it on the rock that had sealed the tomb. In Luke, we have neither an angel nor a youth, but two men in dazzling apparel.

3. Where there is someone at the tomb (remember that in John there is no one) we have disagreement about what was said. In general we are told that Jesus is risen. In Mark and Matthew the women are told to tell the disciples that Jesus will appear to them in Galilee. According to Matthew, Jesus does meet them there. We have no appearances in the authentic ending of Mark. The assertion that Jesus will meet them in Galilee is omitted from Luke, since for Luke the resurrection appearances must occur not in Galilee but in Jerusalem.

4. As we have seen there is no messenger in John, so it is Mary Magdalene who speaks to the two disciples, thinking that the body has been stolen. They come to see the tomb and go home. In Mark, Luke, and Matthew there is a commission to tell the others. According to Mark, the women tell no one anything. In Luke they do tell the disciples, who don't believe a word of it. According to Matthew, their return to the disciples is interrupted by Jesus himself, and when they report to the disciples, they are sufficiently believed that these go to Galilee to meet Jesus.

Now what are we to make of all this? Clearly the accounts are irreconcilable. The only apparent historical "kernel" is that Mary Magdalene (and others) discover after a lapse of about 40 hours, that Jesus' tomb is open and empty. Everything else is determined by the theological point of view of the author.

When we inquire about the points being made by the narrators we find that despite enormous disagreement over details they do make at least one point in common: the empty tomb proves precisely nothing. The point is made in startlingly different ways. In Mark's Gospel the women are overcome with fear and say nothing. In Luke they carry the message but are simply not believed. In John, Mary Magdalene draws the reasonable conclusion that the grave has been robbed. In Matthew, where we have an enormous amount of detail about an earthquake (the second in less than 40 hours) and an angel, the end result is the same, since the Romans and the priests cook up a story that the disciples stole the body—a tale that Matthew tells us is still widely believed many decades later. Thus, in quite different ways each of these narratives makes the point that the empty tomb is not the gospel, a point re-enforced by the disparity between the differing accounts themselves and by the absence of any such tradition in the writings of Paul (especially the already traditional formula of 1 Corinthians 15:1-10), the earliest texts we have.

In the narrative unfolding of the Gospels the empty tomb serves to mark the transition from passion narrative to appearance narrative. It "opens the door" to that which follows. In the case of the Gospel of Mark that which follows is left to the decision of the reader. In Matthew, Luke, and John that which follows is a narrative concerning the appearance of Jesus to his followers. But as we shall see, this will by no means solve the "mystery of the resurrection."

2. THE APPEARANCES

The Gospel of Mark in its original form gives us no appearance narrative following the crucifixion of Jesus.

The Gospel of Matthew has Jesus appear twice. The first appearance is to the women who are returning with the message given them by the angel. Here Jesus merely repeats what the angel has already told them, namely, that he will appear to his disciples in Galilee. Thus, the first appearance seems to be redundant to the appearance of the heavenly messenger. The second appearance is the one promised both by the angel and by Jesus—on a mountain in Galilee. Since, as we shall see, this final account of Matthew combines motifs sometimes distributed between resurrection, ascension, and even Pentecost we may say that for Matthew it is intended to be the only resurrection appearance. This also seems to be what Mark would have done had Mark wished to recount an appearance story, since for Mark, as well as for Matthew, Jesus is to appear in Galilee.

When we turn to the Gospel of Luke we have a very different picture. Here Jesus does not appear in Galilee at all. Instead, the appearances are located in and around Jerusalem. Although the number of appearances in Luke (two) corresponds to what we find in Matthew, they are narrated at much greater length (thirty-six verses as opposed to six). The first of these concerns Cleopas and another unnamed follower (24:13-35) on the road to Emmaus (about six miles from Jerusalem), while the second occurs in Jerusalem on the same day as Jesus' appearance to the eleven "and those gathered with them." This appearance concludes with Jesus leading them back out toward Bethany and his ascension. Interestingly, Luke (if, as virtually all assume, Luke is the author of both the Gospel and of Acts) is not interested in maintaining the literal accuracy of the narrative. In Acts 1:3 we hear that Jesus appeared to the disciples for a period of forty days, while the narrative of the Gospel has the ascension occurring on the evening of the day of the resurrection.

The long ending of Mark appears to attempt to harmonize the

Matthean and Lukan resurrection narratives. Rather than taking sides between the Galilean tradition (represented by Mark and Matthew) and the Jerusalem tradition (represented by Luke), the long ending leaves the location unspecified. This is not really very useful, however, since the only appearances listed are those that could be plausibly located in and around Jerusalem. Thus we have appearances to Mary Magdalene, two walking in the country, and the eleven at table, after which Jesus ascends, thus terminating the resurrection appearances. Thus the long ending of Mark contradicts the expectation of the Gospel of Mark that Jesus will appear (only) in Galilee.

The Gospel of John has two concluding chapters. In the first of these we have three appearance narratives. In the first Jesus appears to Mary Magdalene in the cemetery after Peter and the other disciple had gone home from the empty tomb. That same evening Jesus appears to his disciples in the house in Jerusalem. Instead of ascending (there is no ascension narrative in John) as he does in Luke, he returns eight days later to the same house to encounter Thomas, who for some reason had not been present at the earlier meeting.

In the second concluding chapter of the Gospel, Jesus appears to eight of his followers who are out fishing on the sea of Galilee (or Tiberias, as it is here called). Thus we do finally have an appearance in Galilee but it is not on a mountain (as in Matthew) but on the lakeshore.

Once again we find ourselves in the situation of irreconcilable differences not only between accounts, but also within the same account. Just exactly where and to whom does Jesus appear after his execution? There appears to be even less agreement here than in the case of the empty tomb. Even the location (Galilee or Jerusalem) is entirely determined by kerygmatic and theological considerations. Neither Mark or Matthew will permit an appearance to the disciples in Jerusalem (although Matthew will permit a redundant appearance to the women there). Luke will absolutely not permit an appearance in the Galilee; the disciples *must* stay in Jerusalem until Pentecost (and so until after the ascension has put an end to resurrection appearances altogether). In the Gospel of Luke all the appearances take place on a single day. But in Acts (presumably by the same author) we are told that the appearances occur over a period of forty days. In John the resurrection appearances appear to be an open-ended series.

It is little help to add the earliest account of resurrection appearances available to us—the list that we find in 1 Corinthians 15. Here we find the following list: (a) Cephas, (b) the twelve, (c) the five hundred, (d) James, (e) all the apostles, (f) Paul. This list bears no relation whatever to the Gospel narratives, in which we have no account of an initial appearance to Peter; indeed this is flatly contradicted by Luke,

Matthew, John, and the longer ending of Mark. There is no appearance in the Gospels to the "twelve," although we do have appearances to the "eleven" in Jerusalem according to Luke and the longer ending of Mark and a final appearance to the eleven in Matthew (although in Galilee rather than Jerusalem). Indeed, an appearance to the twelve seems impossible, at least for Luke, for the twelve are not reconstituted until after the ascension.

We have no account of anything like an appearance to the five hundred which in any case seems impossible for Luke and the longer ending of Mark, although possible for Acts and John. It is not clear what is meant by all the apostles since it appears to be a category different either from the twelve or the five hundred. An appearance to Paul entails a more or less open-ended sequence beyond the forty days of Acts. This would seem to be permissible only for the Gospel of John. From the standpoint of Acts this would not be a resurrection appearance at all, but a vision of the ascended Lord like that reported by Stephen. But while Paul here lists several resurrection appearances either unknown to or excluded by the evangelists, he omits any mention of those appearances that play an important role in the Gospels. He does not mention an appearance to Mary Magdalene (with or without sisters) as reported by Matthew, longer Mark, and John. Nor does he mention the "two" to whom Luke gives such prominence and who are also mentioned in the longer ending of Mark. Nor does he mention the appearance by the lake shore that occupies the entire final chapter of John.

Once again, if we were attempting to get at the "facts" behind the accounts we would be in a hopeless position. Apart from the assertion that Jesus appears to some followers somewhere and at sometime following his execution, there is not a single point of agreement and there are, as we have seen, a good many flat contradictions. The poor historian who seeks to arrive at a plausible kernel of fact here is in dire straits, as is the fundamentalist. But we are theologians, not historians, and so were the authors of our texts. The texts are not histories, but sermons. They are concerned not with what lies behind the story, but with what stands in front of them.

There is a word that we find on the lips of Jesus in the Gospel of John when Jesus appears to Mary Magdalene in the cemetery: "Don't hold me . . . ." The attempt to "get hold" of the resurrection is prohibited. But this prohibition is followed by a command: "go to my brothers and tell them . . . ." It is in the "going" of proclamation and not in the "holding" of history that the significance of the resurrection, whether as empty tomb or as appearance, is to be discerned.

3. MEANING

When we approach the resurrection appearance narratives asking not what lies behind them, but what lies before them as the meaning they are "driving at" and "driving home," we find a number of themes that are of great importance for faith.

Mystery

The first theme is the inconceivability of the event itself. Whatever is meant by resurrection it absolutely exceeds the capacity of language to explicate and so to domesticate. This theme is expressed in a number of ways in the New Testament accounts. There are at least three basic reactions on the part of Jesus' friends which especially draw our attention to this inconceivability. They are fear, unbelief, and non-recognition.

1. The reaction of fear and dismay is the only reaction we encounter in the original narrative of Mark.[14] The reaction of the women to hearing the news of Jesus' resurrection is one of panic, speechlessness, and terror. This is scarcely the reaction one is led to expect from all those confident and more or less implausible Easter sermons we hear in the course of a lifetime in the Church. Easter sermons regularly try to tell us that everything is fine, not to worry, that things turn out well in the end. Scarcely the stuff of the nightmarish panic that we encounter in the Gospel of Mark. Those who run away in panic are not Jesus' enemies, whom he has confounded by appearing, but his dearest friends who are there because they love him and wish to do him honor. They are not reassured, but terrified by the announcement of resurrection.

A resurrection message that is not in some way terrifying is not the message of the resurrection of Jesus. There is something going on here which, far from reassuring Jesus' friends and making them feel smug in their Easter finery, shakes them to their foundations and sends them running in speechless panic.

It is not only in Mark that we find this reaction (although in Mark it is the only reaction). In Matthew the reaction of the soldiers to the appearance of the messenger of the resurrection is also one of panic—although this might be expected perhaps due to earthquakes and guilty consciences. But the messenger also has to tell the women not to be afraid (Matthew 28:5), and even then they depart still very frightened (28:8), although now the fear is mingled with joy. In the Gospel of Luke, when Jesus appears to the eleven and "those who were gathered with them," the immediate reaction is again one of terror, "supposing they saw a ghost" (24:37).

Now what is the meaning of this terror? To an important degree its

135

meaning depends on the narrative context within which it is located. Yet we may still put forward a general thesis: the terror marks the apparition of that which cannot be grasped or assimilated. When the categories of our experience and expectation are shattered, the mind and heart panic. The earth upon which we so confidently stood begins to tremble and it seems that nothing can stand. As Matthew suggests, the resurrection of Jesus is something like an earthquake which throws us to the quivering ground and takes away our ability to stand or understand. Far from confirming in us our beliefs and assumptions, the resurrection throws everything into question.

2. The second expression of this theme of unintelligibility is that of unbelief. It is not the unbelief of outsiders which is at stake here, but the unbelief of Jesus' closest friends and most stalwart followers.

In the Gospel of Luke, the disciples simply reject out of hand the Easter message brought them by the first apostles, Mary Magdalene and Joanna, Mary the mother of James, and the other women who were with them. They regard it as an "idle tale" (Luke 24:10-11).

In the long ending to Mark we find that neither Mary Magdalene nor even "the two men walking in the country" were believed by the rest (Mark 16:11-12). Thus it is not only the women who are disbelieved. In Matthew at the final resurrection appearance of Jesus on the mountain in Galilee we hear that while some worshiped him, others doubted what they seemed to see with their own eyes! Until now the doubters had been those who did not see. But even seeing is not believing.

In the Gospel of John we also encounter the doubt of the friends of Jesus, this time in the account of "doubting Thomas." As we have seen, church tradition gives Thomas a "bum rap." When it comes to not believing the Easter message he has lots of company: all of Jesus' other friends. When people today say that they find the resurrection hard to believe, it should not simply be attributed to modern post-mythological consciousness. It is a reaction inscribed already in the earliest resurrection narratives.

3. The third expression of this theme of inconceivability is that of the non-recognition of the risen Jesus. Here we come to what may be the most difficult (and also universal) characteristic of these traditions. This is especially difficult for those who suppose that there is an obvious and literal meaning for the resurrection narratives. Jesus appears and is simply not recognized. This alone should demonstrate that we are not dealing with a legend about a resuscitated corpse. No one has any trouble recognizing Lazarus or the daughter of Jairus or the youngster in Nain or even Eutychus. But they do not recognize Jesus.

This is the point of Luke's extraordinary narrative about the two "apostles" (Cleopas and the anonymous one) who meet a stranger on the road, talk with him at great length while they walk, and invite him to supper. In all of this they still don't recognize him. When they do recognize him (how they do so is something to which we will return to later), he vanishes from sight.

In what is probably a reference to the same story, the longer ending to Mark says that Jesus appeared to the two "in another form." This is somewhat at variance with Luke's explanation ("their eyes were kept from recognizing him") but the end result is the same.

This same theme is echoed not once, but four times by the Gospel of John (that is, in connection with every resurrection narrative in the Gospel). In the cemetery Mary Magdalene has a conversation with a man she takes to be a groundskeeper. Only after he calls her by name does she recognize him. When Jesus subsequently appears to the disciples they also seem not to recognize him until he shows them the marks of the cross, and the same is true of Thomas eight days later. In the final chapter Jesus stands on the beach talking to his friends about fishing. If we were to take the narrative order seriously here it would mean that these same friends have seen the risen Jesus twice before, yet even now they don't recognize him. Only when the net nearly bursts with one hundred and fifty-three large fish does "the disciple Jesus loved" finally recognize him. According to John, Jesus' closest female and male friends have trouble recognizing him.[15]

We have noticed three ways in which the resurrection narratives draw attention to the inconceivability of that which they are narrating. The terror, unbelief, and non-recognition which are found in these narratives all point us away from a simple-minded or literal-minded interpretation of the resurrection appearances. Each in its own way is concerned to narrate something that exceeds all categories of explanation. We should then not be surprised that there is so little agreement among the narratives about what actually happened. The irreconcilability of the narratives points us in the same direction as the terror, unbelief, and non-recognition which is narrated.

Now if the matter were left here we might suppose that we had an indeterminant "x" here in place of the resurrection. This in itself would be preferable to those misunderstandings that begin by assuming what must be meant by resurrection and so fail to take into account its most characteristic feature.

Yet this is by no means the only feature of these varied accounts. If they point to the mystery and inconceivability of this resurrection, they also point to its "materiality" or definiteness. They do this in at least two ways. One is to insist on the relation of the resurrection to the crucified one. The other is to speak of eating and drinking. Are these merely crude materialistic concessions to a mythological world view, or are they instead driving at something of fundamental importance for faith?

The Resurrection of the Crucified

The gospel concerning the cross may be understood as the revocation of the negative verdict of the historical cross.[16] Historically the cross represents the power of domination and division. Thus the gospel of the cross represents reconciliation and liberation. Historically the cross represents the power of the law to condemn; theologically it is the message of the grace and mercy of God.

This revocation or reversal is the positive meaning of the resurrection. It has the form of the reversal of death by life. This transformation is proclaimed by the Christian community as the divine reversal of the worldly judgment that imposes the cross as the correct punishment for Jesus. In the first Christian sermon according to Acts, Peter gives this as the meaning of the resurrection:

> This Jesus, delivered up according to the definite plan and foreknowledge of God, you crucified and killed by the hands of lawless men. But God raised him up, having loosed the pangs of death . . . . (Acts 2:23-24)

Thus, the reversal of the worldly verdict is not arbitrary or speculative but rather based in the event of the resurrection. In order to understand the resurrection it is necessary to understand it in rigorous relation to the cross. There is no resurrection that is not the resurrection of the crucified.[17] If without the resurrection the cross indicates the power of the forces of domination and division, of hostility and the law, then without the cross the resurrection becomes just another happy ending which can make us acquiesce in these same powers. When the Church forgets this rigorous relationship between cross and resurrection, it loses its way and begins to worship illusions and superstitions with no relation to the gospel. In order to show the importance of this relationship, we may briefly indicate some of the ways it is expressed in the New Testament.

1. We have seen that the Gospels relate various anticipations (sometimes called predictions) of the passion. Here we draw attention to the fact that in every case in which rejection and suffering and death are mentioned as the appropriate or fitting end of the Son of man (or "new humanity"), we also hear of resurrection "after three days." We have in the Gospel of Mark three of these anticipations (8:31; 9:31; 10:34). In this way the Gospel of Mark (as well as Matthew and Luke) establish that cross and resurrection must be understood together as one destiny, even as a single event.

2. The references to the passion of Jesus in the Gospel of John are always and at the same time references to the resurrection. This unity is expressed in the double entendre "lifted up" (John 3:14, 8:28, 12:32-34), a phrase which unites cross and resurrection in a single event.

3. The accounts of the crucifixion of Jesus are also used to express this relation to the resurrection. This is especially remarkable in the account from Matthew of Jesus' death, where we are told that when Jesus gave up his spirit, the graves were opened and many bodies of the saints who had fallen asleep were raised up (Matthew 27:52). This remarkable story appears in no other account of the death of Jesus. But like the other accounts, this one demonstrates an intimate relation between the cross of Jesus and the resurrection.[18]

4. But the most important expression of this intimate relation is found in the resurrection accounts themselves. In the announcement at the empty tomb (in Mark, Matthew, and Luke), the messenger (remember that it seems to be a different messenger in each story) reminds the women that Jesus had said that he must die and that he must be raised. The initial announcement of the resurrection is the announcement of the resurrection of the crucified.

5. In the Gospel of Luke the long encounter between Jesus and Cleopas and the other disciple is largely concerned with the unrecognized Jesus explaining the importance of the cross. The "content" of the resurrection appearance is precisely this clarification of the significance of the crucifixion.

6. In the next Lukan account of the appearances to his disciples, Jesus again explicates the unity of cross and resurrection, "showing how it was necessary that the Christ should suffer and be raised from the dead on the third day" (Luke 24:46). But the disciples only actually recognize Jesus when he shows them the marks of his crucifixion (24:39).

7. Finally, in the Gospel of John the insistence that the resurrection of Jesus must be understood as the resurrection of the crucified is highlighted in the story of Thomas' doubt, as well as of his being persuaded. It is the mark of the cross that demonstrates the identity of the risen one.

8. Although it is not a part of the narrative tradition we are considering, we should not fail to mention that the connection between cross and resurrection is also emphasized by Paul. For him it is always the resurrection of the crucified that is important. Thus Paul can simply subsume resurrection into the message of the cross.

On the basis of this summary we can affirm that the resurrection of Jesus must not be understood in isolation from the cross. We may even say that the resurrection of Jesus appears to have no other content than that of the cross. It is the exclamation mark that follows the cross and so gives it its distinctive emphasis. By means of the resurrection of Jesus we do not believe in yet another resuscitated body, but in the reversal of the verdict of the powers of this world, the powers of division and domination, a reversal that leads to the proclamation of the God of love and of the ultimate reality of justice, liberty, and love. When we do not believe in the radical and total transformation of the structures of the world we do not rely upon the cross or the resurrection, but on an illusion.

It is true that we often encounter a proclamation of the resurrection that does not have this rigorous relation to the cross. The proclamation of the resurrection apart from the cross leads to another myth of success that seeks to evade the reality of conflict, suffering, and martyrdom. This is the myth and cult that we so often encounter in North American Protestantism. It leads us to believe in a Jesus who is a kind of legendary hero who, in spite of difficulties, is able to win out and have earthly success. This is a pagan faith in spite of its promiscuous use of names like Jesus, Lord, and Saviour.

Alongside this new myth of success we also encounter a more ancient myth, that of the god who dies and rises. Many of the religions of the Hellenistic world spoke of a dying and rising god. As this myth was well known in the world within which Christianity developed, it was possible for Christianity to appropriate features of it to express its own faith. But the difference between Christianity and these cults was the memory of a human being in the historical and public sphere: Jesus of Nazareth, whose destiny was the cross. Thus we do not proclaim a resurrection in general (on the order of, say, the coming of the spring after the winter) but rather the resurrection of the one who suffered and was crucified under the power of Pontius Pilate. When this is forgotten, the cross and the resurrection are understood in a merely allegorical or "spiritual" sense. In this case "spiritual" means to have no relation to the historical or public sphere but only to interiority and the "other" world. This cross means nothing other than death in general and has no reference to the real powers of division and domination, of Pontius Pilate or the law. But without this groundedness in the earth which the historical cross provides, our talk of the cross has no root in reality and the resurrection merely suggests a spiritual victory without a transformation of reality. Many Christians suppose that this sort of faith is more spiritual and so more Christian. The irony is that this sort of faith is precisely that faith represented by the pagan cults that were the earliest opponents of Christianity. Now these pagan cults are resuscitated by Christians themselves.

Thus it is urgent in our time to recall that we do not announce our faith in and loyalty to just any god (for, as Paul says, there are many gods). Rather, we rely upon and are loyal to one Lord Jesus Christ. This is not an empty name for which we may supply any sort of religious or mythic content. It is not possible to use terms like cross and resurrection without reference to the precise realities that are the basis of our faith. The Jesus in whom we trust and to whom we proclaim our loyalty is the one who was crucified under the power of Pontius Pilate. The resurrection we proclaim is the resurrection of the crucified. Thus we rely on the love of God which is not abstract but concrete, on the grace of God that seeks neither to escape nor to explain the world, but to transform it.

4. EATING AND DRINKING, THE ANTICIPATION OF THE VICTORY OF GOD

In all their diversity, the resurrection narratives point backward to the cross and insist that the resurrection with which we are concerned is none other than the resurrection of the crucified. But there is a second point of agreement between many of these accounts which signals the eschatological communion of Jesus with his followers.

In the Gospel of Luke when Jesus encounters the two disciples walking to Emmaus he not only explains from Scripture the meaning of the cross and its tie to the resurrection, he also accompanies them into the wayside tavern to share a meal with them. It is precisely as he breaks bread with them that they recognize him (Luke 24:30-31).

Subsequently, when Jesus appears to the disciples in their Jerusalem hideout he not only seeks to quell their initial panic by showing them the marks of the cross, but also inquires whether they have anything to eat. They find him some leftovers (24:41-43), and it is again in eating with them that he is recognized.

Finally, in the final appended chapter of the Gospel of John Jesus prepares a fish fry on the beach for his followers (John 21:9-13). Clearly the resurrection has something to do with eating and drinking. This connection is re-enforced when we recall that the raising of Jairus' daughter concludes with Jesus asking the parents to give the girl something to eat (Mark 5:43).

What is going on here? We should recall that eating and drinking with friends and strangers was one of the characteristic activities of Jesus' ministry—so much so that his opponents accused him of being a drunk and a glutton. When he spoke of the reign of God it was often to speak of an invitation to a party. In his mission to the multitudes he not only healed and taught them, but also fed them in the wilderness.

Thus it is no accident that the resurrection not only points to the cross, but also includes this characteristic reference to eating and drinking. It is in the conjunction of these images, that of the cross and that of the party or fiesta of the reign of God, that we come closest to the heart of the meaning of Jesus' resurrection.

It is of course true that this aspect of the resurrection puts us in mind of the Eucharist. But the Eucharist is not only the recollection of Jesus' death, but also the celebration of his victory over the powers of death. That is, it is not only the "Last Supper" remembered (and so the Lord's Supper), it is also Eucharist: celebration and thanksgiving.

We must beware of speaking of the Eucharist in a one-sidedly "cultic" way. There is nothing cultic about stopping over at a tavern, having leftovers in the hideout, or making breakfast on the beach. The resurrection is expressed not in the closed confines of the liturgical act of the sacramental space, but rather in the open friendship of Jesus that celebrates the coming of the reign of God. For this, the Eucharist may serve as a kind of summary, a sort of sketch or blueprint, but it may not become a substitute for the real thing. The real thing is the celebration of the coming of the reign of God which is anticipated whenever the companionship of the mission is celebrated, whenever the hungry are fed, whenever God's fiesta overcomes the "everydayness" of the reign of anxiety and avarice.

As the anticipation of the messianic fiesta, the resurrection of Jesus is the beginning of the general resurrection of the dead. The overcoming of enmity and separation by friendship, and of lack by the sharing of bread points to the overcoming of death by resurrection life. According to Paul, the resurrection of Jesus is but the beginning of the resurrection of the dead. It is the "first fruits" that herald the beginning of the eschatological harvest of the general triumph of God over the powers of death. It is this which Paul stressed primarily in 1 Corinthians 15: the resurrection of Jesus entails our own.

The notion of the resurrection of the dead will be the theme of discussion when we come to that clause of the Creed. Here what is important to notice is that the resurrection of Jesus is not an isolated event. It heralds the resurrection which marks the transformation of history. It signals not the general "immortality of the soul," but the final resurrection of the dead. The resurrection of Jesus points to the final consummation of all things when the last enemy is overthrown.[19]

Thus, the resurrection of Jesus points not only to the past as the resurrection of the crucified, but also to the future for us and for the world, a future whose meaning is the resurrection of the dead already begun in the resurrection of Jesus. This future is already present in the eating together (com-pan-ionship) of the risen Jesus with his followers. We will have occasion to clarify this present and this future in subsequent clauses of this article (is seated, will come) as well as in the third article of the Creed.

The resurrection of Jesus is affirmed in nearly every text of the New

Testament. Yet it is affirmed in such a way as to clearly elude discursive or narrative comprehension. It eludes speech at the same time that it provokes speech. Yet despite this elusive character it has clear coordinates with the cross and with the companionship that anticipates the aim of the resurrection of the dead.

CHAPTER FOURTEEN

ASCENDED INTO HEAVEN

The ascension of Jesus marks the transition from the past of Jesus to the present and future. Thus the resurrection is marked off as a definite set of events with a determinant significance. In this way the resurrection is prevented from becoming a vague and contentless apparition—as is threatened with Paul's inclusion of Jesus' appearance to him within the set of resurrection appearances.

The ascension of Jesus is actually narrated only in Luke and Acts and in the apparently dependent longer ending of Mark. But it seems also to be presupposed by the Gospel of John. As we shall see, the meaning of the ascension as the commission of Jesus to his followers is also present in texts which do not have an ascension narrative.

The three accounts of the ascension present the following picture:

> And when he had said this, as they were looking on, he was lifted up, and a cloud took him out of their sight. (Acts 1:9)

> While he blessed them, he was parted from them. (Luke 24:51)

> So then the Lord Jesus, after he had spoken to them, was taken up into heaven, and sat down at the right hand of God. (Mark 16:19)

What is the meaning of this odd event which is told in such a strange way?

From the standpoint of the Gospel of John the ascension of Jesus, though not actually narrated, is presupposed as the aim of Jesus' cross and resurrection. Thus, the way in which John refers to the complex of cross and resurrection as "being lifted up" also includes the ascension as the culmination of this upward movement. From this point of view the resurrection itself is simply a kind of transitional moment which aims at the ascension. This is made clear, for example, in Jesus' initial resurrection appearance to Mary Magdalene. There, Jesus responds to her belated recognition of him with the warning "Do not hold me, for I have not yet ascended to the Father" (John 20:17).

In Luke and Acts the ascension serves to put a limit to the resurrection appearances. In Luke these appearances are limited to the "first day" which includes the appearances to Mary, to the two disciples, and to the eleven. This series is concluded, apparently on the same day, by Jesus leading the disciples out toward Bethany where he ascends. In the Acts of the Apostles the ascension is said to occur "forty days" after the beginning of the resurrection appearances. Whether this forty days is to be understood as a definite number or as simply an indication of symmetry (as in forty days in the wilderness[20]) is not clear. In any case the ascension serves to put a limit to the resurrection appearances which are thereby marked off as belonging decidedly to the past, rather than being an open-ended series.

In the Gospel of Mark, where there is no narration of the ascension (except in the appended longer ending), we get some idea of the attitude toward the resurrection appearances which may have played a role in the limitation of them, or their treatment as a transitional moment. In Jesus' farewell discourse we encounter the warning against what may be taken as false resurrection appearance reports:

> Many will come in my name, saying, "I am he!" and they will lead many astray. (Mark 13:6)

> And then if anyone says to you, "Look, here is the Christ!" or "Look, there he is!" do not believe it. False Christs and false prophets will arise and show signs and wonders, to lead astray, if possible, the elect. (Mark 13:21-22)

These warnings seem to point to the possibility of false resurrection appearances ("I am he") and false reports of such appearances ("here is the Christ"). The reason for discounting such events is to prevent the community from being led astray by those who make use of the gullibility associated with appearance reports. It would appear that there was some actual danger that reports of encounters with the risen Lord could be manipulated in order to lend credence to distortions (from Mark's point of view) of the gospel. This suspicion of the way in which such reports could be used to subvert the gospel may help to explain why Mark has no post-crucifixion appearances of Jesus. In this respect then it is possible that the Luke-Acts limitation of the resurrection appearances through the ascension and John's relativizing of them as provisional and transitional are less radical versions of a shared strategy aimed at preventing the misappropriation of the resurrection for ideological purposes within the community.

Up to this point we have considered the ascension from the standpoint of its relation to the resurrection. But do the accounts of the ascension have no independent or at least "proper" significance?

THE COMMISSION

When we persist in asking this question we see that in every case the ascension is linked with an account of Jesus commissioning the disciples, his understudies in ministry and mission, to continue the work that he had taught them by word and example.

Thus in Acts: "and you shall be my witnesses in Jerusalem and in all Judea and Samaria and to the end of the earth" (1:8); and in the Gospel of Luke: "and that repentance and forgiveness of sins should be preached in his name to all nations, beginning from Jerusalem. You are witnesses of these things" (24:47-48). In the long ending to the Gospel of Mark we have something similar: "Go into all the world and preach the gospel to the whole creation" (16:15).

Each of the accounts carries with it the commissioning of the disciples. The positive content of the ascension narratives seems to be this commission to represent Jesus and the gospel.

We remember that the first thing Jesus did in his ministry was to call disciples to be his understudies. He teaches them, he takes them with him. He gets them to try their wings by sending them out two by two. He tells them that his own death will help them face the inevitable trials and persecutions which they will encounter. And even following his resurrection, he continues to instruct them about the gospel they must carry forward.

Jesus' ascension means that his ministry and mission is entrusted to his disciples. He has shown them what is to be done, he has taught them how to conduct themselves, he has instructed them in the ways of life that represent the coming of God's reign of justice and generosity and joy. Now it is their turn, now it is their responsibility.

In a way their responsibility seems even greater. Before the ascension Jesus' ministry was confined to a single place, a single nation, a single time in history. Jesus carried out his ministry and mission in Palestine. He showed them there how it was to be done. But following the ascension the mission of Jesus suddenly becomes liberated. It now reaches out to all nations, to all time, to every place. It is suddenly multiplied. It becomes something that can be encountered not only in first-century Palestine, but in every nation, in every era, in every place and time. It breaks the bounds, the limits of place and time, to become the universal good news available to all and available always.

The ascension, then, has the significance of the dissemination of the gospel across the boundaries of place and time. The time of this dissemination is the entire period from Jesus' ascension until his coming "to judge the living and the dead."

When this commissioning and so this dissemination is seen to be the significance of the ascension, then two other texts normally associated with the resurrection become essential to the presentation of this theme. First, this reminds us of the ending of the Gospel of Matthew which seems to combine Jesus' resurrection and ascension, and in which Jesus says to the disciples:

> Go therefore and make disciples of all nations, baptizing them in the name of the Father and of the Son and of the Holy Spirit, teaching them to observe all that I have commanded you. (28:19-20)

The commission here includes the themes of sending and the indication of the extent of this sending (all nations). The distinctive emphasis of Matthew lies in the charge to baptize, as well as in the command to teach, which corresponds to the distinctive emphasis of this Gospel on Jesus as teacher.

The second text that comes into play here is the penultimate resurrection appearance of John 20.[21] There Jesus encounters his disciples (except for Thomas), shows them "his hands and his side," and then says: "Peace be with you. As the Father has sent me, even so I sent you" (John 20:21). The sending which is the distinctive theme of the ascension is here made comprehensive and definitive, for it becomes evident that the disciples are indeed commissioned to carry on Jesus' ministry and mission in every respect, to imitate the word and action of the Father. This account also includes John's version of the reception of the Holy Spirit (verse 22) and the further specification of the authorization of the disciples to exercise authority with respect to the forgiveness (and "retaining") of sin (verse 23).

The commissioning of the disciples in each of these accounts implies that the significance of the ascension is that the past of Jesus now becomes the pattern for the activity of the disciples or understudies. They are now fully responsible for the continuation of Jesus' ministry and mission, which on this account, escapes the confines of space and time to become universal.

In the third article of the Creed we will have occasion to speak of the Holy Spirit as the capacitation for this task, of the Church and the communion of saints as the context of this mission, and of the forgiveness of sins as the characteristic feature of this activity. But here what is in view is simply the continuation of the ministry and mission of Jesus. This provides a certain critique of a kind of ecclesio-centrism which would make of the Church an independent theme, rather than subsuming it clearly and decisively under the theme of the continuation of the mission and ministry of Jesus.

The commissioning of the disciples to continue the mission and ministry of Jesus is also the restoration of the primal commission of humans to be the image and likeness of God, and so to be those who represent and reflect the being and activity of God in the world.

We began by noting the relation between the ascension and the resurrection. This relation is not only a negative one of placing a limit or term to the resurrection appearances, but also entails a positive and confirmatory relation as well. We noted that it is characteristic of both empty tomb and appearance traditions concerning the resurrection to insist on the incomprehensibility of the resurrection, an incomprehensibility to which the incompatibility of the various accounts also gives testimony. The ascension points to the only way in which the resurrection can be verified in such a way as to be credible. It is precisely in the activity of those who have been commissioned to continue the mission and ministry of the crucified. While Bultmann's formula that Christ is risen into the proclamation of the community is questionable, it does seem fair to say that Jesus is "ascended" into the proclamation and witness of the followers. And it is insofar as this witness really does continue in such a way as to bear recognizable relation to the mission of the crucified, that the resurrection acquires credibility.

THE PROMISE

Viewed as the limit and term of the resurrection appearances, the ascension may appear to signal the absence of Jesus. But this impression is countered by a further theme of the ascension/commission narratives, the theme of the promise of Jesus, his blessing and empowerment of the disciples so that they are capable of doing what they are called to do.

In Acts, Jesus promises that the disciples will receive power from on high to continue the mission. In Luke, Jesus lifts up his hands to bless those who continue in his mission. In Mark, Jesus promises the followers that their following will be accompanied by signs of Jesus' continuing presence with them. Perhaps the most clear expression of this blessing and promise are the final words of Jesus in the Gospel of Matthew: "And lo, I am with you always, to the close [end] of the age" (Matthew 28:20*b*). That he is with us is an indispensable part of the message of the ascension.

The ascension focuses not on the absence, but rather on the presence of Jesus.[22] It concerns his promise to accompany his disciples as they follow him, to be present to them as they represent him, to empower them as they continue in his mission and ministry.

In this way the accounts of the ascension point us clearly toward the way in which Jesus exercises authority in the present (is seated) and to the way in which the disciples are empowered to continue this ministry and mission (the Holy Spirit).

A consideration of the ascension narratives confirms that what is of greatest importance here is not the undoubtedly spectacular features of a literal disappearance into the clouds, but rather the identification of Jesus' on-going presence in the world—in the mission and ministry entrusted to his followers. That the spectacular myth-like features of this clause are not its basic point is also illustrated in Acts when the disciples are chastised for staring open-mouthed at the skies into which Jesus has so impressively disappeared. The messenger's word to them points them back to terra firma and to the mission for which they have been commissioned and for which they will shortly be empowered.

CHAPTER FIFTEEN

SITS AT THE RIGHT HAND

With this clause of the Creed a dramatic shift occurs from the past to the present. In the long central section of the Creed we have celebrated the "dangerous memory" of faith which is directed toward Jesus as the Son of God and the Lord of the community. This memory is recited with verbs in the past tense which are the drumbeat of faith: conceived, born, suffered, crucified, dead, buried, descended, rose, ascended. This emphatic rhythmic iteration of memory is now suddenly broken by a verb in the present tense, "is seated." The accumulated force of this memory suddenly lights up the present: the present of Jesus, the present of the community, the present of the world.

Yet it is remarkable that it is only here and in this curious way that the second article of the Creed refers to the present. For immediately afterward we are directed to the future of Jesus and so to our future as those who are loyal to him ("from whence he shall come to judge the living and the dead.") Thus it is only here and in this odd phrase that the presence of Jesus is spoken of directly. Of course, in another sense we have always been speaking of the present, of our present as those who do rely upon this God (the Father Almighty) and this Jesus, and as those whose lives are determined by the loyalty we here announce and confess. Thus, in speaking of the past of Jesus we have been speaking of a past that discloses the identity of the one upon whom we rely and to whom we seek to be loyal. In this way that past determines our present identity.

Nevertheless, it is altogether remarkable that the present is directly spoken of as the present of Jesus and the Father only at this point and in this way. Indeed, even here, it is by no means an independent clause that stands on its own, but is instead a fleeting transitional clause linking together the past of the ascension and the future of the return. This is in itself surprising, for from another point of view the present between the life and death of Jesus and his "return" seems altogether more weighty and significant than this brief and glancing mention in the Creed would suggest. It is, after all, the time of history in which already nearly two thousand years have passed, and in which we now still stand. Yet in the Creed, all of this is collapsed into a fleeting transitional clause.

We will have occasion in the third article of the Creed to speak of Spirit and Church and the forgiveness of sins, all of which bear upon this present, and shape it. Yet it is well to remember that from the standpoint of this central and fundamental article of the Creed, the present, and especially the present of faith and the Church is but a fleeting and transitional moment whose meaning is wholly determined by the past which it remembers and the future for which it hopes. The present has no independent status, not even, as we shall see, the present of the Spirit.

This is an especially salutary warning both to the Church and to faith. We are forever experiencing the temptation to give to both the Church and faith an independent and permanent status, permitting the past to recede to a shadowy time of origin, while the future becomes a mere appendix marked off as "eschatology." In this view all that is really important takes place "between." It is in this way that we come to preoccupy ourselves with the structures and strategies of Church life, of ecclesiastical authority, sacraments, orders, liturgies, and with institutional extension, preservation, and program. Similarly it is here, in this space opened up by a receding past and an equally receding future that we allow ourselves leisure to become preoccupied with the analysis of faith, conversion, and our own holiness. Both institutional and individualistic distortions of faith are made possible by this wide and inviting space between the past and the future. But within the structure of the Creed, all of this is rendered highly problematic and indeed, fundamentally impossible. For here, this wide and inviting space of the "between" is rendered as a brief, transitional, and dependent clause.

I do not mean to imply that the present, and especially the present of history, is here rendered insignificant. On the contrary, the meaning of the present (and of the historical present between the past and future of Jesus) is completely specified. But it is specified as dependent upon and determined by the past and the future of Jesus. It is in the light shed by this past and this future that we live in the "twilight" (double light) of the present and so of history. That this does not rob us of the present and of history, the world and the body as some in the tradition of the Church have supposed is made clear precisely by what past and future, and by whose past and future we rely upon and are loyal to in the present. Already we have seen with what insistence the Creed has spoken of the past as the past of Jesus, which directs us to the real world of history and of humanity. Later, we will speak again of the future, but here we must confirm that the present in which we stand is the present determined by the memory of Jesus: conceived, born, suffered, crucified, dead, buried, descended, raised, ascended.

Even when we recognize the reason for and significance of the brief and fleeting nature of this reference to the present and restrain ourselves from leaping over this impediment to speak at length about Church and faith, we may still be dismayed, if not at the brevity, then at the strange, "mythological," and uncongenial way in which the Creed speaks of the present as the present of Jesus "who is seated at the right hand of God the Father Almighty." What is the meaning of this curious phrase and how does it disclose for us the meaning of the "between" in which we live?

We must first notice that while the phrase does not occur often in the New Testament, it does occur at crucial points both early and late. It occurs only once in the letters of Paul, but in such a way as to be highly significant for our reflections on the Creed: the compressed, hymnic, and semi-creedal formula which introduces the triumphant anthem of assurance that concludes the eighth chapter of Romans.

> It is God who justifies; who is to condemn? Is it Christ Jesus, who died, yes, who was raised from the dead, who is at the right hand of God, who indeed intercedes for us? Who shall separate us from the love of Christ? (8:33-35)

Thus we see that this way of describing the present of Jesus is recorded quite early and is already formulated in terms of the definitive events of cross and resurrection. Moreover, we also have here an explication of the meaning of this phrase, for it clearly suggests to Paul the ground of a completely triumphant confidence in the power of Christ's love. Already we are warned against viewing this clause as a merely speculative, or even "mythological" depiction of the location of Jesus, but rather as an assertion concerning the ground of our confidence in God made possible in and through Jesus "who died, who was raised, who sits, who intercedes."

This phrase is found in a variety of other texts. In Colossians it serves as the basis for an admonition to discover our identity precisely in the identity of Christ who is "seated at the right hand of God" (3:1). This then serves as the basis of an admonition to shun evil and to put on the character of love. In Ephesians 1:20-21 it designates the complete authority of Christ "far above all rule and authority and power and dominion" in a way that is reminiscent of the Romans passage.

Similarly in 1 Peter 3:22 the assertion that Jesus is "at the right hand of God" stands in the context of an appeal for steadfastness in faith, endurance in hope, apparently in the face of persecution at the hands of those who appear to rule the world. The two references in Hebrews (1:3; 10:12) have in view the authority of Jesus which is understood against the background of the cross as "purification of sins." It, too, is a call to confidence in this Jesus whose work is understood in this way.

The phrase is also included in the long ending of Mark (16:19); in Peter's first sermon (Acts 2:33), where it is associated with the gift of the Spirit; and in Stephen's dying vision (Acts 7:56).

It is quite possible that these allusions have as their background an eschatological depiction of the "New Human" (the Son of man). This is the character of the saying that we find in the Synoptic Gospels in which Jesus, in response to his interrogation by the high priest, speaks of this "New Human" sitting at the right hand of God (Mark 14:62; Matthew 26:64; Luke 22:69). In this context the saying refers to the future and to the Son of man in the third person. For the confession of faith (see Stephen's vision) that future has become present and the new humanity is already inaugurated in and through Jesus.[23]

But all of this only demonstrates that this phrase is one which is firmly rooted in New Testament tradition. It does not yet explain its meaning. In order to do this it may be helpful to reflect first on the significance of "sitting" and then on that of the "right hand." This apparently childishly literal language points us in the direction of a profound truth without which our understanding of faith would be incomplete.

For the biblical world, sitting is the posture or "body language" of authority.[24] In the Gospel of Matthew, when Jesus instructs the crowds he first takes up this posture of authority (Matthew 5:1; 13:1-2). This image still survives in the reference to a court or legislature as "sitting," by which is meant that they are at work, exercising legitimate authority. Similarly, we may indicate the authority of a ruler by referring to the "throne," or to the authority of a professor by referring to the "chair" of philosophy, or speak of authoritative pronouncements of the pope as *ex cathedra*—as "from the chair." In more mundane contexts, we speak of the one who presides over a meeting or a group as the "chair."

To speak of Jesus as "sitting," then, designates not inactivity but activity, not retirement from the world, but the exercise of authority. Thus when the disciples wished for special privilege and authority this was expressed as the right "to sit" (Matthew 20:21). And the parable of the Last Judgment refers to the king who pronounces judgment as "sitting" (Matthew 25:31). Indeed, in the Gospel of Luke this posture is already appropriate to Jesus as a child who was discovered "sitting among the teachers" (Luke 2:46).

But to sit has another meaning in this context; it is also the posture of fellowship, of intimate friendship. Thus, Jesus speaks of the fellowship of the Gentiles with Abraham, Isaac, and Jacob in the reign of God (Matthew

8:11). Matthew follows this saying with the scene of Jesus sitting at table with tax collectors and sinners (9:10). Sitting at table signifies the fellowship of those who eat and drink together in the messianic banquet. When Jesus is said to be sitting at the right hand of God, it is ordinarily his authority which is in view. But, as in the case of Romans 8:34, what is also in view is the intimacy of Jesus' relationship with the Father that anticipates the universal intimacy of the messianic banquet.

The "right hand" of God is the power of God to deliver. In the song of Moses (Exodus 15:1-18) it is the right hand of God that delivers the Hebrew people from bondage to Pharaoh (15:6). This image of the right hand as the work of deliverance is echoed in Psalm 118:15-16 where the history of God with Israel is recapitulated. To be at the right hand of God, then, means both to be delivered (Matthew 25:33), and to be the instrument of deliverance. Thus, when Jesus is referred to as "at the right hand" it refers both to his own deliverance through resurrection (Colossians, Ephesians), and his role as deliverer through the cross (Romans, Hebrews, etc.).

We are now in a position to consider the meaning of this strange expression in which we comprehend the fleeting, yet for us quite important, "between" which separates the death and resurrection of Jesus from his return. What is expressed here is that it is this same Jesus who was conceived, born, suffered, crucified, dead and buried, who is the actual, albeit yet hidden, Lord of history; the actual, if not yet fully apparent, authority to which all else is subjected and being subjected.

Certainly it must appear to all the world that nothing has fundamentally or finally changed since the event of Jesus of Nazareth. Earthly authority still appears handed over to the powers of division and domination and death. Yet the glad affirmation of faith is that these principalities and powers are even now being brought into subjection to the only true and legitimate Lord of history. This claim is expressed in the resurrection/ascension account of Matthew, where Jesus prefaces the sending of the disciples with the extraordinary assertion "I have been put in charge of everything." The audacity of this claim cannot be minimized. And it is "verified" only in the actual taking up of Jesus' ministry and mission in the world.

Yet we must take care when we speak of Jesus as the true Lord of history that we do not forget which Jesus it is who is meant here. We must not lose sight of *who* it is that sits in authority at the right hand of God. This is the meaning of that long succession of clauses in the past tense. They remind us not to substitute some lordly figure of myth or dream for the one who truly and legitimately exercises authority and power.[25]

This necessity is magnificently expressed in the startling image of the Apocalypse of John of the "Lamb slain from the foundation of the [earth]" (Revelation 13:8 KJV). For the Lord of history reigns not as some cosmic emperor, but as the Lamb. It is precisely as the one who suffered under Pontius Pilate that he is known to us as the Lamb who is "Lord of lords and King of kings" (Revelation 17:14). It is as the victim of the forces of history that he is acclaimed: "worthy is the Lamb that was slain to receive power, and riches, and wisdom, and strength, and honor, and glory, and blessing" (Revelation 5:12 KJV). Because he is history's victim he is acclaimed worthy of lordship. It is in this way and only in this way that the divine sovereignty and authority is exercised.

One of the catastrophes to which Church and theology have fallen victim is that we have sometimes displaced the Lamb with a cosmic and transcendent emperor of our own imagining. We forget that it is not some deified Persian emperor to whom we refer as King of kings and Lord of lords, but the one who hung upon the cross and above whose head was the title "King of the Jews." Or we suppose that the executor of divine authority was someone other than the one who ate and drank with tax collectors and sinners.

When we imagine for ourselves some other lord and authority, then the advice of the author of Colossians to "seek the things that are above, where Christ is seated at the right hand of God" (3:1) becomes deadly. For we seek then either to flee the real world which is the scene of his birth and death and resurrection (and so to escape into some imaginary realm), or to model ourselves after this imaginary heaven of pomp and power. Thus, it is urgently necessary to recall *who* is said to be "sitting at the right hand." Only in this way do we even begin to glimpse the audacity of faith that affirms that the meaning of our history, of our present, is to be found in none other than the same Jesus who was born, suffered, crucified, dead and buried.[26]

Far from proposing to us some mythological imagery of heavenly power, this image of Jesus as seated at the right hand of God the Father Almighty serves to break the fascination of all such myths, and to claim that the true power and authority for the history in which we live and the earth on which we live is Jesus, "the Lamb slain from the foundation of the world."

That it is none other than Jesus who is our Lord and the hidden Lord, authority, and significance of history is manifested by the way we live in "between." It is by fixing our attention on the one who is the true authority for life and history that we learn to turn away from a life of compulsion (Colossians 3:5) and division (3:8) and deceit (3:9) and turn instead to a life formed by forgiveness, peace, and gratitude (3:12-17). The life that reflects the one who sits at the right hand is the life of love.

This clause of the Creed returns us to the discussion of the Father

Almighty which predominates the first article of the Creed. Here again it becomes evident that what is at stake in the first article of the Creed is precisely the identity of the one who is the Father of Jesus, and thus the one who graciously liberates us from bondage to the principalities and powers, adopting us and making us the heirs of the divine rule. It is in this sense that the "Almightiness" of the Father is also to be understood, for the power of God is not displayed in analogies to military might or political tyranny, but through the "weakness" of the cross. The repetition here of the name "God the Father Almighty" should have served to correct false interpretations of the meaning both of Father and of Almighty. Unfortunately this has not usually been true in the theological exegesis of the Creed.

CHAPTER SIXTEEN

WILL COME TO JUDGE

W e are not permitted to linger long with the vision of Jesus who is seated at the right hand of God the Father Almighty, but are directed immediately to the future of Jesus, and so to our future and that of our world. In turning toward the future we come to the conclusion and climax of the central section of the Creed. As is so often true of a narrative sequence, the conclusion is not only the end, but also the aim or goal which determines the meaning of the entire sequence. Thus, we must be prepared to see in this reference to the future the significance of this long recital of the memory of faith.

That a creedal narrative such as the one we have been considering should include a reference to the future is by no means self-evident. The creedal narratives of Israel refer only to the past as the sphere of the divine action (Deuteronomy 26:5-9).[27] Moreover, it is often the characteristic of other sacred narratives to be concerned with a more or less mythic past whose function is to explain and legitimate present institutions and realities.

However, in the case of the later prophets of Israel and the emergence of Jewish apocalyptic, an orientation toward the future becomes decisive. This orientation remains the fundamental horizon of Christian faith and is given expression in the Creed by reference to the future of Jesus (as it will also be expressed later in the conclusion to the Creed).

For many Christians today this orientation toward the future expressed as the "coming again" of Jesus has become a dispensable, and indeed, an unintelligible phrase of the Creed. For others, it has assumed a kind of independent significance which permits it to be understood in a narrowly individualistic sense. It is therefore crucial to obtain a correct understanding of this phrase of the Creed if the hope which it expresses is not to be rendered unintelligible or arbitrary.

Accordingly, it is necessary first to see this phrase as the point of the others that precede it and thus found it and ground it. On that basis it will be possible to say how the phrase may shape and give expression to our actual faith and hope.

This clause of the Creed makes explicit what is already implicit in the name which introduces the second article of the Creed as a whole: Jesus Christ. To name Jesus as the Christ is to identify him as the one who is to come. Thus, from the very beginning we have been turned toward the future. Indeed, as both Moltmann and Pannenberg have shown, faith remembers because it hopes.[28] Without hope there would be no cause for remembering. If the past had no future it would not concern us. It is because the past of Jesus has a future and because it shapes our future that we have occasion to recall that past and to rely upon it and to remain faithful to it. But the reverse is also true in that the hope we have is a hope that is rooted in and given shape by a particular past, in this case most decisively and fundamentally in the past of Jesus who, as the Christ, is the one who will come.

As we have seen, the ministry and message of Jesus is wholly determined by the orientation toward the long-expected arrival of the reign of God. In parable and in healing, in exorcism and in companionship, in instruction and in forgiving, all is oriented in such a way as to be transparent to the coming of God, of God's rule. Thus, when Matthew and Luke write of the birth of Jesus, they do so in such a way as to show that the birth is itself but a beginning—the beginning of the breaking in of the divine rule through the power of the Spirit. The trial of Jesus as the scene of his suffering is the location of the saying that directs us to the coming of the Son of man—the messianic figure immediately linked by early Christian faith to Jesus. He is crucified with the ironic placard "King of the Jews" announcing his messianic agenda. The account given by Matthew of Jesus' death, in which the tombs of the "saints" are opened, demonstrates the anticipation of the general resurrection of the dead (Matthew 27:51-54).[29] And when Jesus is raised we are pointed forward to the general resurrection of the dead, which his resurrection anticipates and inaugurates (1 Corinthians 15:20). Even when we speak of him as "sitting at the right hand" we are directed forward to the manifestation of the authority which is now hidden in this time between resurrection and return.

WILL COME

At every point along the way in the recitation of the *kerygma* we are directed insistently toward the future of Jesus as determinative also of our future. Without this direction and orientation there is simply no memory of Jesus. When faith loses this orientation toward the future as the future of Jesus it turns the past of Jesus into a kind of myth that explains and legitimates the present. It may do this in the form of a pious and moral (or perhaps even "charismatic") individualism which sees the past of Jesus as that which legitimates and founds one's own piety, moralism, or charism, but which is by no means in any position to challenge or to relativize it. Something similar happens on the broader scale of institutionalism, for which the story of Jesus is understood as the founding myth that legitimates the power and authority of the Church as the inheritor of the power and authority of Jesus. But faith that is expressed in the Creed and in the Bible is a faith that is oriented toward a future which absolutely exceeds every present and every past. In the light cast by this future, faith and Church are both but obscure images in a mirror of that which is to be. Thus faith and Church are prevented from absolutizing themselves by being directed toward the future as the future of Jesus.

The future spoken of here is neither the future of faith as such, nor the future of the Church as such, but the future of Jesus. Thus, that form of faith (perilously close to unbelief) that only wants to hear about its own immortality may with good reason be chagrined to hear no mention of this. Similarly, the Church that expects to hear about its own triumph and vindication may be no less embarrassed here. The future of which we speak is the future of Jesus, and it is only insofar as it is the future of Jesus that it is also in any way our future as well.

But we should also note that we are present in this clause of the Creed only because we are among those who are either living or dead, not because of our piety or our churchliness. The future of Jesus is one with a global or universal horizon. The future of Jesus is at the same time the future of all who are either living or dead, that is, it is the future of all equally. Nothing is said here about the coming of Jesus to the faithful or to the Church but to the living and the dead—to all.

Now we may put this another way. The shape of the future, not only for us but for all, has already been disclosed in the mission and ministry, the death and destiny of Jesus of Nazareth. The point of the long recitation of the past is to clarify that the future we expect, the future for which we hope and upon which we rely is the future of precisely *this* Jesus. The future is "Jesus-shaped." We must not permit the specific features of apocalyptic expectation to distract us from the essential audacity of this faith and hope. For we live in a world in which the question of the shape of the future has become one of absolute urgency. The prospects of cataclysm have moved from the fringes of apocalyptic imagination to assume palpable and grisly shapes. The threat of planetary starvation grows every day with the population explosion. The land upon which we depend for food is poisoned, the air itself so contaminated that the rain brings corrosive acid rather than healing water. The protective umbrella of the atmosphere is pierced by the products of our greed and carelessness; the rivers and streams are so polluted that to swim in one is to risk multiple and deadly disease. These are not isolated breakdowns in local ecology, but the signs of the collapse of the ecology of the planet itself. Perhaps even more urgent is the laceration of the human community by divisions between East and West, North and South, which appear to point inexorably to an uncontrolled cycle of violence. Even in the moment when the "super powers" are taking halting steps to reduce this danger, the proliferation of nuclear, chemical, and biological weapons, the implacable hatreds and cycles of violence keep the earth in constant danger of unleashing an apocalyptic paroxysm that will destroy the conditions of life on the planet. Yet in the face of this catastrophe all nations on earth divert more and more of their resources away from the needs of a swelling population and a wounded planet toward the acquisition of more instruments of domination and death.

There are other images of the future that also seize our imagination, images of technological advance that will cure all ills, of automation that will produce life-enhancing leisure, of economic development that will produce prosperity, of revolutions that will produce justice. To live in the modern (or "post-modern") world is to live in a world constantly subjected to and distracted by a bewildering succession of images of the future.

In the midst of this bewilderment about the future, Christian faith announces its confidence that the future will be shaped like Jesus.[30] Indeed, more strongly and accurately put, if there is to be any future at all it will be shaped like Jesus. For this planet there can be no future that does not begin with justice for the poor; there can be no future that does not lay aside the implements of violence; there can be no future without the end of avarice in generosity, the end of bitterness in forgiveness, the end of enmity in reconciliation.[31]

We are not speaking here of pipe dreams, but of the bare minimum essentials for the survival of our planet and of life on this planet. Where there is no hope for and no commitment to the reign of justice and generosity, of peace and joy for all there is no hope at all, only the mad acceleration toward annihilation. When Christian faith affirms its reliance upon and loyalty to Jesus who "will come again," it affirms that the love and grace that was manifest in him belongs not only to the past, but is the shape of any possible future.[32] And once again we remind ourselves that we are speaking here not of a future that concerns pious individuals alone, or the Church alone, but the world as such, the world of the "living and the dead."

It is a dreadful irony that today, just as the question of a future for the planet, for all humanity and for life itself has become so urgent, just as it becomes more evident with every passing day that apart from the reign of justice, generosity, and peace there can be no future, that the Church and faith are tempted to give up on this hope and to settle for a preoccupation with individual salvation and institutional preservation. The Church is the Church of Jesus Christ only insofar as it is the bearer of this planetary hope, and faith is faith in Jesus only when it includes the turn toward this planetary hope which includes all the living and the dead.

TO JUDGE

No consideration of this clause of the Creed would be appropriate that did not take with full seriousness the image of the judgment that is executed by Jesus and that constitutes the aim and goal of this future of Jesus. This image has certainly occupied the imagination of faith and the Church since its inception. The most varied conceptions and most lurid depictions have been occasioned by this hope and by the fear that is sometimes made to accompany it.

We must remind ourselves therefore, initially, that the affirmation that it is Jesus who is the judge is fundamentally nothing other than gospel, the astonishing good news that is announced to all. Where much Christian eschatology both official and unofficial has gone wrong is in its failure to be clear that there is no other judge than Jesus. When Christianity emerged there were many who supposed that there would be a final judgment. Christianity accepts this expectation, but with the radical and total revolution entailed by the affirmation that there is no other judge than Jesus. Thus all uncertainty, all forms of spiritual terrorism (so often associated with scenes of judgment) are specifically and fundamentally excluded. Jesus who healed the sick, who fed the multitudes, who announced good news to the poor and freedom for the oppressed, who celebrated intimate friendship with sinners and publicans; this Jesus and no other is the judge.[33] For the poor, the broken, the imprisoned and tortured, the scorned and despised, for all those deprived of dignity, for all those who yearn for friendship and justice, and hunger and thirst for the justice of God, this affirmation is nothing but light and joy. This is the meaning of the Beatitudes pronounced by Jesus:

Blessed are you poor, for yours is the [reign] of God.
Blessed are you that hunger now, for you shall be satisfied.
Blessed are you that weep now, for you shall laugh.

> Blessed are you when men hate you, and when they exclude you and revile you, and cast out your name as evil, on account of the [Human]. Rejoice in that day, and leap for joy, for behold, your reward is great in heaven; for so their fathers did to the prophets. (Luke 6:20-23).

If only this most basic and fundamental principle had been kept firmly in mind, no fatal ambiguity, confusion, or terror could have crept into this announcement and affirmation. Yet such ambiguity has crept in and taken possession of this theme of final judgment. Accordingly, some additional considerations may be brought forward to further strengthen our resolve to understand this aspect of our confession correctly.

It is first of all necessary to remind ourselves of the meaning of judgment. The basic and fundamental meaning is that of salvation and deliverance. It is for this reason that the legendary heroes of Israel, including Deborah, Gideon, and Samson, were called judges of Israel. They are judges not because they hand out rewards and punishments, but because they rescue the people of Israel from the power of those who would crush the people and return them to bondage and captivity. Similarly, when Israel became a kingdom it was the role of the judges to defend the poor and helpless from the greed and cruelty of the rich and powerful. The task of the judge is to take up the cause of the weak, the poor, the helpless. Moreover, where breaches in the life of the community threaten to embroil the community in enmity and division, it is the task of the judge to effect fair reconciliation on the basis of a just compensation for injury suffered. The judge delivers from enmity, from injustice, from the power of those who would destroy.

It is only because and insofar as the judge delivers, that the judge also condemns. By delivering the weak, the judge comes into opposition to the powerful; by delivering the poor, the judge comes into opposition to the greed of the rich; in serving the cause of peace, the judge comes into opposition with those who seek to sow strife and enmity. Thus, the reversal of the Beatitudes with corresponding woes: Luke 6:24-26. This image and role of the judge remains constant even when it takes on an apocalyptic character. For here again it is the apocalyptic judge who will deliver the people from imperial rule, who will deliver the poor from their greedy and violent oppressors (Ezekiel 34:11-31). This is especially the point of view that we find in the Apocalypse of John. While some of these images take on the character of a simple revenge on the part of the marginalized against their oppressors, the emphasis on deliverance still remains clear. When Jesus is announced as the judge, the one who suffers under Pontius Pilate, who is friend of publicans, and who healed the daughter of the centurion, then these images are or should be purged of every element of revenge and be focused on the theme of deliverance and salvation, which is their true core. The pairing of the Beatitudes and woes in Luke makes this quite clear. For they are followed by the instruction: "love your enemies, do good to those who hate you, bless those who curse you, pray for those who abuse you" (Luke 6:27-28). This is actually demonstrated in the word that Luke (alone) reports from the cross: "Father, forgive them, for they know not what they do" (Luke 23:34).[34]

Yet in this process of clarification, the possibility of a renewed misunderstanding arises. We say, and quite rightly, that deliverance is dependent only on a complete reliance upon and loyalty to Jesus. But what does this mean? All of our reflections on the Creed have been designed to clarify this faith. Accordingly, we will have to be content with brief summary remarks.

To rely on Jesus is to rely on the one we have been describing. It is to have no other cause than the cause of Jesus; the cause of God who comes to set at liberty, to heal and forgive, to bring life where there was death, to bring reconciliation where there was estrangement and enmity. As Paul indicates, this faith was already present in Abraham who turned himself toward the future that God promised and, as the author of Hebrews notes, this faith is also attested in all those who, long before the coming of Jesus, nevertheless made common cause with the promises of God (Hebrews 11). Moreover, the New Testament reminds us that pious or dogmatic claims about Jesus are not what is at stake here, for "not every one who says to me, 'Lord, Lord' . . . , but [the one] who does the will of my Father" (Matthew 7:21). Nor are we left in any doubt about the specific character of this will. As Jesus' parable of the Last Judgment illustrates, it is precisely the action that offers concrete help and assistance to those who are hungry, naked, oppressed that characterizes the Father's will (Matthew 25:31-46).

Above all what is at stake in loyalty to the one who "will come to judge" is precisely solidarity with his mission and ministry, his open friendship with all who are despised and marginalized. Thus, the Synoptic Gospels repeatedly assure us that solidarity with this cause in the present has eschatological consequences: "For whoever is ashamed of me and of my words in this adulterous and sinful generation, of him will the [Human] also be ashamed, when he comes in the glory of his Father with the holy angels" (Mark 8:38. Compare Matthew 10:32-33). This is by no means limited to the attitude taken to Jesus' own mission, but to the continuation of that mission on the part of those who truly follow in his path (Mark 9:37, 41).

To rely utterly upon Jesus with undivided loyalty is to take up his cause in the world, the cause of that divine love which abolishes division, domination, despair, and death. The act that most dramatically represents this transformation of human relationships is that of the forgiveness of one another. The Gospel of Matthew is especially insistent that the followers of Jesus exhibit this mutual forgiveness, going so far as to insist that our relation to God is dependent upon the practice of openhearted and persistent forgiveness of one another (see, for example, Matthew 6:14-15; 18:35).

In the Creed we say that we believe in Jesus, who is the future both for us and for the world. In the face of all terror and uncertainty and illusion about the future we gladly point to Jesus and say that he is the future. And to all those who seek a future in division and domination, in spiritual arrogance, political violence, or economic avarice we say that there is no future in that direction, that it is a road that leads only to annihilation and death. Thus we call all to share in the hope for the triumph of love and generosity, of justice and joy, of gratitude and peace. We do this in the name of Jesus "who will come again to judge the living and the dead."

ARTICLE THREE

CHAPTER SEVENTEEN

THE HOLY SPIRIT

W e come now to the "Third Article" of the Creed, pertaining to the Holy Spirit. This doctrine raises a number of difficulties for the theologian since one finds so many different possible explications of its meaning in the course of the life of the Church.

Initially, we should realize that this doctrine does not yet have the rigorous form that we find in a number of other doctrines. In the course of the first few centuries of the life of the Church, theological attention was focused on the clarification of christological problems concerning the identity of Jesus as the Son of God. Typically, the doctrine of the Holy Spirit was merely an appendix that sought to "fill out" the triune identity of God. Often it is not made clear why we should speak of three, rather than two "persons" in the identity of God.[1] After the sixth century, these fragmentary reflections on the Trinity were accepted without being further developed. The theological questions of the Middle Ages were focused on the identity of the Church and the sacraments, and the Holy Spirit was often simply understood within the context of a reflection on these themes. After the twelfth century, the most important questions were the relation between God and the world and the possibility of acquiring a knowledge of God as creator, as theology sought to come to terms with classical philosophy mediated through the great Islamic schools of thought. In this context, the doctrine of the Spirit was dealt with in terms of the problematic of reason and revelation.

The reformation of the Church in the sixteenth century focused on the life of faith. Accordingly, the Spirit was understood principally as the origin or source of the life of faith, through such doctrines as regeneration and sanctification. In the modern period, the most important problems have been the theories of knowledge and the relation of faith to culture. Accordingly, spirit was understood as the principle of knowledge associated with the understanding of Scripture or interior illumination, or as the possibility for the development of a speculative or philosophical understanding as per Hegel.

Thus, the doctrine of the Spirit has been made to embrace the most varied religious and theological meanings and cultural and philosophical trends. Our own epoch is characterized by a considerable increase in the attention given to this doctrine without, however, reaching any degree of clarification or precision. Thus, the task of developing a rigorous and comprehensible conception of this doctrine is an important one for contemporary theology. Above all, it is important to understand this doctrine within the context of a trinitarian reflection on the identity of God. Only in this way will it be possible to avoid confusion about the work or function of this Spirit as the Spirit of the Father and the Spirit of Christ.

In order to acquire a clear understanding of the Holy Spirit it is important to ask, who is the Spirit? As we have seen before it is not sufficient to say that we believe in God. As Paul says there are many (so-called) gods (1 Corinthians 8:5-6). Rather, it is important to clarify in which God we believe, upon which God we rely. In this way we have sought to interpret the content of the first and second articles of the Creed. There are many who are called liberators, saviors, lords. It is not sufficient to believe in any lord or savior, but in the Jesus whose identity is the subject of the clauses of the second article of the Creed. This same method must be employed in order to clarify the third article of the Creed.

That method is an attempted reconstruction of the doctrine on the basis of a careful consideration of the relevant biblical texts. This will mean that we also attempt to define the relation between this article and the two that precede it. Because of the complexity of the issues involved in this process of construction, it will be possible here only to indicate some of the most basic characteristics of the Spirit.

As in the first two articles of the Creed, here, too, the consideration of the Holy Spirit begins with the clause that first mentions this theme. However, subsequent clauses of the article will further serve to clarify the identity of the Spirit of God.

1. SPIRIT AND POWER (THE ETYMOLOGICAL BASIS)

The word in Hebrew that we translate as spirit is *ruah*. This word has a somewhat different range of meaning than that of the English word "spirit." In the first place, *ruah* is used for "wind" to name the strong movements of the air that bring storm and tempest, rain and fair weather. In this sense, the *ruaḥ* of God is the wind of God that is the manifest power of the air which carries important changes in the conditions of our lives.

Ruaḥ is not only the name for the movement of the air; but also the name for that less dramatic, but no less essential movement that we call breath (English has something of this in the word re-spir-ation, that includes the root for spirit). As respiration or breath, *ruaḥ* suggests the power of life. The first human received life when, according to Genesis 2:7, God breathed into the nostrils of Adam. Thus, it can also be said that the length of our lives depends on the limitation of *ruaḥ* (Genesis 6:3). All animals are described as those that have "the breath of life in their nostrils" (Genesis 7:22).

Thus, both wind and breath are *ruaḥ* and this suggests that both are expressions of vital and mysterious power. This power called *ruaḥ* may be understood as something that overwhelms the life of the person or community. In this rather general sense of that which overpowers, we find things like a "spirit of fornication" (Hosea 4:12), or of dizziness (Isaiah 19:14), or of sleep (Isaiah 29:10), or of lying (1 Kings 22:22), of wisdom (Isaiah 11:2), or jealousy (Numbers 5:14). Thus, spirit could signify a power that overwhelms or overpowers the human being. As this partial list reveals, spirit is not a moral force, but rather any sort of mysterious power or force.

Alongside this view of spirit we find the sense of *ruaḥ* as a power that enables or empowers someone to accept a responsibility or perform a task or mission. We encounter this meaning of spirit in the distribution of the spirit that was with Moses to the seventy elders (Numbers 11:16-30). We encounter it also in the story of the spirit that empowers Samson to save the tribes of Israel from the Canaanites (Judges 13:25–16:31). David also received the spirit that remained with him (1 Samuel 16:13) to make him capable of being the king of Israel. Elisha received the power (spirit) of Elijah and was enabled to perform miracles and continue with the mission of Elijah (2 Kings 2:9-15).

Thus, the *ruaḥ* of God seems to indicate a surprising and even excessive power. In some cases this *ruaḥ overpowers*, in others it *empowers*. But whether as empowering or overpowering, it always indicates an astonishing or surprising excess of power.

In the New Testament we find the Greek term *pneuma*, a word with a range of meaning similar to that of the Hebrew *ruaḥ*. We find in *pneuma* a similar reference to "wind," "breath," or "spirit." A good example of this range of meanings is found in the discussion between Jesus and Nicodemus in John 3:5-8 and in the resurrection appearance of Jesus to his disciples in John 20:21-23. In order to translate these passages literally

169

it is necessary to make up words to illustrate the play of meanings. Thus, when Jesus speaks of those who are born of the spirit being like the wind, the same word is translated both as spirit and as wind. The same is true of Jesus breathing the spirit upon the disciples. Terms like "inspiration" convey something of what is meant here.

In the New Testament we also encounter "evil spirits" in Mark 1:23-27, 3:11; 5:2-13 and so on.[2] The use of evil spirit in this connection always indicates a power that overwhelms an individual in order to produce, for example, madness. Thus, in the New Testament the spirit that overpowers is the spirit of evil. In contrast, the Spirit of God is the spirit that empowers, that enables and capacitates persons to do that which anticipates or represents the reign of God. This is an important advance in clarity over the range of meanings one finds in the Old Testament.

On the basis of this brief etymological and lexicological study we may say that biblical texts that refer to spirit indicate power. This power is that which is necessary for life, making the spirit the power of life itself (as breath). On this basis, it is possible to speak of spirit as overpowering or empowering. New Testament usage distinguishes between that which overpowers (evil spirit) and that which empowers (Holy Spirit). Consequently, it becomes all the more conclusive that Holy Spirit indicates life-giving power or energy par excellence.

2. THE SPIRIT OF GOD THE FATHER

What does it mean to speak of the Spirit as *Holy* Spirit? Since the term "holy" occurs not only here, but also in connection with the "*holy* catholic church" and the "communion of *saints*" it is important to become as comprehensible as possible about this at the outset.

The term "holy" suggests that which pertains to God or the divine. In tribal religions for example, geographic features like mountains, lakes, or particular rocks or trees may be understood as holy because they are located where the god has been revealed or encountered. In the history of Israel we encounter something of this in the notion of the holy mountain (Sinai) where God appeared to give the law. But we also find it in the stories of the patriarchs where shrines were erected at every point where God was decisively encountered. Part of the reform of the cult of Israel was the abolition of these shrines in favor of a single temple erected on the holy mountain of Zion.

In addition, an artifact may be regarded as holy in that it belongs particularly to the god or in some way to the presence of the god. This is true of those artifacts that are called idols by the prophets of Israel, but is also true, for example, of the ark of the covenant, or the temple, or the altar. One also speaks of persons as holy in the sense of being set apart for the divine, or for that which pertains to the divine. In some cultures this may mean someone whose strangeness or unpredictability mirrors that of the gods, as is the case with persons who in other cultures' terms appear crazy or deformed. In certain cultures it is the professional class of priests who are so regarded.

Obviously the notion of holiness varies according to the idea of God. Thus, in order to clarify the holiness of the Spirit it is necessary to clarify its relation to the One we call "Father Almighty."

In the discussion of the first article of the Creed, we have seen that the identity of God is specified as the Father Almighty. This specification of the identity of God envisions the good news that God has graciously determined to set us free from the dominion of the principalities and powers in order to adopt us as God's own sons and daughters, thereby bestowing upon us the dignity and responsibility of God's heirs created in the divine image and likeness.

The announcement of this gracious love and the reception of this message is what produces the acclamation of God as Abba/Pater/Father according to Paul. Because of this connection to the "Father," the Spirit as the Spirit of this God is, as Paul says, the spirit of adoption (Galatians 4:6; Romans 8:15-17) rather than that of fearful bondage. As we have seen in connection with our reflections on the "Father," the result of this adoption is liberation from bondage, and the inheritance of the dignity and responsibility of the adopted daughters and sons of God. Thus, the characteristics of this new life we receive from the spirit are liberty and peace, joy and love. These are the characteristics that demonstrate that it is God who is the Father whose spirit we have received.

Accordingly, the faith provoked through the proclamation is the beginning of the rule of God. It is important however to recognize that it is the beginning and not the end. The scope of God's rule cannot be reduced to the sphere of the intimate and personal without depriving God of lordship over the earth. Our trust in God as Father is a sign that anticipates the consummation of the reign of love. Thus, Paul also maintains that the beginning of faith is to be understood within the horizon of the liberation of the earth itself from its bondage to "futility" (Romans 8:18-22). In this way, the spirit that we experience in the dawn of faith is the spirit of the Father, who is also the creator of heaven and earth. Thus Paul can say that if a person is in Christ, behold: new creation (2 Corinthians 5:17).

The spirit that is the Spirit of the Father is the Spirit of the "Maker of Heaven and Earth" and so is the Spirit that anticipates the transformation of all things. Paul already makes this clear in his reflection on the Spirit of adoption which he interprets as the beginning of the universal or global transformation for which "all creation is groaning" (Romans 8:19). The Spirit must be understood within the framework of this eschatological horizon.

Through the message of the prophets, the faith of Israel was directed more and more toward the future. The prophets conceived this future in a variety of ways: the coming of the Messiah, the restoration of Jerusalem, the new temple and so on. But the most far-reaching of these images was that of a new creation. The creation of life was seen as the gift of Spirit (Genesis 2:7). Concerning the end-time and the consummation of God's action on behalf of Israel, we encounter this oracle of Joel:

> And it shall come to pass afterward, that I will pour out my spirit on all flesh; your sons and your daughters shall prophesy, your old men shall dream dreams, and your young men shall see visions. Even upon the menservants and maidservants in those days, I will pour out my spirit. (Joel 2:28-29)

Thus, the gift of the spirit belongs to the consummation of God's aim in the renovation of the earth.

In the New Testament this relation between the Spirit and the "last days" is even stronger. We can say that the Spirit signifies the presence of the future that God has promised. As we have seen, the mission and ministry of Jesus enacts and announces the coming of the divine reign. Faith has the character of hope that relies upon the promises of God on the basis of the ministry of Jesus. The presence among us within the world of that which pertains to this hoped-for future is what we call the Spirit of God. Thus the proclamation of the New Testament is that the consummation that we hope for is already present as a kind of down payment or "earnest" or anticipation of that future (2 Corinthians 1:22; 5:5; Ephesians 1:4). This anticipation or down payment is always indicated by the use of the name of the Spirit. The Spirit is the presence in advance of the future of God. In the same way, we may speak of Christian life as a new birth by the Spirit (John 3:5-6). This means that our life as a life characterized by faith is itself a sign of the last days of the final fulfillment of the divine promises.

On the one hand, when we speak of the Spirit, we are speaking of this eschatological power that is like a wind blowing from the future of God into our present, giving concrete and dramatic signs of the consummation of God's promise to bring the renovation of creation. These signs are indications that our faith is not in vain, that the promises are not merely fantasies, that our hope is based in reality. On the other hand, it is necessary to remind ourselves that the Spirit of God is not that future itself, but the presence in advance of that future. Thus, the gifts of the Spirit or the fruits of the Spirit have no isolated or autonomous significance, but are meaningful precisely in relation to that future. The Spirit then, as Spirit of "God the Father Almighty, Maker of Heaven and Earth" is the dramatic presence of the divine election that provokes the acclamation of God as Abba/Pater and that anticipates the final victory of the Creator over the forces that subject creation to bondage.

3. THE SPIRIT OF THE SON

Often in the New Testament, the Spirit is called the Spirit of Christ, as for example in Romans 8:9; Galatians 4:6; and Philippians 1:19. Thus the Spirit that is the presence of that which God has promised is also the presence of Jesus Christ, for Jesus is the future of God as person.

The Spiriting of Jesus

In the Gospels, the coming of Jesus is related to the Spirit. Thus, we affirm our loyalty to the Jesus "who was conceived by the Holy Spirit." In the accounts of his baptism, Jesus is depicted as receiving the Spirit who appears as a dove (Mark 1:10). According to Luke (who makes far more use of the Spirit than the other Synoptic Gospels), the result of the baptism is that Jesus is "filled with the Holy Spirit" (Luke 3:22; 4:1). In the same source Jesus' first sermon begins with the text from Isaiah, "The Spirit of the Lord is upon me, because he has anointed me to preach good news to the poor" (4:18).

From the point of view of Paul, the resurrection of Jesus is also to be seen as the inauguration of the ultimate future, and so he may say that the resurrection of Jesus demonstrates the power of the Spirit (Romans 1:4). All of this indicates that we should understand Jesus as the beginning of the eschatological future of God in which the divine promises will find fulfillment. Through Jesus, his ministry and mission, his life and destiny, we know the form and the content of this future—as the consummation of love.

The Spirit Received from Jesus

Jesus who "is seated at the right hand of God the Father Almighty" is the hidden Lord of history and our world. This authority of Jesus is demonstrated through his gift of the Spirit. In the first sermon of Peter, according to Acts, Peter says:

> This Jesus God raised up, and of that we all are witnesses. Being therefore exalted at the right hand of God, and having received from the Father the promise of the Holy Spirit, he has poured out this which you see and hear. (Acts 2:32-33)

Thus, the reception of the Spirit that is experienced at Pentecost is the sign of the authority of Jesus and is the evidence that Jesus truly has been raised and is seated at the right hand of God.

There is another story with a different form but strikingly similar meaning in the Gospel according to John. Prior to his crucifixion, Jesus had promised the Spirit to his followers (John 7:37-39; 14:16 and so on). This promise is fulfilled, according to John, on the evening of the day of Jesus' resurrection:

> On the evening of that day, the first day of the week, the doors being shut where the disciples were, for fear of the Jews, Jesus came and stood among them and said to them, "Peace be with you." When he had said this, he showed them his hands and his side. Then the disciples were glad when they saw the Lord. Jesus said to them again, "Peace be with you. As the Father has sent me, even so I send you." And when he had said this, he breathed on them, and said to them, "Receive the Holy Spirit. If you forgive the sins of any, they are forgiven; if you retain the sins of any, they are retained." (John 20:19-23)

The disciples' reception of the Spirit signifies the beginning of the consummation that Jesus had promised with his words and his deeds. This narrative also indicates that the only Spirit in which we believe and upon which we rely is the Spirit of Jesus.[3] Thus, it is always necessary, as John says, to test the spirits (1 John 4:1). There are many powers, many "spiritual forces," but the only Spirit in which we believe is that of Jesus Christ. This identification can be so strong that Paul, referring to Jesus, can call the "second man" a "life-giving Spirit" (1 Corinthians 15:45).

The Spirit who is the Spirit of Jesus is necessarily the Spirit of the crucified. This is expressed quite clearly in this story from the Gospel of John. Immediately prior to the gift of the Spirit in John's Gospel, Jesus showed the disciples his hands and side. The Spirit that is received by the disciples is the Spirit of the crucified. Thus, we are concerned here not with some anonymous power or force, but with the power of the one who "suffered under Pontius Pilate." This is also the meaning of Peter's sermon in Acts; Jesus who was rejected, condemned, and crucified is the one who bestows the Spirit. Paul's letter to the Corinthians, with its frequent focus on the gifts of the Spirit, begins with the emphasis upon "Christ and him crucified" (1 Corinthians 2:2). This explains how Paul can insist that the basis of the reception of the Spirit by the community of Jesus is Jesus' cross:

174

Christ redeemed us from the curse of the law, having become a curse for us—for it is written, "Cursed be every one who hangs on a tree"—that in Christ Jesus the blessing of Abraham might come upon the Gentiles, that we might receive the promise of the Spirit through faith. (Galatians 3:13-14)

In the Gospel of Mark, the reception of the Holy Spirit by the disciples is determined by their sharing the fate of the crucified. Thus, Jesus' promise of the Spirit is connected to their being arrested and handed over: "And when they bring you to trial and deliver you up, do not be anxious beforehand what you are to say; but say whatever is given you in that hour, for it is not you who speak, but the Holy Spirit" (Mark 13:11). It is precisely as the followers share in the fate of the rejected and crucified that they receive the Spirit, which is thus marked above all as the Spirit of Jesus.

All too often in the Church we encounter a discussion that lacks an awareness of this rigorous relation of the Holy Spirit to Jesus as the crucified. When this happens, we are often dealing with an anonymous spirit that can just as well be the power of our dreams and illusions, our emotions and desires. Thus we must always ask ourselves: What is the relation between what we call spirit and the Jesus who was crucified? A spirit that leads us to forgetfulness of our neighbor, that leads to an escape from the world into the heavens of contemplation or the interiority of piety cannot be the Spirit of Jesus who "suffered under Pontius Pilate." When we are confronted with confusion in the Church concerning the Holy Spirit, we need to test everything by the relation to Jesus who is for us the origin and source of the Holy Spirit.

4. GOD'S SPIRIT AND OURS

One of the striking features of the use of terms like "spirit" and even "holy spirit" in the New Testament is that it is often, indeed usually, difficult to specify whether we are to understand these terms as referring to God's spirit or to ours. The translators generally resolve this difficulty wherever possible in favor of the former by supplying a definite article (the) and capital letters (*Holy Spirit*).

However, this ambiguity should not be so easily and precipitously resolved, for it points to an essential feature of any biblically informed treatment of the Holy Spirit. What is at stake when we talk of holy spirit is not the discrimination of the divine from the human, but the transformation of the human by the divine. This transformation has the effect of animating the human, setting the human in motion toward the

175

divine future in such a way as to make the human a participant in the divine mission actualized by Jesus.[4]

Spirit and Mission

We never receive the Spirit for ourselves alone, to be our own private possession. The Holy Spirit is always the Spirit of mission. "Holy" means that which pertains to or belongs to God. Thus, the Holy Spirit is that which belongs to God, that which pertains to God's will. The will of God, as we know from the ministry and mission of Jesus, is the radical and total transformation of our world. Thus, "holiness" is that which pertains to this transformation, that which manifests and enables it. This is the character of the Holy Spirit.

We recall that in the biblical accounts the Spirit of God is given to persons to make them capable of performing tasks or missions that relate to the community or society as a whole. When Samson received the Spirit, he received the capacity to do that which God wanted—to liberate the people. When David received the Spirit it was in order to undertake the public responsibility of leadership and kingship. The prophets were given the Spirit, not for their own spiritual entertainment, but to enable them to speak clearly and forcefully to the public life of the society as a whole, thereby confronting that social, economic, and political reality with the word of God.

Thus we should say that the Holy Spirit is never separated from public responsibility, and therefore, from mission. We never hear of the gift of the Spirit that is concerned primarily with the interior and private lives of individuals. This is of primary importance, for all too often in the Church, persons speak of the Spirit only or primarily in connection with the interior life, with the life that is personal and private. This idea is so prevalent in the Church that we can speak of such things as "spiritual retreats" and think of spiritual life as that life which is separated from the world. But this is an idea that is completely impossible from the biblical standpoint. A "spiritual retreat" is an oxymoron. The Spirit is that which enables us to engage in mission, that which empowers us to witness and work in the world.

It is possible to see this quite clearly in the two accounts of the reception of the Spirit that we have already noted. In the account of Acts 2, the reception of the Spirit is manifested in that the disciples suddenly proclaim the gospel to all those around them who, in spite of differences of culture and language, each hear that gospel proclaimed in their own language. The reception of the Spirit is that which makes it possible for us to testify to Jesus in spite of differences of culture, nation, and language.

Something similar occurs in the Gospel of John. The disciples receive the Spirit in order to be able to fulfill their commission: "As the Father sent me, so I send you" says Jesus. It is in order to be able to do that which they are called to do that they are given the Spirit. And this is further expressed as the authority and responsibility to forgive sins. The gift of the Spirit, then, has as its aim that we should be enabled to be witnesses in all the world of the liberty of the sons and daughters of God.

It is then no accident that when Paul speaks of the gifts of the Spirit in 1 Corinthians, he emphasizes that these gifts are related to tasks, to concrete service to the neighbor and concrete responsibilities in representing the lordship of Christ.

The Spirit that is Holy Spirit is not a spirit that leads us away from the world, but rather one that leads us and guides us into the world; it is not a spirit that leads to escape into the heavens or the interiority of "spirituality," but rather that which empowers us to fulfill the ascension commission, to continue the mission of Jesus.

The Divinity of the Spirit

It is precisely the reality and significance of this empowerment for mission that ultimately leads the Church to insist upon the "divinity" of the Spirit and so to the intuition of a trinitarian form for the doctrine of God.

The divinity of the Son insists that there can be no separation between the way of the liberation demonstrated in Jesus and the ultimate reality that we call God. There is not some "higher truth" that could somehow supersede this way of the crucified or loyalty to this way. There is not some more "ultimate" way that could be set over against it, limit it or surpass it and therefore enable us to dispense with this loyalty in favor of a more "spiritual" and less costly way, that is more eternal and less "worldly."

In the same way, the divinity of the Spirit that is here only suggested rather than explicitly affirmed, serves to prevent a christological focus from becoming static and formalized and receding into mere historical preoccupation. The doctrine of the Spirit emphasizes the presence and effective power of that which is affirmed concerning Jesus and his mission, and makes clear that the follower is empowered for the continuation of that mission.

The doctrine of the Spirit focuses upon the astonishment that this empowerment actually occurs in spite of the power of sin and death. The way of solidarity and liberation that leads to life is experienced again and again, here and now, in new and astonishing ways. The Spirit is this astonishing presence of power. The older dogmatics spoke of God the Father as transcendent and the Spirit as immanent. The truth in this formulation lies precisely in this present empowerment in the actual life of persons and communities. The interaction of divine and human spirit produces the insistence on the divinity of the Spirit—a trinitarian as opposed to a binitarian doctrine of the divine.

One way this development can be "tracked" is in the response to the proclamation to the Gentiles. The response of the Gentiles must be viewed either as an anomaly or regarded as "of God." The recognition that it is of God, most notably in the successive narratives regarding Peter's vision and subsequent visit to the home of Cornelius (Acts 10–11:18), makes possible the recognition of the imperative to evangelize the nations.

Similarly we note Paul's emphasis on the way in which the proclamation is received with tribulation and joy, and his connection of this with the Spirit (Galatians 4:6-7; Romans 8:15-17; 1 Thessalonians 1:5-6). It is this spirited response to the proclamation that is recognized as divine, as is also the basis of this proclamation (the grace of God) and its content (Christ and him crucified).

The divinity of the Spirit is further recognized in the transformation of people from helpless objects of forces beyond their control (sin and death), into fully active subjects or participants in the ministry and mission of the Church.

The way in which the activity of Jesus is taken up by his followers, to continue his mission in defiance of the principalities and powers, is also seen as their being "spirited" as the real presence of the divine in history. The miracle of Spirit is the way in which Jesus' ministry and mission becomes transitive, incorporating others into itself, and proliferating.

Thus are laid the bases for the view that the Spirit is fully divine and so for the development of the trinitarian form of the Christian doctrine of God. Although this is not yet articulated in the Creed, it is already clearly implicit both in its form and in its formulations.

Above all it must be recognized that the divinity of the Spirit should not be taken as an excuse to separate the divine spirit from the human spirit, or to seek to eliminate the essential ambiguity of those New Testament texts where it is difficult and even inappropriate to decide whether what is in view is the human or the divine spirit. It is precisely as the immanent empowering spirit that the spirit is divine spirit. Thus, the "status" of the spirit corresponds to that of the son. We noted that Jesus is "only son" precisely insofar as Jesus is the first of many brothers and sisters. That is, Jesus' sonship is not one that separates Jesus from his brothers and sisters, but is one that summons them to share in this sonship. In the same way, the divinity of the spirit is the divinity precisely of that spirit that enters into the human to capacitate for participation in the divine mission of transformation.

The Presence and Power of the Spirit

We have thus far only begun to identify the character of the Holy Spirit upon whom we rely and to whom we affirm our loyalty. In the interpretation of the subsequent clauses of this third article of the Creed, we will have occasion to specify further the identity of the Holy Spirit. This corresponds to the second article of the Creed, where the identity of Jesus as Christ, Son, and Lord is further clarified by the subsequent series of verbal clauses, and to the way in which the identity of God is specified in the first article as Father Almighty, and Creator. A brief glance ahead may help to suggest the further dimensions of the identity of the Spirit as the subject of this article as a whole.

The Spirit of God is, in the New Testament, associated with the Church. It is the Church that is commissioned to engage in the mission for which the Spirit empowers it. And this Church is characterized internally as a community in which divisions are overcome. The community as entrusted with this mission and as characterized by this reconciliation is the holy catholic church.

But the Spirit as the Spirit of God must not be restricted to the Church in such a way as to become its own possession, the guarantor of its privilege. Thus, the Creed also speaks of the communion of saints as the solidarity of all who are committed to the coming of God's reign of justice. The Spirit is present not only inside, but also outside the Church.

The overcoming of enmity and division which is signaled by these two spheres of the work of the Spirit has the concrete character of overcoming the dominion of sin and death. Accordingly, we speak of the forgiveness of sins as the action within the community which testifies to the presence and power of the Spirit. This forgiveness of sins aims at overcoming both the guilt and the power of sin. The forgiveness of sins is not only something received by the community, but also something entrusted to it. Thus, mutual forgiveness is the necessary sign of the presence of the Spirit.

If the forgiveness of sins corresponds to the community of faith, then the resurrection of the body corresponds to the communion of saints, in that it is the universal work of the Spirit that signals the overcoming of the reign of death in all creation.

The aim of the forgiveness of sins and of the resurrection of the dead is precisely "life everlasting." The master symbol for the identity of the divine Spirit, and so for the aim of God in Christ, is life. This unrestricted or "everlasting" life is the aim of the Spirit and so identifies the Spirit as the giver of life.

CHAPTER EIGHTEEN

THE HOLY
CATHOLIC CHURCH

The clarification of the identity of the Holy Spirit is carried forward in a decisive way by subsequent clauses of the third article of the Creed. It is of particular importance to note that this occurs primarily through the designation of essentially social or corporate realities—the holy catholic church and the communion of saints. This emphasis on social or corporate reality as the principal domain of the Spirit stands in remarkable contrast to the post-Reformation emphasis on individuality and inwardness as the principal domain of the presence and the power of the Spirit. In the Creed, the Spirit is not to be encountered primarily in the sphere of the inward and personal (whether in terms of interior illumination or special religious experiences or even pious sentiments), but in the public and social sphere designated by the holy catholic church and the communion of saints.

Among these corporate realities priority belongs to that designated as the Church and it is to this that we first turn.

The doctrine of the Church must not be understood as an independent theme, but as a specification of the character of the divine action which is the theme of the Creed as a whole. Thus, we must attempt to develop an understanding of the Church rigorously based upon the identity of God as Father, Son, and Holy Spirit. To this end it is critical to recall that the clause concerning the Church is found in the context of an affirmation of faith in the Holy Spirit. As we have seen, our reliance upon the Holy Spirit is a reliance upon the presence of the reign of God already in the present, a reliance upon the presence in advance of the new creation of God that is anticipated in the acclamation of God as Father. At the same time, the Spirit is the presence of that Jesus who was crucified and raised, and who thus constitutes the realization of the promises of God. Thus, the presence of the past of Jesus and the presence of the future of God characterize the action of the Spirit.[5] This presence of the Spirit is not to be restricted to an interior and "personal" reality, but to the corporate sphere. The corporate presence of the Spirit, the way in which this presence takes on public, social, and visible form is the Church.[6] This double determination of the presence and power of the Spirit is expressed in two basic images of the Church as a domain of the Spirit. The image of the Church as *ekklesia,* or "assembly," emphasizes the effect of the Father's gracious adoption, while the image of the Body of Christ emphasizes the relation of the Church to the ongoing ministry and mission of Jesus. A consideration of these images will prepare the way for the clarification of the catholicity and the holiness of the community of faith.

THE *EKKLESIA* OF GOD THE FATHER

The corporate or social reality that is called the Church is also known in the letters of Paul as the *ekklesia* or assembly of God the Father (1 Thessalonians 1:1). The term *ekklesia* comes from the political lexicon of Greek city-states. The *ekklesia* was the name of the assembly of citizens responsible for discussing and deciding matters related to the welfare of the community as a whole. Such matters included the decision to form alliances with other city-states, to begin or terminate warfare, and to resolve emergencies, like plagues. According to the view of that epoch, all citizens had the responsibility to participate in these discussions and decisions. But who were these citizens? Only those who were regarded as free and responsible. Thus, slaves were excluded, as were women. But this was also the case with merchants who were dominated by private interest, even if they were among the wealthiest inhabitants of the cities. The *ekklesia* was defined as an assembly of those who had the freedom to attend to the public good, the welfare of the community as a whole. Those who were tied to familial, domestic, or private interest could not be expected to have this wider concern and interest. Thus the *ekklesia* was an institution that was based in the free responsibility of citizens for the common good.

When the first Christians began to employ this terminology to describe their community, they were introducing considerable novelty into the term. Their assembly included both women and men, both slave and free, both Greeks and barbarians. In truth, this was a radical innovation. What remained was the notion of free responsibility for the common good. But the manner of understanding and implementing this underwent far-reaching changes.

On what basis was it possible to include such diverse types of people in the assembly? The Christians were understood to be those who had been liberated from anxiety, from self-preoccupation and self-interest. From this point of view, sin is precisely this enslavement to anxiety and self-preoccupation. This slavery is abolished by means of the gracious love of God made manifest in the mission and ministry of Jesus. In place of an existence bound to anxiety and closed in upon itself, we receive a new life based on love that is open to the other. Thus, this liberty is, at the same time, responsibility. The responsibility of the *ekklesia* is a public, indeed, political responsibility. However, the scope is no longer restricted to a single city-state, but extends to include the whole of social reality, the reality included in the promise of the reign of God. This reign of God is not merely a private, interior, and personal reality, but one that includes all life, that takes on public form; it is a reign constituted by justice and peace, love and generosity.

The Church has been given the commission to demonstrate the liberty and the responsibility that is implicit in the coming of the reign of God. The Church is the concrete and public evidence of the truth of the gospel concerning the coming of this divine reign.

The one whom we call God the Father Almighty has acted in such a way as to liberate persons from the dominion of bondage and to summon them into the dignity and responsibility of God's adopted heirs. The *ekklesia* is the corporate sphere of this dignity and responsibility practiced by those who have been thus set free and adopted.

THE BODY OF CHRIST

Another of the principal images of the Church, especially in the writings of Paul, is that of the Body of Christ. In the second article of the Creed we affirm our loyalty to the one who "is seated at the right hand of God the Father Almighty." As we have seen, this clause indicates the hidden authority of Jesus as the Lord of history. This authority (as the authority of the servant) also has a visible and concrete form; that of the Church as the Body of Christ.

Our body *is* our visibility. By virtue of the body we have relations with one another, we can see one another, hear one another, touch one another. Thus, the body is a reality both public and relational. When we speak of the Church we are speaking of this visibility, this relatedness of Jesus in every place and time.

Further, the Church is the presence of the future, of the reign of God. The Church is the concrete and visible presence (although also provisional and partial) of the new creation promised through the prophets and through the ministry and mission of Jesus. The existence of the Church is, or should be, the visible and concrete sign of this reign.

Obviously the Church is not this reign as such. That full and final reign is "not yet"; it belongs to the as-yet unrealized future. But it is already, if ambiguously, present in the world in the visible reality of the Church. The Church is the sign, however partial and provisional, that the reign of God is more than a dream or a utopia. The Church demonstrates that this reign is already taking shape, is already being actualized in our history.

The image of the Body of Christ not only underscores the corporate character of the domain of the Spirit—it also entails that in speaking of the Church we are speaking of a visible reality. There is simply no point in speaking of an invisible body.[7] This means that the distinction beloved of theology between the visible and the invisible church, between the empirical church and the community that is both catholic and holy cannot be of service to us. In terms of our clarification of the holiness and catholicity of the community of faith we must understand that we are dealing with a visible or publicly accessible reality in speaking of the Body of Christ.

THE CATHOLIC CHURCH

The Creed places special emphasis on the catholicity or universality or inclusiveness of the Church. In principle this means that the social reality of the community of faith as assembly and as body is to be present in all nations and cultures, and thus be the incorporation of the full diversity of humanity into the society that is the result and the prolongation of Jesus' mission and the anticipation of the transformation of all reality.

The basis of this catholicity is the universal mission of the Church.[8] As we have seen, the Holy Spirit is the Spirit that capacitates for the mission indicated by the accounts of the ascension of Jesus. It is important to recognize that the sole basis for the existence of the Church is participation in the mission to announce and actualize the drawing near of the divine reign. In its essence the Church is not a religious institution, nor even an institution devoted to worship. These aspects of the Church's life have meaning only insofar as they facilitate the reason for the Church's existence: the commission to participate in the mission of God, and to continue the mission of Jesus under his authority and with the capacitating power of the Holy Spirit. This is the meaning of the Church that we encounter in the conclusion of the Gospel of Matthew.

> And Jesus came and said to them, "All authority in heaven and on earth has been given to me. Go therefore and make disciples of all nations, baptizing them in the name of the Father and of the Son and of the Holy Spirit, teaching them to observe all that I have commanded you; and lo, I am with you always, to the close of the age." (Matthew 28:18-20)

We have seen that this passage combines themes related to ascension (commission) and to "seated at the right hand." The latter indicates the authority of Jesus here represented by Jesus saying, in effect, "I have been put in charge of everything." But this authority "in heaven and on earth" has the concrete form of the mission of the followers. The authority of Jesus and the mission of the followers is linked with the force of the "therefore." The power and authority of Jesus is neither abstract nor mythic, but concrete and historical: it is the mission of the disciples. Precisely this mission is the expression of the authority of Jesus as it is also the testimony to his identity.

It is of great importance to realize that we do not encounter here an emphasis on worship or institutional life. The emphasis falls on the mission, summed up in the command "Go." The church exists only in and through this mission.

In addition we find the promise "and lo, I am with you always." It is of particular importance to recall that this promise of the presence of Jesus is related to the task of mission. It is not in our devotions, nor in our worship that we are promised the presence of Jesus, but rather in the carrying on of his mission. Jesus is not with us in the temple, nor in our interiority, but rather in our mission. The presence of Christ in our meditation or worship then depends upon the way in which these are oriented to mission.[9]

This mission is directed to "all nations." Thus, the universality of the Church is given as a task. In speaking of the Church in this way we are not using the language of permanent or metaphysical characteristics but are indicating concrete actions, tasks, missions, vocations.

The universal horizon of the mission of the community is expressed with dramatic clarity in the account of the origin of this mission that we find in Acts.

> And they were all filled with the Holy Spirit and began to speak in other tongues, as the Spirit gave them utterance. Now there were dwelling in Jerusalem Jews, devout men from every nation under heaven. And at this sound the multitude came together, and they were bewildered, because each one heard them speaking in his own language. And they were amazed and wondered, saying, "Are not all these who are speaking Galileans? And how is it that we hear, each of us in [our] own native language? Parthians and Medes and Elamites and residents of Mesopotamia, Judea and Cappadocia, Pontus and Asia, Phrygia and Pamphylia, Egypt and the parts of Libya belonging to Cyrene, and visitors from Rome, both Jews and proselytes, Cretans and Arabians, we hear them telling in our own tongues the mighty works of God." (Acts 2:4-11)

There are a number of important features of this passage, but the most important for purposes of clarifying the nature of the Church as mission is the proclamation of the gospel within the idiom of diverse cultures. Here the "other tongues" which are mentioned are clearly the languages of "every nation under heaven." The miracle of Pentecost is that the disciples are able to communicate the gospel in such a way that, despite the diversity of culture and idiom, each finds the gospel intelligible in terms of her or his own language. The "gift of tongues" here is not a supernatural tongue unintelligible to mere mortals, but precisely the rendering intelligible of the gospel to every nation.[10]

In this way the event of Pentecost is one that suggests a new creation. We recall the corruption of the first creation, expressed in the story of the tower of Babel and resulting in the division of human beings by a diversity of languages (Genesis 11:1-9). But here the gospel is the instrument for the unification of this diversity as each hears the gospel in her or his own idiom.

This narrative in Acts serves as an anticipation of the proclamation to all nations. In Acts those who hear are Jews and proselytes from every nation. This restriction to international Judaism is overcome in the course of the narrative so that what occurs is an anticipation of the unrestricted mission, not only to the Jews of all nations, but also to the pagans of these nations. This universal horizon of mission is itself but an anticipation of the universality of the reign of God. The reign of God is not the reign of a group, a tribe, or a nation but includes all the earth. Thus the Church as a sign of this reign must be universal, must be present in each culture. Only when this is the case is it possible to proclaim the gospel and to praise God in every language (Acts 2:5). Thus the promise of a universal reign of God spurs the universal mission of the community of followers. This, in turn, is the basis of the history of the Church as a history of this mission. Even today there are cultures and tongues in which the gospel has not yet been effectively expressed. But even when the gospel is present, for example, in the form of full or partial translations of the Bible into the vernacular of a people, the work of penetrating that culture with the gospel has not been accomplished.[11] The universality of the Church entails the gospel's penetration into every group and into the diverse dimensions of each culture. It is necessary to give testimony to the reign of God in every group or subculture, including our own. This mission of proclaiming and actualizing the radical transformation for which we hope is the task of every Christian. In this sense all are called to be "missionaries," for mission is the dynamic form of the existence of the Church.

The story of Pentecost demonstrates quite clearly that the existence of the Church as mission is an expression of the Holy Spirit (Acts 2:2-3). Peter explains this to his hearers with the words of the prophet Joel: "And in the last days it shall be, God declares, that I will pour out my Spirit upon all flesh, and your sons and your daughters shall prophesy, and your young men shall see visions, and your old men shall dream dreams" (2:17). And this prophecy is fulfilled in a surprising way because:

> This Jesus God raised up, and of that we all are witnesses. Being therefore exalted at the right hand of God, and having received from the Father the promise of the Holy Spirit, he has poured out this which you see and hear. (2:32-33)

Thus the mission of the Church is the presence of that which God had promised. The mission of the Church is the expression of the power of the Spirit, the Lord, the Giver of Life.

The universality of the community of faith is an extension of the inclusive character of Jesus' mission and ministry as represented in the Gospel narratives. The outreach to those excluded by considerations of law and purity from participation in the people of God is recalled by the Gospels as decisive for the ministry of Jesus.

The Church embodies this ministry and mission extensively in the mission to "all the nations." But it also does so in terms of the inclusion within particular communities of persons from diverse social positions within a given culture. Thus, the distinguishing characteristic of the inclusive catholicity of the community is the abolition of barriers to human fellowship in the community in which there is neither male nor female, neither Jew nor Greek, neither slave nor free (Galatians 3:28; Colossians 3:11). In this way the new society of the community of faith anticipates the goal of God the Father Almighty, Creator of Heaven and Earth: the new creation in which God will be all in all (1 Corinthians 15:28).

THE HOLY CHURCH

We say that the Church is holy. But what is meant by this holiness? In the course of the history of the Church we find two main interpretations of this holiness. One view is that the Church is somehow "objectively" holy on account of its possession of "holy things"; thus the performance of the sacraments is what makes the Church holy. On the other side is a more "subjective" view that speaks of the personal and moral life of the members of the community as the expression of its holiness. The strength of the objective view is that the holiness of the Church should be publicly visible. The strength of the subjective view is that this holiness should be related to the transformation of existence that pertains to every Christian.

Despite these strengths, these views cannot be accepted. The "objective" view of the holiness of the Church leads inexorably to placing emphasis on the performance of cultic acts and the assignment of privilege to those who are charged with the maintenance of the cultus. This flies in the face of the ministry and mission of Jesus, who abolished the cultic distinction between sacred and profane, between clean and unclean; whose ministry was characterized by the abolition of the ritual meaning of purification, of fasting and of the sabbath; who is condemned for abolishing the temple, whose death rends the veil of the temple that secures the separation between God and humanity. The elevation of some persons to cultic privilege is rendered impossible by Jesus' own insistence on the radical equality of persons and on the abolition of every form of "lording" it over one another on the basis of cultic or other privilege.

It is true, as the objective view maintains, that the holiness of the community of faith must be visible. But the association of the visible holiness with temple, cultus, and priesthood is a catastrophic betrayal of the most obvious features of Jesus' mission and ministry.

The subjective view of the holiness of the Church leads to equally unacceptable results. Stress is placed on a personal holiness that reinstitutes the worst features of Pharisaism, with its distinction between "sinners" (who are to be excluded) and those who comply with the law both in general and in detail. Indeed, one characteristic of "holiness" movements has been the recuperation of the law of Moses and the proliferation of additional attempts to regulate the life of individuals. In many of the churches of the Protestant movement, especially in Latin America, Christianity comes to be associated with obeying such rules: don't smoke, don't drink, don't dance. The inevitable corollary is the exclusion of those who do not comply with these regulations. This is clearly a betrayal of the mission of Jesus which scandalized the Pharisees by including all those who were deemed to be excluded.

The holiness of the community of faith must not be interpreted in ways that seek, consciously or unconsciously, to reverse the most fundamental characteristics of the ministry and mission of Jesus. The community is to be the visibility of not just any religious conception, but as the Body of Christ, the visibility of the mission and ministry of Jesus.

The holiness of the Church is to be understood as its mirroring or reflecting of the activity of God in Christ. In terms of the social reality of the community of faith this is expressed in (a) the inclusion and reconciliation of the diverse peoples and cultures of the earth, (b) the empowerment and incorporation of diverse gifts and ministries in the Body of Christ, and (c) the corresponding abandonment of the ways of division and enmity within the community and the demonstration of those spiritual fruits which produce love within the community. We will deal with each of these dimensions of holiness in turn.

(a) The universality of the Church entails the diversity of the Church. The community of faith ought to be expressed in every language, dialect, culture, and subculture. Thus, there are important differences not only between national and regional expressions of Christianity, but also differences in the way Christianity is manifested in the countryside and in the metropolis, in academia and among the marginalized. Of course, there are also differences between nations. The Church does not have (nor should it have) the same form in Central Africa as in Europe, in Japan as in Mexico, and so on. These differences are not to be regarded as something to be overcome. They testify to the diversity of the divine creation. It has too often been a feature of Christian mission that it has attempted to reduce this diversity, imposing the cultural forms of European or North American Christianity upon other societies. Fortunately, this cultural hegemony is being overcome with indigenizing and contextualizing movements within Christianity.

In spite of this diversity, it is also necessary to speak of the unity of the Church. The unity of the Church is even more difficult to see because of the divisions between Protestants and Catholics, between charismatics and moderates, between conservatives and radicals. From a sociological or historical perspective the Church is not one, but divided. It is important to note that this division is a problem for the identity of the Church. Division is a sign of the power of the world and sin. Division is then the antisign (the countersign) to the reign of God.

The unity of the church is the theme of the letter to the Ephesians. From the point of view of this letter the aim of God from "before the foundation of the world" (Ephesians 1:4) is demonstrated in Jesus through whom we were destined to be adopted as the sons and daughters of God (1:5). And this adoption demonstrates the will of God "to unite all things in him, things in heaven and things on earth" (1:10). Thus this letter indicates that the will of God is the unification of all things. This unity is demonstrated in the mission of Jesus and is realized as a kind of down payment or guarantee (1:14) in the reality of the community of faith. Now the key expression of this preliminary unification of all things is to be found in the Church as the unity between "those who were far off " (the Gentiles or pagans) and "those who were near" (the Jews). The unity in diversity of these peoples anticipates and is an earnest of the unification of all things. Thus the unity of the community of faith reflects the character of God: "one Lord, one faith, one baptism, one God and Father of us all, who is above all and through all and in all" (Ephesians 4:5-6).

(b) The same Spirit who capacitates persons for participation in the ecumenical mission of God that includes all peoples is also the Spirit who gives to each member of the new society of God a role in the life of the community. It is this dimension of the community's spirited life that is given particular emphasis by Paul in his discussion of "spiritual gifts."

For Paul the Spirit is associated first with the spirited response to the proclamation of the good news of the divine mercy and love, the response that acclaims God as Father and Jesus as Lord. But this by no means exhausts the spiritedness of the new society. Paul emphasizes the distinctive character of this society in which all persons are made capable of fulfilling distinctive and significant "callings" within the community and in the outreach of the community to others.

Accordingly, Paul notes the multiplicity of these various tasks and responsibilities:

And God has appointed in the church first apostles, second prophets, third teachers; then deeds of power, then gifts of healing, forms of assistance, forms of leadership, various kinds of tongues. (1 Corinthians 12:28, NRSV; see also Ephesians 4:11)

This is a true diversity, since not all have the same gifts and tasks (1 Corinthians 12:29).

The spiritedness of the community produces a diversity or multiplicity of ministries just as the gift of life in creation produces an astonishing variety of forms of life. But the basic truth about this diverse ministry of all the people of God is that this diversity springs from the presence and power of the Spirit:

Now there are varieties of gifts, but the same Spirit; . . . To one is given through the Spirit the utterance of wisdom, and to another the utterance of knowledge according to the same Spirit, to another faith by the same Spirit, to another gifts of healing by the one Spirit, to another the working of miracles, to another prophecy, to another the discernment of spirits, to another various kinds of tongues, to another the interpretation of tongues. All these are activated by one and the same Spirit, who allots to each one individually just as the Spirit chooses. (1 Corinthians 12:4, 8-11, NRSV)

Paul explains the aim of this prodigal spiriting of the community as follows: "To each is given the manifestation of the Spirit for the common good" (1 Corinthians 12:7). The aim of this spiriting of each and every member of the community, the aim of this diversity of capacities and callings is precisely the good that is common to all. In Ephesians, these gifts are intended "to equip the saints for the work of ministry, for building up the body of Christ" (Ephesians 4:12).

The distinctive way Paul indicates the coordination of these gifts and ministries is to speak of the Body of Christ (Romans 12:4-5; 1 Corinthians 12:12-27; Colossians 3:14; Ephesians 4:14-16). It is precisely as all are equipped for their own distinctive participation in the life, work, ministry, and service of the community that this community takes on the character of being the visible presence of Jesus, the Body of Christ.

That the community of faith truly belongs to God, truly anticipates the ultimate goal of God, truly embodies the action of God in Christ is evident in the liveliness of this body in the distribution of gifts and tasks. Here every person is gifted; every person is summoned to responsible ministry. The aim of this diversity is not competition and confusion, but love and peace: the anticipation here and now of the ultimate harmony in which God will be all in all.

The Church is holy only insofar as it truly corresponds in this way to the divine goal and intention. The liveliness of this corporate body is the liveliness of love (1 Corinthians 13). Only as the embodiment of this lively love is the Church holy, distinctively separated from the world of deadly apathy, bondage, competition, and enmity. As the community of this lively love, it bears unmistakable testimony in the world of the truth of the gospel, the good news that God makes all things new.

(c) The love that is expressed concretely in the inclusiveness of the community and in the lively participation of each and all in its mission and ministry also marks the life of each of its members. If participation in ministry is designated by "gifts" of the Spirit, then the formation of style of life is designated by "fruits" of the Spirit. Yet no absolute distinction is possible between gifts and fruits of the Spirit, since love belongs to both groups and is indeed the foundation of each.

Where we might speak of life-style, Paul speaks of "walking according to the Spirit" and opposes this to walking according to the flesh. It is in this connection that we often encounter Paul's listing of vices and virtues:

> Now the works of the flesh are obvious: fornication, impurity, licentious-ness, idolatry, sorcery, enmities, strife, jealousy, anger, quarrels, dissen-sions, factions, envy, drunkenness, carousing, and things like these . . . .
> By contrast, the fruit of the Spirit is love, joy, peace, patience, kindness, generosity, faithfulness, gentleness, and self-control. (Galatians 5:19-21, 22-23)

These lists give the initial impression of a kind of arbitrary heaping together of good and bad qualities. Undoubtedly there is some of that character to the lists, which may have in part been taken over from popular pagan philosophy. But closer attention shows that Paul is fundamentally concerned with the attitudes and patterns of action that are relevant to the construction of community. The spirited life is that which makes us fit for community, while the "lusts of the flesh" are those activities (envy, dissension, enmity etc.) that destroy community. This indicates that Paul, like other New Testament authors, is not concerned with individual ethics, but with the patterns of life that produce or destroy community.

Holiness of life then is precisely the sort of life that enables us to relate to one another in love. Meanwhile, the "lusts of the flesh" (which is by no means a category of specifically sexual behavior) include anything that provokes enmity and dissension and so destroys human community. The individualistic bias of much Christian ethics is at odds with this basic point of New Testament ethics.

The basic theme of holiness, then, is love. It is this love that makes possible the realization of the new society, the community that reflects and anticipates the divine aim and promise.

It is in this light that we can understand why Paul lays so much stress upon the overcoming of enmity and strife in the community. What is at stake here is something far more than peace and quiet, and quite different from law and order. It is the basic quality of the Christian community as the anticipation of the reign of God. Holiness is not the quality of an individual as such; it is essentially communal in character. This helps to explain how it is that boasting, judging, and mutual condemnation are excluded from the life of the community. These things, while compatible with some conceptions of holiness, are utterly at odds with the sort of holiness that reflects the divine love.

CONCLUSION

The holy catholic church is the community in which divine love is embodied[12] and which carries the divine mission of announcing and enacting this love in all the world. It is this community that is the sphere of the presence and power of the divine Spirit.

Now it must be admitted that much that is called the Church bears little relation to this holy catholic church. It is already clear that the existence of this holy catholic church cannot be determined or defined by the presence of cult or temple, hierarchy or institution. These have no necessary relation to the community that embodies the divine love.

In order to deal with this discontinuity, theologians have often used the distinction between the visible and the invisible church. But this is mistaken, for as the Body of Christ the church is visible or it is nothing. This visibility has nothing to do with monuments and organizational structure, or with the putative identity of doctrine or rite. The visibility of the holy catholic church is the visibility appropriate to love. Love is not invisible. It is visible in word and deed. There is nothing invisible about life-long loyalty, about sacrificial service, about solidarity and generosity. These are not secret sentiments, but visible patterns of behavior, manifest, often strikingly so, to all who come in contact with those who live in this way. The "visible" church is there wherever we encounter these patterns, whether or not they are found within the organizations and edifices commonly called churches. And wherever, in spite of architecture and organizational structure, we do not discern this community, there is no visible church and so no holy catholic church at all. What is visible instead is the religious form of the structure of division and domination: the pious decoration of worldliness.

The point of this analysis is not to set up an invidious contrast between the actual and the ideal church. The holy catholic church is actual, it is there to be seen in ordinary congregations of believers by any who trouble to look. Of course it may not be found in all congregations, nor is it the predominant reality in many, or in enough of them. No doubt many weeds are sown amid the wheat (Matthew 13:24-30). But it is not our task to purge the weeds, for this would be to violate the ethics of community life in the name of "saving" it.

Rather, we are driven to recognize the holy catholic church as both gift and task coming from the divine Spirit. It is gift. It can be discerned and recognized in ordinary congregations where love for the neighbor, for the sister and brother comes to expression. Wherever it is found it is indeed a miracle of the Spirit, for there is much in our community life that conspires to overthrow this rule of love, of mutual respect, of inclusiveness, of mutual ministry of forbearance and generosity.

Thus, it is also task. Against all that limits the inclusiveness of the community, against all that restricts the full participation of all in its life and ministry, against all that produces dissension and enmity we are called to struggle. In this struggle we are armed, not with edicts of compulsion, nor with institutional authority, but solely and simply with the persuasions of love. In this way the constant and inescapable task of the reform of the Church embodies the goal of that reform, which is that the community truly and clearly reflect the holy will of God for all creation.

CHAPTER NINETEEN

THE COMMUNION
OF SAINTS

I n addition to the holy catholic church, the Creed speaks of the communion of saints as the sphere of the activity of the Holy Spirit. The common sense of the theological tradition is that this clause refers to the same domain as that specified as the holy catholic church. Although I will argue that this is a mistaken view, it will be helpful first to indicate briefly the main ways in which the communion of saints has been understood as referring to some or other dimension of the community of faith before proposing an alternative construction of this clause of the Creed.

1. The Eastern Orthodox tradition emphasizes the unity of the Church across the generations in and through its liturgy. Within this context, it is quite natural to understand this clause of the Creed as an expression of the presence of the whole Church in the worship of any congregation. On this view whenever a congregation participates in the liturgy, in reality all Christians of whatever nation and whatever epoch are joined together spiritually in the liturgy. Thus, this clause of the Creed is understood to refer to the communion together of all Christians across the ages, both living and dead, in the liturgy of the community (see Hebrews 12:1-2). Thus the meaning of this clause is that we are surrounded by a great cloud of witnesses, the past generations of Christians.

2. The Roman Catholic Church has interpreted this clause of the Creed in two basic ways:

a) The communion of the saints refers to our relation to the saints, that is, to persons who demonstrate the power to work miracles and whose lives were exemplary of the life of faith. Thus, this clause does not refer to the whole church across the centuries, but to a communion with a select company of Christians—the saints. According to this point of view, the saints are with God in the heavens (see Apocalypse of John, those gathered by the throne). But as the Church still on earth we have or can have an intimate relation with them. They can intercede for us and be instruments of God's will and blessing for us.[13]

b) The second interpretation focuses on the sacraments. According to this view cultic actions such as baptism, Eucharist, confirmation, or ordination are actions that assure the sanctity of the community. Thus, the communion of saints refers to the actions that realize the holiness of the Church. This is the sacramental interpretation of this clause.[14]

3. Protestant churches do not seem to have an official interpretation of this clause of the Creed. Nevertheless, it is possible to say that we often encounter here an interpretation that focuses on the moral holiness of persons. Often this refers to a detailed obedience to the rules and laws of the Church. From this point of view the communion of saints reiterates the importance of holiness within the community, which leads in turn to the exclusion of those who are regarded as living less than holy lives. Of course this view runs into contradiction with the activity of Jesus, who identified with sinners rather than with the pious.

All of these interpretations of this clause of the Creed presuppose that the clause refers to the Church. The differences between them stem from differences in the understanding of the Church. Thus, the orthodox interpretation places the emphasis on the continuity of the Church through the centuries. The Catholic interpretation emphasizes the sacraments. The Protestant interpretation emphasizes the moral or interior life of individual members of the congregation. On the basis of this common emphasis on the Church, it is merely a matter of deciding what aspect of the Church comes into question here.

But the theme common to the diverse interpretations of this clause is itself dubious. We have already affirmed our faith in the holy Church. Why the need for this repetition? Why two clauses with the same meaning and reference? This is especially strange when we recall that we are dealing with a very brief Creed that does not use excessive words to articulate the faith. In raising the question in this way we are driven to doubt the common sense of the tradition.

This clause of the Creed is found for the first time in a commentary by Niceta of Remesiana in the fourth century. Thus, the clause appears together with the initial interpretation of its meaning. Niceta says that the communion of saints refers to all just persons: "From the beginning of the world patriarchs, prophets, martyrs and all other just men who have lived, are living or who will live in the time to come."[15] This commentary indicates that we rely upon or are loyal to the fellowship of all just persons. Here we encounter a meaning of this clause which was lost for many centuries as the Church focused exclusively upon itself as the context of "salvation." It is a meaning that can be of great significance for the contemporary Church, which like the early Church lives in a context of religious, ideological, and philosophical pluralism. The "communion of saints" indicates an intimate relation between persons whether within or without the Church, a solidarity based on their commitment to the justice of God. This solidarity exists in spite of the fact that those who are participants in this solidarity to not know or do not acknowledge the lordship of Jesus in any explicit way.

Another even better known witness to the importance of this solidarity is the African theologian, Augustine of Hippo. In his maturity Augustine wrote the following words clarifying his work "Of True Religion":

> That which today is called the Christian religion existed for centuries and never was absent from the beginning of humanity until the coming of Christ in the flesh. In this epoch the true religion that already existed came to be called, Christianity. (Retractions I, xiii)[16]

This means that true religion is not only found in the Church, but also before and outside the Church, indeed wherever we find a commitment to the will of God and a life of truth and love.

Clearly this refers in the first place to Judaism, especially the patriarchs and prophets. We recall that Paul clearly affirms that the faith of Abraham that relied on the promises of God is the proper pattern for Christian faith, even though Abraham's faith was by no means an explicit commitment to Jesus (Romans 4; Galatians 4:21-31).[17] In addition, the author of Hebrews indicates that all those persons throughout the history of Israel who shared in this reliance upon the promises of God are witnesses to faith (Hebrews 11). Indeed, this author suggests that there is a kind of communion of fellowship between them and ourselves:

> Therefore, since we are surrounded by so great a cloud of witnesses, let us also lay aside every weight and the sin which clings so closely, and let us run with perseverance the race that is set before us, looking to Jesus the pioneer and perfecter of our faith, who for the sake of the joy that was set before him endured the cross, disregarding its shame, and has taken his seat at the right hand of the throne of God. (12:1-2, NRSV)

In this brief passage the author relates this communion of the saints to past history, to the ultimate future, and to the cross of Jesus "who is seated at the right hand." The communion of saints then joins together the past and future in the present of the crucified as the pattern of our faithfulness.

It is important to recognize that this communion or companionship does not only include the Jews but also all "the just." Even here in Hebrews the list of the company of witnesses includes Rahab the whore, who was by no means a Jew.[18] And earlier, the author of Hebrews had included the pagan priest Melchizedek not only as a pattern for us, but also as the pattern for Christ!

In the early Church, especially among the more philosophically inclined interpreters of Christianity, it became commonplace to include among the just those with whom Christians were in essential solidarity— the great philosophers of Greece and Rome who were committed to justice, truth, and the unity of God. This sense of solidarity is already rooted in the view of Paul that we find in Romans. There, speaking of the Gentiles, Paul writes:

> For what can be known about God is plain to them, because God has shown it to them. Ever since the creation of the world his invisible nature, namely, his eternal power and deity, has been clearly perceived in the things that have been made. (Romans 1:19-20)

This passage aims to clarify the responsibility of pagans to the will or law of God: "For he will render to [everyone] according to his works; to those who by patience in well-doing seek for glory and honor and immortality, he will give eternal life" (2:6-7). The pagans will receive eternal life on the basis of their justice even though this justice was actualized on pagan grounds, with pagan motives (glory and honor and immortality). Thus Paul can conclude this portion of the argument as follows:

> For it is not the hearers of the law who are [just] before God, but the doers of the law who will be [made just]. When Gentiles [pagans] who have not the law do by nature what the law requires, they are a law to themselves, even though they do not have the law. They show that what the law requires is written on their hearts, while their conscience also bears witness and their conflicting thoughts accuse or perhaps excuse them on that day when, according to my gospel, God judges the secrets of men by Christ Jesus. (2:13-16)

Here it is quite clear that the norm used to judge all persons is the same: Jesus Christ. Thus, the law or will of God is not something abstract but that which is expressed in Jesus. But this does not mean that all are judged in accordance with whether or not they actually knew Jesus, with whether or not they made an explicit commitment to him. On the contrary, the argument of Paul supposes that there have been persons throughout the course of history and in diverse cultures who have been committed to the will of God even though they knew nothing of Jesus. Their rationale for doing justice may have sprung from philosophical or religious motives.

What matters is that they did, in fact, embody this commitment. Thus Christians, as those who do have this explicit commitment, are in solidarity with these just persons.[19] The name which the Creed gives to this solidarity is the communion of saints. Because of this solidarity between Christians and non-Christians it was possible for Paul to make use of lists of virtues and vices that come from pagan philosophy in order to clarify the sort of life-style that he believed to be congruent with the gospel (Galatians 5:19-23; Romans 12 and 13 and so on).

The attitude of Paul has its root (whether or not Paul was aware of this) in the behavior and attitude of Jesus. Both Mark and Luke report the dispute that arose when the disciples noted someone casting out demons who were not of their number. But Jesus replies that "whoever is not against us is for us" (Mark 9:40). In this way Jesus points to the solidarity between those who are his disciples and those who are not. The basis of this solidarity is that both are engaged in the work that demonstrates the coming of the reign of God by casting out the powers that darken the minds of their fellow creatures. Whoever is committed to this liberating practice is "with us."

There is another saying that appears to say the opposite, "He who is not with me is against me" (Luke 11:23; Matthew 12:50). But this apparent contradiction dissolves when we attend to the context. Once again the subject is the exorcism of demons. In this case the Pharisees are those who disparage this work, saying that it derives not from God but from Satan. Thus, they are opponents of the action that liberates. Here there is no solidarity but only division and opposition.

That which distinguishes the sphere of opposition from that of solidarity, then, is the attitude taken toward the work of setting persons free from demonic structures and forces. Those who participate in this action, on whatever basis, are in solidarity with Jesus. And those who are opponents of this action, however pious, are the enemies of Jesus.

The fundamental principle is that which is enunciated by Jesus when he says: "Not every one who says to me 'Lord, Lord,' will enter the [reign] of heaven, but [the one] who does the will of my Father who is in heaven," (Matthew 7:21). The question of entering the reign of God is further elaborated in Jesus' last parable concerning the great judgment when the ultimate fate of persons will depend not on their having known Jesus, but on their having clothed the naked and cared for the sick and imprisoned (Matthew 25:31-46). Thus, it is quite clear that the basis for the community of the saints as the solidarity of all just persons is the action that demonstrates a commitment to the reign of God. The test of this justice is not religious or doctrinal, but a commitment to the neighbor, especially the poor, the oppressed, the afflicted.

Now it is important to see how this communion of saints is related to the faith in the Holy Spirit. The Spirit designates the anticipation of the accomplishment of the purpose of God (new creation, reign of justice, peace, etc.) as that purpose was announced and enacted by Jesus of Nazareth. The sphere of this presence and power of the Spirit is primarily the Church, which has the responsibility to testify to Jesus through its mission and proclamation. But alongside this sphere is another, that of the communion of saints. The affirmation of the communion of saints confirms that the Spirit of God is not the prisoner of the Church. Rather, the divine spirit is the very wind of God that blows where it will. The gift of life is given by the Spirit to every creature. The work of commitment to life and opposition to the forces and structures of death is also something that is not confined to the Church, but is found everywhere, in all peoples and in every era. Wherever we encounter this commitment, we encounter the work and the gift of the Holy Spirit.

Thus, we can give thanks to God whenever we encounter these just, these "saints." We must not be like the disciples of Luke 9:49 and be jealous and resentful of them as though their justice should somehow diminish us rather than enrich us.[20]

The doctrine of the communion of saints is especially important for us today. We live in a world in which numerous religions encounter one another. The history of our encounter with other religions has too often been characterized on our part by a determination to oppose them and eradicate them. This attitude comes from a failure to celebrate the communion of saints. A recovery of this doctrine will enable us to deal in a more authentic way with other religious traditions, celebrating wherever we find an expression of what Augustine called "true religion." Moreover, in the modern world we encounter a number of groups and movements that are committed to the real transformation of the world, to the realization of justice and opposition to oppression. We are enabled by this doctrine to recognize our essential solidarity with all who are committed to the liberation of humanity from the power of anxiety, division, and domination.

Our solidarity with those who are committed to this cause outside the sphere of the Church does not negate our own responsibility to give testimony to Jesus as the true Lord. We offer to others of "the saints" the glad news that the aim of our hopes, the object of our commitments, has already become flesh in the mission and ministry of Jesus. At the same time, they can help us overcome the provincialism of our formulations of this cause and the partiality of our commitment.

The solidarity among all those who are committed to the reign of love and peace, of justice and generosity, is both gift and task. It is a gift in that it is the Spirit who awakens and capacitates for this commitment both within and without the Church. It is gift as well in that it is the Spirit that permits the recognition of one another's commitment as having a common ground (in the Spirit that we also know as the Spirit of Christ) and a common goal. But this communion and solidarity is also a task to be accomplished. It is the call of the Spirit to place greater confidence in the act of the divine than in our own institutional and ecclesiastical boundaries. The discernment and celebration of this solidarity is one of the most critical tasks facing us in our pluralistic world.

CHAPTER TWENTY

THE FORGIVENESS OF SINS

We turn now from a consideration of the nature and sphere of the Spirit to a consideration of the act and aim of the Spirit. As we have seen, the presence of the Spirit is the mode of Jesus' presence in our lives and world. The presence of Jesus has the form of the presence of that future which is promised and demonstrated in his mission and ministry, his cross and resurrection. The presence of the Spirit as the presence of Jesus and the presence of the reign of God within our history and world is expressed as the holy catholic church. This is the sphere of the Spirit's activity in empowering us for mission. In addition, we encounter the Spirit in the solidarity with all who are committed to the cause of divine justice, whether or not they see the relation between this commitment and the name or person of Jesus. Thus, the holy catholic church and the communion of saints indicate the sphere of the Spirit's operation. It is in this context that we encounter the clause concerning the forgiveness of sins and the resurrection of the body which indicate the distinctive character of this spirited activity.

In order to interpret this clause of the Creed it is essential to bear in mind its context. It is not found in the second article of the Creed dealing with Jesus Christ, the Son of God, our Lord, but in the third article of the Creed concerning the Holy Spirit. Thus, it does not have immediately in view the atoning work of God in Christ, but the capacitating power of the Spirit of God.[21] This capacitating power of the Spirit is that of the Spirit that is sent by Jesus, and that has its definiteness from the mission and ministry of Jesus. But we must avoid the tendency to develop a view of forgiveness that bypasses the work of the Spirit altogether. The work of God in Christ may also be summarized as the forgiveness of sins and we have seen how the cross itself brings to a head Jesus' solidarity with the outcast and despised and so becomes the announcement of the acceptance of sinners. But now what is in view is the activity of the Spirit in empowering those who follow after Jesus. And this empowerment is spoken of as the forgiveness of sins.

In the Nicene Creed this forgiveness of sins will be correlated specifically with baptism ("one baptism for the forgiveness of sins"). The association that we have already noted between the Apostles' Creed and the practice of baptism and the way the Creed as a whole may be understood as a reaffirmation of baptism, serves to make this a plausible connection. However, before reducing this clause of the Creed to a reference to baptism it is important to see in what way the forgiveness of sins as tied to the Holy Spirit is expressed in the biblical witness that the Creed summarizes.

When we consider the forgiveness of sins as the effect of the Spirit's presence and power, we are immediately driven to the account of the "spiriting" of the disciples in the Gospel of John.

> Jesus came and stood among them and said, "Peace be with you." After he said this, he showed them his hands and his side. Then the disciples rejoiced when they saw the Lord. Jesus said to them again, "Peace be with you, As the Father has sent me, so I send you." When he had said this, he breathed on them and said to them, "Receive the Holy Spirit. If you forgive the sins of any, they are forgiven them; if you retain the sins of any, they are retained." (John 20:19b-23, NRSV)

This encounter brings together the cross, the resurrection, the ascension, and Pentecost in a remarkable way. It is the risen Jesus who confers the Spirit upon the disciples. But it is emphasized that the risen Christ is none other than the crucified one ("he showed them his hands and side"). Thus we may say that the whole of the preceding narrative climaxes in such a way that the commissioning of the disciples is the outcome of the events of cross and resurrection, that is, of Jesus' being "lifted up." We have already seen that the commissioning of the disciples is the import of the ascension of Jesus, something not directly narrated by the Gospel of John, but presupposed by it.

The actual commission is itself remarkable in two ways. First, the character of the commission is global. The disciples are sent as Jesus was himself sent ("*as* the Father has sent me, *so* I send you"). Their mission is the prolongation of Jesus' own mission. They who are no longer servants but friends (John 15:15) are now entrusted with the whole of Jesus' mission.

Second, the narrative of the commission is based upon the creation narrative of Genesis 2, just as the prologue to the Gospel is based upon the creation poem of Genesis 1. The breathing upon the disciples here echoes the action of God: "Then the Lord God formed man from the dust of the ground, and breathed into his nostrils the breath of life; and the man became a living being" (Genesis 2:7). The connection here between breath, life, and spirit is mirrored in the commissioning of the disciples by Jesus in the Gospel of John. Thus, the disciples are, as it were, re-created; they become the new human being. The author signals that what is at stake here is the beginning of the new creation as the act of the one who is the creating Word made flesh. Indeed, nothing less than such a re-creation could serve to capacitate persons for the awesome task of continuing the work of God in the Son.

Now the result of this global commissioning and capacitation as re-creation is intimately connected to the forgiveness of sins, or rather to the dual authorization both to release and to retain. Thus, the forgiveness of sins is expressed as the work of the disciples for which they are made ready by Jesus' commissioning and the Spirit's re-creation.

It is clearly this commissioning, creation, and authorization which corresponds to the meaning of this clause of the Creed. That is, we are concerned here not with the forgiving character of God as such, nor the atoning work of God in Christ, but immediately with the authorization of Jesus' followers to engage in the liberating work of releasing from (and retaining) sin.

Before attempting to clarify further the meaning of this authorization, let us first recall that this is by no means the only place in the Gospels that we hear of such a commissioning regarding sin. We find a similar commission repeated twice in the Gospel of Matthew. The first occurrence follows the affirmation of Jesus as Messiah by Peter in Caesarea Philippi. In Matthew's Gospel this confession receives from Jesus the response:

> And I tell you, you are Peter [Rock], and on this rock I will build my church, and the [gates of Hades] shall not prevail against it. I will give you the keys of the [reign] of heaven, and whatever you bind on earth shall be bound in heaven, and whatever you loose on earth shall be loosed in heaven."
> (Matthew 16:18-19)

While this text has sometimes been taken to confer special authority upon Peter, this is rendered impossible by the repetition of this same authority in relation to the disciples as a whole:

> Truly I tell you, whatever you bind on earth will be bound in heaven, and whatever you loose on earth will be loosed in heaven. Again, truly I tell you, if two of you agree on earth about anything you ask, it will be done for you by my Father in heaven. For where two or three are gathered in my name, I am there among them. (Matthew 18:18-20, NRSV)

Here it is clear that the authoritative binding and loosing is the work of any "two of you" and is not concentrated in a person or office. The office of the "keys" is that of the community itself, the community of any two who are gathered in the name of Jesus.[22]

The central notion in each of these texts is a correspondence between the activity of the disciples and the activity of God. It is precisely as if God has entrusted the divine mission into the hands of the followers of Jesus, just as previously that divine mission had been entrusted to Jesus himself. This correspondence is made especially clear in Matthew, where the action of the community precedes and so "produces" the action "in heaven": "whatever you loose . . . *will be* loosed." That is, the divine action awaits the action of the faithful community and follows after it.

Now there is simply no way around the breathtaking audacity of this authorization. It says simply that God has determined to be bound by the decision of the followers of Jesus. What they bind will be bound by God, what they release will be released by God. God agrees to be represented by them so that what they say and do will be true of God's word and deed.[23]

Although Matthew does not refer to the Spirit here, he scarcely ever does. John's tying of this commission to the Spirit is appropriate since, as we have seen, the Spirit designates the presence and power of the divine in the human so as to make it often difficult to distinguish in biblical texts whether we are dealing with the divine or the human spirit.

Here it is clear that the overcoming of the separation between creator and creature in the incarnation is by no means isolated, but takes on the more radical (if such is possible) form of the identification of the divine with the decision and action of the community of Jesus' followers. God becomes human in Jesus. God becomes humanity in the "spiriting" of the community.

When we confront the staggering claim of identity between the decision and action of the community and that of God, we are aware of the awful nearness of idolatry and blasphemy. Would it not be far better to insist on the radical transcendence of God as the best way to avoid the divinizing of the all-too-human institution of the Church and the corresponding temptation to assume tyrannical power? The history of Christianity provides more than ample illustration of the terrible consequences of the elevation of the authority of the Church and its institutions, an elevation sometimes accompanied by an interpretation of one or more of the passages here cited that emphasize the authority of the Church and especially of its hierarchy.

Against this cautionary note we must first insist that an emphasis on the transcendence of God that seeks to separate the divine and the human is, however well justified, nevertheless fundamentally impossible on the basis of both the second and the third articles of the Creed. To introduce this note into a discussion of the Spirit is to eliminate its characteristic features entirely. The Spirit of God is God's presence with us, God's empowerment of us.

But we must also emphasize that what is at stake in this authorization has nothing to do with the granting of special authority to any institution whatever.[24] This commission, capacitation, and authorization is given to the followers simply as followers. It has nothing whatever to do with any structure, let alone the development of a distinction between priest and laity, still less a hierarchically arranged priesthood or "ministry." No provision is made here for the delegation of this authority to another, for the restriction of this authority to some few, still less the usurpation of this authority by a special class, however constituted, named, or ordained.

Furthermore, there is no basis in the texts themselves for the spiritual arrogance that insists on its own privilege and authority. The community summoned into being by Jesus is the community of companions who follow him in seeking to serve humanity. No arrogance can possibly comport with the discipleship which is the object of this commission, the recipient of this promise and capacitation. It is the following of the one who came not to be served, but to serve and to give his life as a ransom for many.

If we were to read these commissions out of their context in the Gospels we might conclude that we were faced with two equal and balanced possibilities: loosing and binding—that those who are commissioned to follow Jesus may equally decide to accept and to forbid, to reject and to accept, to release and to retain. But the context makes such an interpretation impossible. In the case of John this is evident above all in the way in which the commissioning of the disciples is a prolongation of the mission of Jesus. The Gospel has made it quite clear that for that mission the ultimate and basic aim is release, forgiveness, and life (John 3:16-17). Condemnation and death is what one brings on oneself by rejecting life and forgiveness (John 3:18). The encounter with the word of Jesus is a crisis that can result in death, but it is this precisely because it is a call to life that can be rejected or repudiated (John 5:25 ff.).[25]

The relation between binding and loosing is defined quite clearly in the mission and ministry of Jesus who "binds the strong man" and lets the oppressed and despised go free. The "strong man" is above all the principalities and powers that hold humanity captive: economic systems that rob the poor, political systems that extort the loyalty of those they oppress and above all, the religious and moral systems that exclude the unclean and the sinners. In the Gospels it is primarily the religious and the respectable who are bound while their captives, those held prisoner to systems of condemnation and rejection, are set free. In short, the accusers are bound, the accused set free. That is why Jesus condemns not the publicans and the prostitutes, but the scribes and the Pharisees.

It must be admitted that our confusion here has reached catastrophic proportions. For all too often we pass over in silence the structures that dishonor and disfigure the divine image, releasing the avaricious and the violent from the divine claim while condemning the weak and despised. We ferret out the peccadillos of the faltering and shrug at the violations of humanity and the earth perpetrated by the powerful. But the example of the mission of Jesus abundantly reveals that it is the "strong" who are to be bound and the weak who are to be released. The commission to bind and loose is by no means a license for "God's bullies," but a call to the imitation of the divine mercy demonstrated in Christ.

This same point is made in a different way in the Gospel of Matthew, where the authorization of the disciples is found in the context of a teaching concerning the necessity of forgiving the neighbor "seventy times seven" and the teaching that those who do not forgive will not be forgiven by God. Those who are commissioned to bind and to loose, then, are those who constantly forgive one another, whose forgiveness knows no impatience or limitation. To no other community is it promised that whatever you bind on earth will be bound in heaven, only to the community that practices this constant forgiving.

And lest this be misunderstood, Matthew at several points makes clear that those who do not forgive are themselves not forgiven, that those who do not forgive the other will not be forgiven by God. It is evident that regarding the gospel there can be no balancing or equivalence between binding and loosing, retaining and releasing, forgiving and rejecting. There is never any positive command to bind. But the command to forgive is insistently underscored in the most impressive ways. Thus we do not consider two equal possibilities, but only one possibility and its "shadow."

With these important delimitations of the meaning of the clause we may avoid some of the worst misunderstandings, but it is still necessary to discern the positive content of the clause. Given the commission and authorization to loose and to bind, what does it mean to rely on the forgiveness of sins; to be loyal to the Spirit that capacitates us for this task?

The release from sin means the release from the burden of brokenness and bondage that is the power of the past. This power is admirably summarized by Paul as the "flesh." The activity of those who continue the mission of Jesus is that of releasing humanity from this bondage and brokenness, and so from the repetition of the past through the inbreaking of the new that is designated as Spirit.

When we speak of the forgiveness of sins we are speaking of the liberation of persons from the dead weight of the past, and from the forms of brokenness and bondage that disfigure and dishonor God's image and likeness on earth. In our life with others we are drawn into a tangled web of complicity in our own bondage and brokenness. This brokenness and bondage may take many forms. It may be the accumulated guilt that flows from the consequences (intended or otherwise) of our actions in relationship to others. It may be the weight of guilt imposed by tradition and the accusation of those who represent that tradition. It may be the compulsive behavior that drives us to repeated attempts at self-destruction, dishonoring ourselves and our neighbors.

Whatever the character of this bondage and brokenness, it has the form of an inescapable past that throttles the present and condemns the future to a repetition of the past. The forgiveness of sins is simply release from this past and an opening toward the future, a future not marred with the compulsion to repeat the past.

Often the forgiveness of sins is related to the repeal of the guilt and the release from the debt of the past. But it is also important to speak, as did Wesley, not only of release from the guilt, but also of release from the power of sin. What the gospel has in view is not simply a forensic transaction that occurs "above us" but a transformation that occurs within us. The past that paralyzes is to be genuinely overcome in such a way as to truly mobilize us toward a fundamentally different life, a life characterized by freedom instead of compulsion, joy in place of anxiety, love instead of egoism and hostility.

The message of the love of God cuts the root of sin in our personal and public life. When we know that we are loved, that this love has no limit but is indeed directed precisely to "sinners" and that nothing can separate us from the love of God manifested in Jesus, then the root of anxiety suffers a fatal blow. The breaking of the chain of anxiety in turn cuts the nerve of self-preoccupation, both of pride and despair. The compulsion to use things or persons to build up the tokens of life loses its hypnotic appeal, for the value of life and of ourselves has a far more secure foundation than can be afforded by these means. As these chains are cut we can begin to feel free, set free from compulsion and obsession. This lifting of the burden produces joy and peace.

Of course we know that the anxiety of the flesh is not so easily dissipated. We still know anxiety and its fruit in our lives. We are still "sinners." But the word of the grace or favor of God is also taking form and having effects in our lives. We are not (yet) perfect. Thus we have not yet reached the point where this message has become dispensable for us. And we must continue to see the fruit of this message in our own lives and in that of those around us. That is why the community of faith and the community of the just remains essential for us. By dwelling in these spheres of the Spirit we have the opportunity of witnessing constantly the effects of this liberating and gracious word.

Loyalty to the life-giving Spirit means that we persist in the practice of the forgiveness of sins to which we have been summoned and for which we have been re-created. This practice has many forms in the life of the community of faith. As we noted at the outset, the Nicene Creed will place special emphasis upon baptism as the principal expression of this commission to forgive sins. This power of forgiveness is dramatically expressed in the act of baptism though that is by no means the only meaning of baptism, certainly not the only or primary meaning of baptism in the earliest Church. Baptism also expresses the divine favor that adopts us and makes us God's sons and daughters. It expresses the renunciation of all other lords in favor of the lordship of Jesus, who is the Christ. Nevertheless, it is true that one of the meanings of baptism as an act of the community of faith is release from the weight of the past of brokenness and bondage and the entry into the life of free responsibility in which the person to be baptized becomes a part of the community that baptizes.

This practice of the forgiveness of sins is also expressed in the Eucharist, where the participation in the meal is also a "drinking of the spirit" as Paul maintains and is a capacitation for the "spirited" life of the community of the new age.

Indeed the confession and forgiveness of sins is an inescapable part of the worship of the community of faith. This worship serves to model the basic structure of our life in the world as witnesses to the gospel and so to the coming of the reign of justice and generosity and joy. This constant liturgical practice of the forgiveness of sins demonstrates that this community has indeed received this commission and continues this ministry and mission.[26]

In spite of the importance of these liturgical expressions of the forgiveness of sins, this theme can by no means be reduced to a sacramental or liturgical expression. The theme of the forgiveness of sins is also a summary indication of the meaning of the proclamation of this community in its mission to the world. In the Gospel of Luke, the risen Jesus instructs the disciples in the necessity of the suffering and resurrection of the Messiah,

> And that repentance and forgiveness of sins is to be proclaimed in his name
> to all nations, beginning from Jerusalem . . . . And see, I am sending upon

you what my Father promised; so stay here in the city until you have been clothed with power from on high. (Luke 24:47, 49, NRSV)

As in the parallel passage in the Gospel of John, the cross and resurrection appear as the basis for a commission having to do with the forgiveness of sins. In addition, this announcement of forgiveness is dependent upon empowerment through the Holy Spirit. Thus, in spite of the remarkable differences between these two Gospels, in both the commission of the disciples focuses on the forgiveness of sins based on the resurrection of the crucified and the empowerment of the divine Spirit.

What Luke adds to this is the specification of the forgiveness of sins as the content of the community's proclamation. This indicates that any attempt to reduce the forgiveness of sins to the internal life of the community, and to its liturgical practices, is interdicted. The forgiveness of sins is the content of the ongoing participation of the community in the proclamation and mission of Jesus.[27] The proclamation of the gospel is here identified as the announcement that God grants to a humanity burdened by the failures of the past, a new future of freedom and responsibility.

As important as it is that the forgiveness of sins be represented in the internal or liturgical life of the community and that this be understood as the basic content of the community's proclamation to the nations, it is even more important that the community of faith and the lives of the faithful clearly exhibit the constant practice of the forgiveness of sins.[28] This is the regular emphasis of the Gospel of Matthew. The forgiveness of sins must become the form of life of those who are a part of the community. Only the community that forgives can be the community that receives forgiveness. The forgiveness that we exhibit must be like the divine forgiveness in that it knows no limit. Thus the life of the community in which the practice of condemning and judging one another has been replaced by mutual forgiveness is the community that is truly loyal to the Spirit that capacitates us for this task and responsibility. Where grudges are held, where patience is short, where resentment and enmity prevail, where persons are excluded and condemned we see the rule not of the spirit of life, but of the power of death.

The forgiveness of sins serves as a comprehensive designation for what is done through the Spirit by and within the community of faith. It is the act of the Spirit in and through us. The reality of this release from bondage and brokenness is expressed liturgically in the practice of baptism, Eucharist, and the confession and forgiveness of sins. It is expressed kerygmatically as the form and content of Christian proclamation. And it is expressed in the life of the community as the liberated zone of the divine mercy in which mutual forgiveness is constantly practiced.

What stands out in the meaning of the forgiveness of sins as expressed in the Creed and in the texts that serve as the basis of the Creed, is the audacious claim that God has entrusted this authority to human beings. With this claim the ground is cut from under the religious handling of human brokenness and bondage which had maintained that only God could forgive sin. That assertion served as the legitimation for the development of sacrificial systems that controlled people by rationing forgiveness on condition of participation in the cultus, and support of those who maintained this cultus. The affirmation that the forgiveness of sins is entrusted to all who follow Jesus, to all who continue his mission of solidarity with sinners and opposition to all that dishonors and disfigures the divine image, serves to render the religious establishment obsolete.

We should not hide from ourselves the audacity of the affirmation that this responsibility of releasing and binding is entrusted to us. This affirmation means that the divine mercy is expressed concretely insofar as it is expressed in the life of the followers of Jesus. Where we do not discharge the task of releasing from bondage and brokenness, no release is actual. The will of the Father is gracious and merciful; the ministry of the Son is solidarity with sinners. But this only actually releases persons from bondage when it is concretely mediated by those who follow Jesus through the empowerment of the Spirit. Only where it is actually articulated (proclamation), dramatically enacted (liturgy and sacrament), and above all, lived out (seventy times seven), do persons experience that release and liberation willed by God the Father and demonstrated in Christ. If we fail to practice this forgiveness either through timidity and uncertainty, or through arrogance, then the divine pardon does not become efficacious in the lives of persons. We really are entrusted with a staggering and awesome responsibility. That is what it means to be heirs of the Father and companions of the Son. The only possibility for carrying out this responsibility is through the empowerment of the Spirit that re-creates and so capacitates us for this task.

CHAPTER TWENTY-ONE

THE RESURRECTION
OF THE DEAD

T he forgiveness of sins corresponds to the holy catholic church. It
is the epitome of the spirited action and responsibility of the new
people of God. The theme of the resurrection of the dead,
however returns us to the universal horizon of the Spirit previously
indicated by the communion of saints. In the forgiveness of sins persons
are liberated from the weight of the past and so are given a new future. In
the resurrection of the dead those who have become past or who are fated
to become past are "awakened" to a future that includes "all flesh."

As we have seen, Christian faith is directed toward the future as the
future of God. Even in the first article of the Creed we have seen that God
is known as creator because God has promised a new creation, a new
heaven and a new earth. This suggests a total transformation of the world
through which all the structures of the world are overcome by or
subordinated to the gracious will of God. Through the second article of
the Creed we have seen that our orientation to the future is an orientation
to Jesus who "will come to judge the living and the dead." This
affirmation indicates that the future is the future of Jesus, the future of
the crucified; that is, the future of the one who suffered under Pontius
Pilate and was raised by the power of the Spirit of divine love. Thus, we
know that the future of Jesus is based in the history of Jesus, a history that
demonstrates the love of God as the future of heaven and earth.

We now encounter that same future from the standpoint of the third
article of the Creed, concerning the Holy Spirit. This article speaks of the
Spirit as the presence of Jesus who is seated at the right hand of God the
Father Almighty, and so of the presence of the divine reign that was
demonstrated and proclaimed in the mission and ministry of Jesus.

At the end of this article we find two phrases that speak of this future
under the aspect of the Holy Spirit. The first is the resurrection of the

dead; the second is the life everlasting. The first speaks of the overthrow of the rule of death; the second speaks of life unmenaced by death. The first phrase is, in a certain sense, negative or at least conflictive. It is the uprising against the "last enemy." The second phrase is positive, indicating the result of this victory. These two phrases together indicate two sides of the same phenomenon. Some New Testament texts emphasize the conflict between life and death and the victory over death, as for example, the letters of Paul and the Apocalypse of John. Others place more stress on the result of this victory, for example, the Gospel of John. In order to understand the intimate relation between these two phrases and so these two aspects of the future of the Spirit as our future, we will first attempt to clarify the resurrection and then the result of the resurrection as the life unthreatened by death.

Of what are we speaking when we speak of the resurrection of the body? In the world of philosophy and of religion it is more common to speak of something like "the immortality of the soul." From this traditional point of view we think of some aspect of human being that is "naturally" or essentially "immortal," that is, some part of human existence which is essentially untouched and untouchable by death. Such ideas are found in diverse cultures, but come to most impressive formulation in the philosophy of ancient Greece.

But to speak of the resurrection of the body is to speak of something quite different from the immortality of the soul. The immortality of the soul is neither miracle nor gift, but is something natural. In contrast, the resurrection of the dead points to a break from the natural, the merely given, the status quo. It is not the prolongation of the existing, but the break with the existing or evident structures of experience.

THE MYSTERY OF THE RESURRECTION

For this reason the phrase "the resurrection of the body" is a metaphor. It is not and cannot be literal. Literal language is used to describe that which is within the sphere of the natural, of the "status quo." But that which breaks with the merely given cannot be described within the terms of the given save by means of metaphor. The phrase "resurrection of the dead" speaks of death as if it were sleep. Resurrection means to wake up or to get up from sleep, from the bed, from dreams. But this isn't literal (death isn't the same as sleep). The phrase points to a miracle that exceeds the possibilities of the status quo, of nature, of everyday experience.

When we understand that the resurrection is something that exceeds and escapes the possibilities of descriptive language we can then understand why the Bible can use such distinct and even contradictory images to speak of the resurrection. Paul can speak of the resurrection of Jesus as something that belongs to the category of a vision (see 1 Corinthians 15:1-12, compared with Acts 9:3-6). In the Gospels, the empty tomb and the eating traditions point to a physical event on the order of the resuscitation of a corpse. We also find distinct ways of indicating the time of the resurrection. For Matthew it seems to already occur with the death of Jesus (Matthew 27:52-53) and in the Gospel of Luke, Jesus says to the bandit crucified with him, "today you will be with me in Paradise" (Luke 23:43). Paul clearly supposes that the resurrection is a future event that comes with the last events of history (1 Corinthians 15; 1 Thessalonians 4:13–5:10). Of course, we could attempt to develop a theory in which there were several successive resurrections in order to attempt to fit in all that we encounter on this topic in the New Testament, but this theory would itself be quite distinct from anything we encounter in biblical literature; it would be our own construction.

It is better to accept the tensions and apparent contradictions as warnings against the attempt to develop such a theory. For such a theory would, as it were, "naturalize" the resurrection, domesticating it within the categories of experience. It is precisely these tensions and contradictions within the biblical discourse that demonstrate that the resurrection is something that exceeds every attempt to grasp or to domesticate it. The resurrection is something that belongs to the action of God, and so cannot be captured by theoretical construction.

Nevertheless, this does not mean that the resurrection is completely foreign to experience, that it cannot be understood at all. Even though this event exceeds the categories of thought it is an event with its own characteristics and dimensions. Indeed, one of its principle characteristics is what we have just been indicating: it exceeds the categories of thought. But there are other characteristics of this way of speaking that together help us to get at the distinctive features of a hope in the resurrection of the dead.

THE INSURRECTION OF THE EXECUTED

We can approach an understanding of the resurrection of the dead if we pay attention to the way in which this hope emerges in the faith of Israel. In its origin, the hope for the resurrection of the dead is tied to the opposition to and subversion of the structures of power and privilege in the world.

The hope for the resurrection of the dead explicitly enters the faith of Israel for the first time in the visions attributed to the prophet Daniel. These visions deal with the crisis occasioned by the Hellenizing policy of Antiochus Epiphanes in the second century before Christ. The books of First and Second Maccabees provide us with a description of the struggle for the survival of Israel's faith that ensued from this crisis.

As a part of his attempt to unify this empire, the Greek emperor Antiochus Epiphanes sought to eliminate the practice of Judaism. He prohibited the Hebrew Scriptures, the cultic practices of the people, and the Temple sacrifices. Those who resisted these policies were executed. Even the possession of the Hebrew Scriptures was an offense punishable by death. The Temple itself was converted to a center of pagan sacrifice, an event called "the desolating sacrilege." Although many of the powerful and wealthy of Israel, especially of Jerusalem, accepted this policy, the poor, especially of the countryside, refused to obey. Their resistance led to the execution of many who maintained their loyalty to the law and the prophets of the God of their fathers. Outrage at this campaign of terror sparked outright revolt and a prolonged guerrilla war which eventually routed the Greek forces and their collaborators.

Those who refused to surrender the faith of Israel and thus who died in this struggle were the "saints of Israel." It was from the midst of this struggle that the book of Daniel arose. The book has the aim of calling people to a loyalty which extends even unto death, using the example of the steadfastness of Daniel during the previous crisis for the survival of Israel in the Babylonian captivity (Daniel 1–6). But the visions of chapters 7–12 are even more radical in character. The accounts of these visions were written in Aramaic, using a symbolism difficult for the officials of the Greek empire to understand. The visions are symbolic descriptions of the empires that have previously menaced the people of God: Assyria, Babylon, Persia, and the Greek empire from Alexander the Great to the reign of Antiochus Epiphanes. The message, in brief, was that God had destroyed the previous enemies of Israel and that the days of this last and most virulent enemy were numbered.

It is precisely within this subversive context that we encounter the resurrection of the saints of Israel (Daniel 12:2-3). This was by no means a speculative doctrine, but rather a protest against the fate of those who were slain on account of their loyalty to the God of the living. The resurrection of the executed is the hope for the divine justice that will overthrow the dominion of the tyrant.

Thus the resurrection of the dead is the insurrection of the executed against the power of imperial oppression and the collaborators with that policy of oppression and repression. This insurrection of the slain is the act of God "Almighty" who will use the executed as the judges of the murderous tyrants, thereby demonstrating that the powers of the world are rebels against the justice of God.

It is in this way that the belief in the resurrection of the dead was accepted by the ideological descendants of the Maccabees, the Pharisees and the assortment of resistance groups often lumped together as "zealots."[29] Ironically, the belief in the resurrection of the dead was rejected by the Sadducees and priests (Mark 12:18-27) who had been the beneficiaries of the revolt. But it is not without significance that those who rejected the belief in the resurrection were also those who collaborated with Roman occupation in order to preserve their own religious and social institutions. The hope for the resurrection of the executed is the ideology of resistance to the religious and social legitimation of the status quo.

In the New Testament we encounter a further development of the idea of the resurrection of the dead. This is focused again on the resurrection of the executed, that is, the resurrection of Jesus who was rejected by the official leadership of his own people and was executed by the Roman Empire.

The resurrection of Jesus was understood as the reversal of the verdict of the powerful over against him. As the reversal of their verdict, the resurrection shows the powerful to be in rebellion against God. Now in the case of Jesus, the resurrection of the dead as the resurrection of the executed is no longer an event of expectation, but of memory. That is, the executed one, the crucified, has already returned from death. Thus, in the resurrection of Jesus the principalities and powers of the world are already judged and condemned as rebels against the just rule of God.[30]

One finds this same view of the resurrection of the dead as the divine insurrection against the political and social powers of death in the Apocalypse of John. Here once again the proclamation of the resurrection of the dead has the thoroughly subversive meaning of the overthrow of the Roman Empire (the successor of the empire of Antiochus Epiphanes). Throughout the Apocalypse we encounter the hope for the resurrection of the executed as the victory of the martyrs led by "the Lamb slain from the foundations of the earth."

Thus, a reading of the biblical hope of the resurrection of the dead shows that this doctrine has a decidedly subversive aspect. The powers of the world rely upon their power to kill as the ultimate sanction for their dominion. This is the ultimate weapon of oppression: "If you don't obey, you will die." But the confidence in the resurrection of the dead disarms the powers of this threat. They can no longer subjugate others relying on the threat of death because death "has been swallowed up in victory" (1 Corinthians 15:54). The martyrs are those who can cry out with the taunt "Where, O death, is your victory? Where, O death, is your sting?" (1 Corinthians 15:55). With this hope, based on the resurrection of the crucified, the Church of the martyrs testifies with blood and with joy against the power of the empire of death. This testimony continues through the ages into our own day where Christians still rely upon the one who threw down the powerful from their thrones and exalted the humiliated (Luke 1:52).

THE RESURRECTION OF *ALL* THE DEAD

Although the root and the heart of the hope for the resurrection of the dead is the uprising of the executed (the saints/witnesses/martyrs), the gospel extends the notion to include the resurrection of the dead as such. This extension to include the dead as such, depends on two other doctrines. The first is that humanity is burdened by the forces of powerful oppression: the law, sin, and death. The uprising of the executed then become by extension the uprising of those who are oppressed by death, conceived on the analogy to the mortal power of the forces of oppression. This extension is made possible by the understanding of God as the God of grace and love, rather than wrath and vengeance. The openness of the divine compassion then extends to all who suffer under the oppressive power of death. The evangelical form of the uprising of the executed thus becomes the resurrection of the dead as such.

We already encounter this extension of the doctrine in the thought of Paul, above all in 1 Corinthians 15 and in Romans 5. From the perspective developed in these letters, humanity has been subjected to the oppressive power of death and sin since the time of Adam. The liberating action of God in Christ is an action that entails the liberation of all. The dominion of sin and death will be destroyed because Adam will be set free from their power.

> For as in Adam all die, so also in Christ shall *all* be made alive. (1 Corinthians 15:22)

> Thus as by the transgression of one came condemnation upon all humanity, in the same way through the justice of one came to *all* humanity justification of life. (Romans 5:18, author paraphrase)

> Because God subjected all to disobedience in order to have mercy on *all*. (Romans 11:32, author paraphrase)

Thus the understanding of the grace of God and the poverty and weakness of human beings results in the extension of the uprising of the executed to the resurrection of the dead. Only thus is it possible to speak adequately of the magnitude of the grace of God who has mercy even upon sinners.[31]

THE RESURRECTION OF THE BODY

The God who is liberator (and thus raises the executed) and who is the loving Father (and thus raises the dead) is at the same time Creator of heaven and earth. Because this is true we speak of the resurrection of the *body*.

The body is the possibility and the reality of having relationships with one another. Thanks to the body we are able to see, to hear, to touch. By virtue of the body we have a "place" in the world as one of the creatures of God. By virtue of the body we are related to other creatures and to one another. Precisely this system of relations is also the "world." Thus body and world are correlative notions.

Both world and body can be understood as realities dominated by anxiety (flesh) by avarice and violence, by enmity and death. The body and the world as thus dominated by sin and death must be overcome that justice and life may have dominion.

This point of view can be understood as the basis of a negation of the body and of the world. This is what characterized Mannichean and Gnostic positions in the time of the emergence of Christianity. These movements could think of salvation as a release from the body and the world in order that the immortal spirit of the human be reunited with the immortal essence of the divine.

It is true that the New Testament is able to make use of ideas which seem to belong to this world view. Thus we have in Romans 7 the cry "who will liberate me from this body of death?" But the use of this terminology was never permitted to lead to an acceptance of the Gnostic world view. The reason was the recollection that God is creator of heaven and earth.

Thus, neither the body nor the world may be destroyed to make way for the rescue of a certain number of spirits or souls. The Christian hope is not for the destruction of the body, but rather the resurrection of the body. Only so was it possible to testify to the victory of the God who is "creator of heaven and earth."

Therefore we find, above all in 1 Corinthians 15, the attempt to explain this key dimension of the doctrine of the resurrection (See 1 Corinthians 15:35-50). Here Paul uses two images. The first is that of a seed which, sown into the ground, emerges with a different form. For example, a seed becomes a plant, an acorn a tree and so on. Note that the transformation is in one sense natural, in that it does not mean the substitution of one thing for another but a transformation which actualizes that which was "only" a seed. The complementary image is that of different forms of "bodies." Here Paul focuses attention on the "heavenly bodies" that seem to possess an astonishing radiance or glory, like the stars. Combining these images Paul speaks of the resurrection of the body as the transformation of the human body of flesh and blood into a body of glory or light. In this way the body that was formerly decaying with anxiety and enmity, a body of sin and death, is transformed to become a body of light and glory. The body will be raised, but at the same time transformed. Thus, our human reality is transformed to become a faithful reflection of the glory of God.

The doctrine of the resurrection as the transformation of the body rather than its destruction testifies to the victory of the creator whose right to the body and to the world will be vindicated not by destruction, but by transformation and glorification.

This then entails that the resurrection of the body is thought of as part and parcel of the liberation of the whole creation, as in Romans 8:19-21:

> For the creation waits with eager longing for the revealing of the [sons and daughters] of God; for the creation was subjected to futility, not of its own will but by the will of [the one] who subjected it in hope; because the creation itself will be set free from its bondage to decay and obtain the glorious liberty of the [daughters and sons] of God.

Thus to speak of the resurrection of the dead is at the same time to speak of the transformation of heaven and earth.[32] The preoccupation with our own personal and private destiny, so often encouraged by talk of the immortality of the soul, is here radically thrown into question. The destiny of the person is tied to the destiny of the earth. The doctrine of the resurrection of the dead, then, entails a profound solidarity with the earth. In this way we testify to the victory of the God who is the Father Almighty, Maker of heaven and earth.

The resurrection of the dead is already begun in the uprising of the crucified. We live in a world dominated by the principalities and powers; nevertheless we rely upon the resurrection of the dead, in the ultimate victory of God inaugurated in Jesus the Christ. Even now in the world, where the powers of death seek to destroy life and where faith takes the form of resistance to these powers, we celebrate the victory of God as the resurrection of the dead.

The resurrection of the dead is the final victory of spirit over the weakness of flesh, the victory of life over death, the definitive bestowal of a future on all that becomes past. In the Creed we affirm our loyalty to precisely this Spirit, the Spirit that overcomes the power of death. This overcoming of death is already experienced in the forgiveness of sins that breaks open the prison of the past to confer a new future upon humanity. In the practice of this forgiveness of sins we already glimpse the victory of spirit over death that is the resurrection of the dead.

CHAPTER TWENTY-TWO

THE LIFE EVERLASTING

From its beginnings Israel knew that God is "the God of the living not of the dead" (see Mark 12:27). This represents the affirmation of life that is present at every stage of the development of faith. From the beginning it was clear that God is not neutral with respect to life and death, but rather unequivocally on the side of life against death.

The creation of all living things by God "in the beginning" bears testimony to the intervention of God on the side of life from the origin. This commitment to life is expressed as the spirit, as the life-giving power of God (Genesis 2:7).[33]

It is clear that for the early theologians who reflected on this commitment of Yahweh, death had to be viewed not as a "natural part of life" but as an intrusion and an interruption. Thus, the certainty that Adam will die comes as a consequence of the fall (Genesis 3:19). It is then scarcely surprising that the author of Ecclesiastes, when all other symbols of faith seem to have lost their interpretive power, could still claim that "even a living dog is better [off] than a dead lion" (Ecclesiastes 9:4). Even in its deepest cynicism, the shadow of Israel's commitment to the God of the living and its affirmation of life itself, remains clearly visible.

This commitment to life is expressed as the meaning not only of creation, but also of the action of God in history, above all in the giving of the law. The law is aimed precisely at the protection of life. The choice of the way of God is the choice of the way of life. To this choice corresponds the renunciation of death and all that leads to death (Deuteronomy 30:15ff.; Proverbs 11:19). The aim of the commandment is life and represents the intervention of the God of the living into the history of death in order to defend and promote the cause of life.

This intervention continues and gathers force in the prophets, who insist that the oppression of the poor is the choice of death. That is, the prophets sought to turn Israel away from a cultic form of faith that maintains the status quo. This status quo is marked by the suffering and death of the poor. Thus religious, social, economic, and political structures or systems that benefit the prosperous at the expense of the poor are regarded as the representatives of death. The consequence of such systems is the death of Israel as the chosen of God, as the representative of the God of life. Only by "turning" toward God, toward justice, and away from the religious mystifications of injustice can Israel truly choose life.

In the face of the calamities that befall Israel and Judah in consequence of their abandonment of the God of the living, it becomes necessary for the prophets to again make clear that the death and destruction that has overtaken the people is not the choice of God, but that God remains on the side of life. Thus it is not the will of God that any should be lost (Ezekiel 18:32). This renewed affirmation of life brings with it the broadening of the vision of life so that it becomes necessary to speak of the renewal of the living creation. Thus the giving life again to the dry bones of Israel is announced by Ezekiel (chapter 37) and taken up and amplified by Isaiah as the renovation of the creation as a whole (43:18). In all of this what is at stake is the outpouring of the divine, life-giving Spirit (Isaiah 44:3), the spirit of life that has aimed at life from the beginning. It is on account of this focus upon life as the aim of God not only in creation, but also in history that the writer of Daniel can introduce into the faith of Israel the Persian notion of the resurrection of the dead as the resurrection of the executed, the martyred who stood with God against the empire of death.

If the God of Israel is clearly marked as the God of the living, this comes to renewed and intensified expression in the New Testament. The messianic action of Jesus is clearly a siding with life, against the dominion of death. This is expressed first in the accounts of healing and exorcism that concretely oppose the intrusion of death into life. It is expressed in the celebration of life that makes the fiesta the symbol of the reign of God, the messianic party in which wine gladdens the heart and to which all are invited. In all of the Gospels this is expressed in terms of the decisive act of raising the dead modeled, perhaps, on the act of Elijah and Elisha in the beginning of the history of prophecy. The raising of Jairus' daughter, of the son of the widow of Nain, and of Lazarus all unmistakably illustrate that the messianic mission of Jesus is directed toward life and against death. The disciples or understudies are likewise summoned to undertake this mission, not only in terms of healing the sick, casting out demons, and the anticipation of the messianic banquet, but also, as Matthew indicates (10:8) and the narrative of Acts verifies (9:36ff.), in the raising of the dead and in the preliminary victory of life over death.

It is thus wholly in keeping with the narrated character of the mission of Jesus when Paul, in contrasting him to the first Adam can call him a "life-giving spirit" (1 Corinthians 15:45).

The messianic mission of Jesus departs fundamentally even from the prophetic faith of Israel in the direct taking on of death. In the faith of Israel there seems to be little possibility of celebrating the noble death. In spite of the impression of a celebration of a warrior god in the traditions of Israel there is no celebration of the death of the hero. Unlike the Greeks who could think of death as heroic, for Israel the only acceptable death is that of one who is full of years, one who has lived life to the full. However, the execution of Jesus at the hands of imperial authority dramatically alters the view of death that is incorporated into Christianity. Death remains the enemy and is not at all taken as a friend; but the choosing of death for the sake of the victory of life becomes a possibility, indeed a normative practice. Thus martyrdom becomes the choice of following the way of Jesus.

This does not mean that death is less opposed but rather that death is opposed precisely by robbing it of its power to terrify or to bribe us into collaboration with its surrogates: the structures of domination and division, of violence and arrogance. The aim remains the overcoming of the rule of death.

It is this commitment to life as the sum of the divine act in the mission and ministry of Jesus that is expressed most clearly in the Gospel of John. In the prologue to the Gospel we are told that that which is expressed in the word "is life, and the life was the light of [people]" (John 1:4-5). The effect of Jesus' message is such that those who hear have already "passed from death to life" (5:24). Thus the aim of Christ's coming is "that they may have life" (10:10).

The life that is spoken of here is life unlimited by death. It is "abundance" of life, overflowing or excess of life. As life unrestricted by death, it is everlasting life.

Now it is clear that the aim of the God who chooses Israel and defends the poor is life. The action of God in history as in creation is life. The aim of the messianic mission of the Son is also life, life that conquers death.

But it is above all in terms of the Spirit of God that the symbol of life, the empowerment of life comes to strongest expression. It is thus appropriate that the Creed as a whole and the article concerning the Spirit should reach their climax in the celebration of life released from all restrictions, of life at last liberated from the shadow and dominion of death. We have seen that the Spirit is that which gives life to every living creature, and that the gift of life is at the same time a task. In natural life, the task is expressed as procreation. In historical (human) life the gift of the spirit is at the same time the empowerment for the task to protect and facilitate the life of the people. Thus, there are judges, kings, and above all, prophets who call the people to choose paths that lead to life rather than death.

We have seen that this call to life is found in two related spheres: that of the holy catholic church and that of the communion of the just. These are the spheres within which we encounter persons and groups that are signs of the reign of God. In the Church we find a public commitment to Jesus the Christ that seeks holiness and universality and that publicly testifies to Jesus as the one who comes. In the communion of saints we find a similar commitment to the ways of life, but without restriction to those who explicitly affirm their loyalty to Jesus. This demonstrates that neither God nor the Spirit are limited by the boundaries of the Church, but rather awaken faith in the form of a commitment to liberty and justice and dignity in every culture and epoch. This testifies to the power of the Spirit in all the earth.

We have seen as well that the presence of the Spirit is shown in actions that concretely liberate persons from the dominion of death, from bondage to anxiety, from the power of sin. These actions have the form of the forgiveness of sins that treats not only the symptoms, but also the root of sin in every sphere of our life.

Thus the Spirit is indeed, as the Nicene Creed will say, "The Lord, the Giver of Life."

Now in this clause, this orientation to life becomes the orientation to the future of life, and a confidence in and reliance upon the resurrection of the dead and the life everlasting. Here we are dealing with life as the astonishing power that overcomes death. Thus we are speaking of the same Spirit of Life.

The God who creates is at the same time the Spirit, the Lord and Giver of Life.[34] In its origin creation was the gift of life and the new creation will be "life everlasting."

Thus the affirmation of everlasting life is an affirmation concerning life now liberated from the dominion of death and therefore everlasting, abundant, eternal. This life is the desire and the aim or goal of God for all creation. And in every creature made by this God we encounter the same desire for life that is unmenaced by death. Through sin this desire becomes the slave of anxiety rather than confidence and so places life under the power of sin and death. But the victory of God is the victory over the corruption, the perversion of the creature. Thus the abolition of this corruption is the abolition of the dominion of death over the life of the creature. Its result then is life unmenaced by death: everlasting or abundant or excessive life.

That the article concerning the Spirit, and that the Creed as a whole concludes with this invocation of life, is then appropriate. But it is also necessary to clarify the character and the function of this declaration.

The notion of unrestricted life, of abundant and everlasting life remains within the framework of the gospel of divine grace. It does not coincide with the Greek notion of the immortality of the soul. The notion of everlasting life is always that of life that has passed through death, and of life as essentially miraculous, just as miraculous as birth or even creation itself. What is at stake here is not the natural immortality of a part of the human being, or the prolongation of life as expression of the inherent indestructibility of the human spirit. The human is flesh, utterly dependent upon God for life. This remains true even when we speak of everlasting life. There are no illusions about the reality of death, no attempt to claim that death is a mere appearance, a natural passage into some other realm. The celebration of life that is characteristic of Israel will not accept the trivializing of death. Death remains the last enemy even when its defeat is assured. Life that is unrestricted by death is not the product of a higher consciousness that comes to terms with death or minimizes it. Rather it is the consequence of the defeat of death as the enemy of life.

Whether we speak of "natural life" or of the new life in Christ or of the unrestricted everlasting life of hope it remains true that life is the gift of God and that the creature has no claim on this gift, but receives it from God.

The point of this affirmation of everlasting life is not to engage in a speculative description of life "beyond death" but is rather to clarify the aim of God as Father, Son, and Holy Spirit. The clarification of this aim asserts that God is not neutral in bestowing life and death upon the creature as two equal possibilities, but rather is wholly committed to life. Loyalty to this God as Father, Son, and Holy Spirit, then, is likewise a commitment to life and an unwavering opposition to death in all its masks and surrogates.

This loyalty to life means that we stand with all that fosters and nurtures life. This means that the life of creation and of each and all of the creatures is precious to us. This commitment to the life of creation is an urgent task in our own day of threatened and actual ecological disaster. Whether the human will be the instrument of death for creation, or will in fact represent and reflect the creator and preserver of life is an open question. The choice between life and death was already urgent in the time of Deuteronomy, but it has now assumed global proportions then scarce dreamed of.

Commitment to life also means the fostering of human life, the commitment to those most vulnerable to the forces of death in the world. This commitment to life means, as the prophets already saw, that we oppose that which menaces the life of the most vulnerable: the rule of avarice and violence among the nations. The systems of avarice (consumer capitalism) and of violence (militarism, nationalism, and imperialism) conspire to maintain the life of the few at the expense of condemning the majority to early death. The commitment to life means above all unrelenting opposition to these forces of mass death masquerading as life in our world. Paradoxically this commitment to life takes the form of a willingness to die on behalf of life.

In spite of the high cost of a commitment to life, the community of faith celebrates life already in the midst of the history of death. It refuses the temptation to limit or deny life and liveliness. We will not be allured by the promise of life after death as though this meant the denial of life before death. Already as those committed to live and die for the cause of life, we celebrate life in the anticipatory fiesta. All too often the Christian community has found itself on the side of a suspicion of life and of vitality. This is the option represented not only by the asceticism of John the Baptist, but by all religious currents that seek to make death less horrible by denying its reality and seeking to escape from the body and creation that passes away. But this is by no means the victory of life and liveliness. Rather it is an attempt to extract oneself from mortality. The celebration of unrestricted life stands in contrast to this. The changing of water into wine represents the commitment to liveliness against all counsels of withdrawal from life in the name of avoiding the pain of death.

Death remains the enemy precisely because of this celebration of life. The celebration of life here and now helps us all the more clearly identify by contrast all that menaces and limits life and so to oppose it in the name of the eschatological life and liveliness for which we hope and which even now we begin to celebrate.

It was precisely for this reason that the early Christians, confronted with the terrible reality of persecution, could declare their loyalty to God by means of the Creed. In a certain sense the last clause of the Creed is the basis of all.[35] With this confidence in the resurrection of the dead and the life everlasting it was possible to face down the forces of oppression, injustice, and death with joy and confidence. The contemporary world still needs this testimony to the victory of the Father Almighty, Maker of heaven and earth, the victory of Jesus the crucified and risen Lord, the victory of the Spirit, the giver of life. May the Creed of the saints and the martyrs become again today a public and courageous testimony to the victory of God, Father, Son, and Holy Spirit.

H ymns have been sung, prayers offered, the word of God read and applied. In reply the people stand and with one voice declare their loyalty to God in the words of the Christian's oath:

> I believe in God, the Father Almighty,
>   creator of heaven and earth.
> I believe in Jesus Christ, his only Son, our Lord,
>   who was conceived by the Holy Spirit,
>   born of the Virgin Mary,
>   suffered under Pontius Pilate,
>   was crucified, died, and was buried;
>   he descended to the dead.
>   On the third day he rose again;
>   he ascended into heaven,
>   is seated at the right hand of the Father,
>   and will come again to judge the living and the dead.
> I believe in the Holy Spirit,
>   the holy catholic church,
>   the communion of saints,
>   the forgiveness of sins,
>   the resurrection of the body
>   and the life everlasting.   Amen.

It is a dramatic and impressive moment, this pledging of allegiance to the God who has called them out of darkness and bondage into freedom and responsibility, who summons them and all creation out of futility and into the inheritance prepared for them from the foundation of the earth.

It is extraordinary to hear these voices raised in a vow of loyalty not to just any lord, but to the one who was crucified.

They affirm their loyalty to the divine spirit who summons them to be full participants in the divine mission.

In every nation and culture and language under the sun they stand hurling their defiance against the principalities and powers that demand the sacrifice of Moloch, trumpeting their allegiance to the true Lord of creation, maker of heaven and earth.

What does one mean with this vow of loyalty and this renunciation of other gods, other lords, other spirits?

In defiance of the powers of domination and division I stand with the God who is pure, generous, adopting love, the one who has adopted me by love and so delivered me from the reign of hostility and isolation, of brokenness and bondage.

I will wager my life that this love is almighty, that the love that suffers and dies for the beloved is not impotent, but the true power of liberation.

I claim the earth itself, all creatures, for this love; for it is the power that brings forth life not only for me, but for all that breathes.

To this love I will be loyal, rejecting the temptation to return to bondage, rejecting the allure of force and division, rejecting rapacity toward my fellow creatures and seeking to show myself to be in truth the adopted heir of this love.

I will be loyal to the way of Jesus, the way that leads to the reign of this love in all creation.

I acknowledge him as my only leader and swear to continue his mission until the world is transformed.

I renounce all other gods, I will bow down before no power, however awesome or seductive, pledging my fealty only to the one whose will is inscribed in history by the mission of Jesus.

He is animated by the divine spirit to announce the overthrow of division and domination and death and calls me to be of the same spirit.

In loyalty to the one who is remembered as the child of an unwed mother I will never turn my back on the vulnerable and the despised.

In loyalty to the one who suffers at the hands of the representatives of earthly power, I will make no compromise with the forces of violence and avarice.

In loyalty to the one who is executed as a subversive, I will stand with all those who hunger and thirst for justice, with all those who are excluded by racial or social privilege, with all those who are branded as outcast by moral and religious authority, with all who are abandoned by the gods of this world.

In loyalty to the one who was dead and buried, I will not shrink from solidarity with all that is mortal.

In loyalty to the one of whom it is attested that he descended into Sheol, I will never write off anyone as without a future.

In loyalty to the crucified who rose on the third day, I will accept no limits to my hope nor make any compromises for my own survival.

In loyalty to the one who ascended, I will continue his ministry and mission in the confidence that he lives in the witness to the coming of the reign of love.

In loyalty to this one seated at the right hand, I will acknowledge him alone as the legitimate ruler of hearts and nations.

I hope to see the future that shall bear his image and fulfill his vision.

I will be loyal to the spirit that gives life, rejecting the many masks of death. I will demonstrate the presence of this power through the continued commitment to the mission of life.

I will celebrate the community of sacrificial service and generosity as the beginning of the reign of God, claiming zones of liberation from the power of death and despair.

I will celebrate solidarity with all those who seek justice, acknowledging the freedom of the Spirit by not restricting solidarity to those who claim the name of Jesus, but embracing all who resist the powers of darkness.

I will faithfully discharge the spirited responsibility of releasing my fellow creatures from the bondage of sin and injustice and establish the reign of peace with all who are my brothers and sisters by heartily showing the divine compassion toward them.

I will await the final triumph of life over all the forces of death, offering hope to all creation for the manifestation of the liberty of the children of God.

I will accept no victory short of unrestricted life in the name of the Lord of life.

To this I pledge my life and my death.

The words of loyalty are said. Will they have effect? Will they in truth become the form of life that we exhibit to the world?

Let the people say, Amen.

NOTES

CHAPTER 1: CREDO

1. This study therefore forms a part of what I began several years ago as a theology for the church based on the actions of worship performed by the church. On other occasions I have offered reflections on the activities of prayer and praise, and on confession and forgiveness of sins. These reflections on the Creed serve to further extend that project of a theology for the church based on the elements of the worship of the community of faith.

2. The connection between the Creed and renunciation of "Satan and all his works" is explicit, for example, in Niceta of Remesiana, *An Explanation of the Creed* (FC vol. 7, p. 43), and in Cyril of Jerusalem, *Catechetical Lecture* XIX (NPNF series 2, vol. VII, pp. 144-46).

3. Cyril of Jerusalem likens the faith expressed in the Creed to marriage as follows: "By faith the laws of marriage yoke together those who have lived as strangers: and because of the faith in marriage contracts a stranger is made partner of a stranger's person and possessions" (*Lecture* V, p. 29).

4. Wilfred Cantwell Smith, *Faith and the Creed* (Princeton: Princeton University Press, 1979).

5. Ibid., p. 76.

6. As far as I know, only David Bailey Harned among more recent commentators on the Creed has noticed the position of Smith. Unfortunately, Harned simply dismisses it without argument in order to develop a notion of personal identity as the meaning of the Creed. See David Bailey Harned, *Creed and Personal Identity: The Meaning of the Apostles' Creed* (Philadelphia: Fortress, 1981), pp. 16-19.

7. So Peter Chrysologus, in Sermon 61, concludes "let your memory retain it, but no paper know it. Do not let any secretary learn of it lest the sacred mystery of the faith be divulged in public and the secret of the faith scattered to the infidel" (FC vol. 17, p. 114).

8. For Augustine on not writing the Creed see Sermon 212 (FC vol 38, p. 120), and Sermon 214 (ibid., pp. 130-31). See also Augustine's *On the Creed* (NPNF series 1, vol. III, p. 369).

9. Augustine writes "For this reason the creed is called a symbolum because in it the approved belief of our fellowship is contained and by its profession, as by a password, the faithful Christian is recognized" (Sermon 214, p. 142). But Augustine can also use the example of a merchant's contract to render this notion intelligible when the need for secrecy had already passed in the life of the church: "merchants draw up for themselves a symbolum by which their alliance is held bound as by a pact of fidelity" (Sermon 212, p. 117). Even here the notion of alliance and loyalty remains determinative for the meaning of the Creed.

10. Even in the Middle Ages this character of the Creed was recalled by Ivo of Chartres in

his *Sermon on the Apostles' Creed*: "It is known to you, beloved, that soldiers of this life, when about to receive temporal benefices from temporal lords, are first bound by soldiers' oaths, and make profession that they will keep faith with their lords. How much more ought those about to fight for the eternal King and to receive eternal rewards, to be bound by heavenly oaths, and publicly profess the faith through which they are going to please him!" See George E. McCracken, ed., *The Library of Christian Classics*, Vol. IX, *Early Medieval Theology*, (Philadelphia: Westminster, 1957), p. 323.

11. After giving us one of the earliest descriptions of Christian baptismal practice Tertullian, in *De Corona*, develops this notion of conflicting loyalties at some length. Some of these contrasts demonstrate what is at stake here: "Do we believe it lawful for a human oath to be superadded to one divine, for a man to come under promise to another master after Christ? Shall he carry a flag, too, hostile to Christ? And shall he ask a watchword from the emperor who has already received one from God?" (ANF III pp. 99-100). Thus Tertullian concludes that martyrdom is preferable to betrayal of one's loyalty to Christ.

12. Thus Augustine refers to "The Creed of most holy martyrdom" (Sermon 215, p. 142).

13. Ludwig Fenerbach, *Lectures on the Essence of Religion*, trans. Ralph Manheim (New York: Harper & Row, 1967), pp. 178-81.

14. Wilfred Cantwell Smith maintains: "Contrary to modern impressions, the classical creeds of the Church include no propositional statements" (*Faith and the Creed*, p. 77).

15. Cyril of Jerusalem notes: "For since all cannot read the Scriptures, some being hindered as to the knowledge of them by want of learning, and others by a want of leisure, in order that the soul may not perish from ignorance, we comprise the whole doctrine of the Faith in a few lines" (*Lecture* V, p. 32). But Cyril also expects to confirm his interpretation of the Creed from a close exegesis: "So for the present listen while I simply say the Creed, and commit it to memory; but at the proper season expect the confirmation out of Holy Scripture of each part of the contents" (Ibid).

ARTICLE 1

1. "Accordingly, believing in God the Father Almighty we ought to believe that there is no creature which has not been created by his omnipotence." See J. H. S. Burleigh, ed., *The Library of Christian Classics*, Vol.VI, *Augustine: Earlier Writings*, (Philadelphia: Westminster, 1953), p. 355.

2. That these cannot be the basis of our theological reflection is further suggested by the great difference between the paucity of reference to God as Father in these traditions, and the great prominence which this designation acquires in Christianity. Even where we may suppose there to be some direct relationship between Christian and Jewish identification of God as Father, we should be cautious, for if the election of Israel is the basis of this title for God in Judaism, it cannot be assumed that this is simply transferable to Christianity. In the case of Greek thought, it will have to be seen to what extent the notion of God as a universal principle of origin has any relation to the specifically Christian use of this term.

3. "When you hear the word Father, you must understand by this father of a Son" (Rufinus, *Commentary on the Apostles' Creed*, NPNF series 2, vol. III, p. 544).

4. Karl Barth maintains: "This first article of the Creed [is] in no respect a playground for Natural Theology." See Karl Barth, *Credo* (New York: Charles Scribner's Sons, 1962), p. 19.

5. There is no basis for the familiar notion that "abba" is used to designate an especially intimate relation between Jesus and the Father. This is one of the myths of the scholars that has had a wide homiletic appeal but is groundless. See also Ernst Käsemann, *Commentary on Romans* (Grand Rapids: William B. Eerdmans, 1980), p. 228.

6. Thus Ivo of Chartres correctly places the discussion of adoption prior to that of creation: "But let us who through the adoption of grace are sons of God, say 'I believe in God the Father Almighty'" (McCracken, *Early Medieval Theology*, p. 324).

7. Cyril of Jerusalem states correctly: "For we call Him Father, not as having been by nature begotten of Our Father which is in heaven; but having been transferred from servitude to sonship by the grace of the Father, through the Son and the Holy Spirit, we are permitted so to speak by ineffable loving-kindness" (*Lecture* VII, p. 46).

8. Note here that Father does not mean "source" as it does for Sirach and for Plato, but rather denotes the liberator and adopter. And this is consistent with the traditions of Israel. There as well God was the Father of Israel in the sense of the one who liberates and elects Israel.

9. So, Cyprian: "when we call God Father we ought to act as God's children" (*On the Lord's Prayer* 11, ANF V, p. 450). This consequence is also drawn by Cyril of Jerusalem: "Knowing this, therefore, let us walk spiritually, that we may be counted worthy of God's adoption" (*Lecture* VII, p. 47).

10. Hans Urs von Balthasar remarks: "he will be the Creator of man and woman, and thus contains the primal qualities of woman in himself in the same simultaneously transcending way as those of man." He also notes: "The Greek *gennao* can imply both siring and bearing, as can the word for to come into being: *ginomai*." See *Credo: Meditations on the Apostles' Creed* (New York: Crossroad, 1990), p. 30; see also p. 78.

11. See Virginia Ramey Mollenkott, *The Divine Feminine: The Biblical Imagery of God as Feminine* (New York: Crossroad, 1985) and Phyllis Trible, *God and the Rhetoric of Sexuality* (Philadelphia: Fortress, 1978). For a wealth of information concerning feminine imagery for God and for Jesus in later and especially medieval theology, see Carolyn Walker Bynum, *Jesus as Mother: Studies in the Spirituality of the High Middle Ages* (Berkeley: University of California Press, 1982).

12. It should be noted, however, that images which have an important place in theology are even scarcer; the idea of the image and likeness of God, for example, or that of the trinity.

13. Thus Jan Milic Lochman avers that "The father of Jesus Christ is an utterly unpaternalistic father." See Jan Milic Lochman, *The Faith We Confess* (Philadelphia: Fortress, 1984), p. 51. Pannenberg acknowledges that the name Father was "connected with patriarchal structures of society" but "on the lips of Jesus the name 'Father' is no longer the symbol of the God of patriarchal society." See Wolfhart Pannenberg, *The Apostles' Creed: In Light of Today's Questions* (Philadelphia: Westminster, 1972), p. 32.

14. Here we deal primarily with the relation between Christianity and Judaism as it is focused on the issue of election or adoption. Subsequently we will have to deal with this question in relation to the specifically christological claims of Christianity.

15. Pannenberg indicates that his earlier supposition (in *Jesus: God and Man*) that Judaism is abolished in the cross must be revised (*The Apostles' Creed*, p. viii). He subsequently notes: "Confession of faith in Christ carries with it the bond between Christian faith and the history and hopes of the people of Israel" (Ibid., p. 59).

16. Karl Barth rightly affirms that "the conception 'Almighty' receives its light from the conception 'Father' and not vice versa" (*Credo*, p. 19). But Barth develops the notion of divine power as authority over life and death in advance of clarification of "Father" thereby violating the principle he has correctly affirmed (Ibid., pp. 19-21).

17. This abstract definition of power is to be found in Rufinus: "God is called Almighty because he possesses rule and dominion over all things" (*Commentary*, NPNF series 2, vol. III, p. 545).

18. Thus Augustine attempts to head off these conundrums in his *Sermon to the Catechumens* (NPNF series 1, vol. III, p. 369): "God is Almighty, and yet, though Almighty He cannot die, cannot be deceived, cannot lie; and as the Apostle says, 'cannot deny Himself.' How many things that He cannot do, and yet is Almighty! Yea therefore God is Almighty, because he cannot do these things" (Ibid., p. 369).

19. For a discussion of the differences between and relation among these diverse forms of God-language, see my *Beyond Theism: A Grammar of God-Language* (Oxford, New York 1986), pp. 186ff.

20. Thus Lochman writes of "the omnipotence of non-violent love" (*The Faith We Confess*, p. 55), and von Balthasar maintains: "It is therefore essential, in the first instance, to see the unimaginable power of the Father in the form of his self-surrender, that is, of his love, and not, for example, in his being able to do this or that as he chooses" (*Credo*, p. 31).

21. See Karl Barth, *Church Dogmatics* III, 3 (Edinburgh: T & T Clark, 1960), pp. 3f.

22. For further reflection on this petition of the Lord's Prayer, see my *Life as Worship:*

Prayer and Praise in Jesus' Name (Grand Rapids: William B. Eerdmans, 1982), pp. 54-56.
23. Ibid., pp. 102-5.

24. "Jesus is then to be understood as the mediator of creation in so far as he is the end of all things and in as much as the end of all things has already appeared in him—the end which decides creation's true nature" (Pannenberg, *The Apostles' Creed*, p. 65).

25. For Israel's elaboration of the laws of the sabbath year and the jubilee, see Leviticus 25.

26. Barth, *Church Dogmatics* II, 2, pp. 3-506.

ARTICLE 2

PART 1: CHRISTOLOGY

1. Thus Karl Barth notes: "With these words we step into the great centre of the Christian Creed. And here decisions are made. For instance, our understanding of the second Article decides whether we rightly understand the first and the third, and therefore whether we understand the whole as Christian creed" (*Credo*, p. 39).

2. This is the theme which Ernst Käsemann, following Adolf Schlatter, emphasizes in his book, *Jesus Means Freedom* (Philadelphia: Fortress, 1969), p. 21.

3. For a helpful discussion of this literature, see Klaus Koch, *The Rediscovery of Apocalyptic* (Naperville: Alec R Anderson Inc., 1970).

4. See Hendrikus W. Boers, *Who Was Jesus?* (New York: Harper & Row, 1989), pp. 31-50, for a most helpful discussion of the relation between Jesus and John.

5. This situation may be rather different in relation to the Nicene Creed which, in this as in other respects, requires a separate treatment.

6. Virtually all interpreters of this phrase seek to drive a wedge between Jesus and his followers. The exception is Jan Milic Lochman: "To speak of the 'son' means to speak of 'sons' and 'daughters.' The 'only' son does not remain solitary" (*The Faith We Confess*, p. 91).

7. Thus Barth notes that "the Lordship of Christ is not only a so-called religious Lordship; as that, it is very much an ethical, yes, a political Lordship" (*Credo*, p. 56). Lochman goes somewhat further: "When the Christian community confesses 'Jesus is Lord' all other powers totter and fall—at least in the sense of being denied any ultimate legitimacy, or any totalitarian claim" (*The Faith We Confess*, p. 97).

8. "As 'our Lord' Jesus was opposed in the faith of the early Christian church to the numerous 'lords' known to the Hellenistic world—on the one hand the Roman emperors (who were given the title 'kyrios' in Greek), and on the other the gods of the mystery religions" (Pannenberg, *The Apostles' Creed*, p. 70).

PART 2: DANGEROUS MEMORY

1. The development of the notion of a "dangerous memory" is a contribution of J. B. Metz. See *Faith in History and Society: Toward a Practical Fundamental Theology* (New York: Seabury, 1980).

2. The discussion of the character and action of the Holy Spirit is deferred to the third article of the Creed.

3. It should be noted that these legends of the divine conception of heroes are less reticent than the New Testament narratives speaking as they do of "gods" rather than of holy spirit.

4. Thus Peter Chrysologus: "Precisely thus [of the Holy Spirit] is Christ born for you in such a way that he may change your own manner of birth. . . . He wants you to have a new birth of life" (Sermon 57, p. 107). And Niceta of Remesiana notes a similar connection: "And so he was born of the holy and immaculate virgin to initiate holy rebirth in us" (*Explanation*, p. 45).

5. See Herman Waetjen, *A Reordering of Power* (Minneapolis: Fortress, 1989), pp. 66-67.

6. For an extensive treatment of this theme, see Jane Schaberg, *The Illegitimacy of Jesus* (New York: Harper & Row, 1987).

7. Note that this is not something to be rejected by Protestants; it is part and parcel of what it means to acclaim Jesus as the Son of God.

8. According to Pannenberg, "in the early church of the first centuries the virgin birth counted as being the special token of Jesus' true humanity, in opposition to the gnostics" (*The Apostles' Creed*), p. 71.

9. Augustine supplies an additional significance: "That dispensation did honor to both sexes male and female, and showed that both had a part in God's care; not only that which he assumed, but that also through which he assumed it, being a man born of a woman" (Burleigh, *Augustine: Earlier Writings*, p. 358).

10. This is the standard explanation for the presence of Pilate in the Creed. Augustine notes: "The name of the judge had to be added to mark the date" (Ibid., #11, p. 359). Ivo of Chartres writes: "The reference to Pilate involves an indication of the time, not an ennoblement of the person" (McCracken, *Early Medieval Theology*, p. 325). Niceta of Remesiana (*Explanation*, p. 47) and Peter Chrysologus (Sermon 57, p. 108) use the same explanation, as does Barth (*Credo*, p. 79).

11. Jan Milic Lochman notes: "What is long overdue and would really be helpful is a concentrated study of the foundations of the Christian faith—including, above all, the role of Pilate in the Creed—that would include intense reflection on its historical and political components" (*The Faith We Confess*, p. 123). But Lochman still develops a "metaphysical" rather than a political interpretation of Jesus' suffering (pp. 127-28). He repeats his call for a political interpretation of the cross (p. 139) but carries this no further.

12. Rufinus notes: "The cross of Christ then, brought those who had wrongfully abused the authority which they had received into subjection to those who had before been in subjection to them. But us, that is mankind, it teaches to first of all to resist sin even unto death, and willingly to die for the sake of religion" (*Commentary*, NPNF series 2, vol. III, p. 549). In spite of the mythological language of this section Rufinus recognizes the connection between the overthrow of the powers by the cross and the way of martyrdom.

13. It has been suggested that this portrait was motivated by the desire to avoid or diminish conflict with the Roman authorities—but while elements of the portrayal of Pilate may be motivated in this way, the overall picture is by no means inconsistent with what we know of Roman provincial administration generally.

14. Thus Pannenberg: "The rule of God, understood in Jesus' exclusive sense, robs every political order of its absolute claim on the people living under it" (*The Apostles' Creed*, p. 85).

15. "Take therefore first, as an indestructible foundation, the Cross, and build upon it the other articles of the faith" (Cyril of Jerusalem, *Lecture* XIII, p. 92).

16. "He was crucified as a rebel, as a messianic pretender; so much is certain from the inscription on the cross" (Pannenberg, *The Apostles' Creed*, p. 80).

17. Cyril of Jerusalem asks: "and wilt thou not be crucified for Him who was crucified for thee?" (*Lecture* XIII, p. 88). And after the time of persecution had begun to fade from memory Augustine could write: "This extremist form of death He chose, that not any kind of death might make his martyrs afraid" (*On the Creed*, NPNF series 1, vol. III, p. 372).

18. "He who was then crucified by one nation is now fixed in the hearts of all nations" (Augustine, Sermon 215, p. 147).

19. This has been a difficult thing to learn in the last two centuries. The collaboration of the Church in structures of segregation in the United States and in apartheid in South Africa can only be understood as repudiations of the lordship of Jesus and thus as open apostasy. But these extreme examples are not exceptional, for most congregations are still constituted as homogeneous groups. As long as this is so the witness to the lordship of the crucified is at best distorted and at worst denied.

20. "You perceive that He was buried, that His death may not be deemed something merely feigned" (Peter Chrysologus, Sermon 57, p. 108; see also Sermon 61, p. 113). Cyril of Jerusalem explains that this is basic to Christian hope: "His death was not a mere show, for then is our salvation also fabulous" (*Lecture* XIII, p. 83).

21. So, Hans Urs von Balthasar says that Jesus: "died a death in companionship with all sinners" (*Credo*, p. 53).

22. "To say that he was buried is the most unambiguous way in which it is possible to stamp a being as a true actual man" (Barth, *Credo*, p. 85).

23. Indeed Karl Barth takes "was buried" as the fundamental point of this article of the Creed determining the interpretation of both cross and resurrection. (See *Credo*, pp. 83-87.)

24. Ivo of Chartres declares: "He therefore died a true death, as he was born by a true birth, so that he might free us from eternal death" (McCracken, *Early Medieval Theology*, p. 325). And Niceta of Remesiana says: "Christ died that he might destroy the rights of death" (*Explanation*, p. 47).

25. In the Gospel of Luke the rending of the temple veil occurs before Jesus' death, that is, immediately before he gives up "his spirit." The Gospel of John does not mention this and neither Luke nor John repeat Matthew's curious tale of the earthquake and the opening of the tombs.

26. "Because Jesus gathers up our dying into his own, the character of our dying changes. In communion with Jesus it loses its hopelessness" (Pannenberg, *The Apostles' Creed*, p. 89).

27. The early church had a wonderfully dramatic way of depicting this death of death. Rufinus speaks of the divinity of the son as a "hook" concealed within the bait of his humanity, so that he "might lure the Prince of this world to a conflict, to whom offering his flesh as a bait, His divinity underneath might catch and hold him fast with its hook, through the shedding of his immaculate blood" (*Commentary*, NPNF series 2, vol. III, p. 550). Cyril of Jerusalem uses a similar analogy: "His body therefore was made a bait to death, that the dragon, hoping to devour it, might disgorge those also who had been already devoured" (*Lecture* XII, p. 76).

PART 3: FROM MEMORY TO HOPE

1. In the early fourth century Rufinus noted that this clause was not found in either the Roman or Oriental churches although it was used in his own and he found it implied in the others (*Commentary*, NPNF series 2, vol. III, p. 550). For other early references to the significance of this clause, see Peter Chrysologus (who speaks of Christ redeeming "those beneath the earth" in Sermon 57, p. 108) and Cyril of Jerusalem (*Lecture* XIV, p. 99).

2. Early Christianity was legal in much of the empire only as a "burial society." In this way its gatherings were often cemeteries (such as the catacombs). Because of this focus on grave sites and the importance of martyrs in the time of persecution, it was nearly inevitable that Christianity should take the form of an apparent "cult" of the "saints."

3. For further clarification of the relation between Yahweh and the dead, see Gerhard von Rad, *Old Testament Theology* I (New York: Harper & Row, 1962), pp. 387-91.

4. See Pannenberg, *The Apostles' Creed*, p. 91.

5. This is also indicated by Matthew's linking of the death of Jesus with the resuscitation of the "saints" (Matthew 27:52).

6. In this connection, see also the view that the humiliation of the divine entails the undermining or bringing into submission of the principalities and powers (Philippians 2:5-11). See also Rufinus, *Commentary*, NPNF series 2, vol. III, p. 550.

7. "For, tell me, couldst thou wish the living only to enjoy His grace, and that, though most of them are unholy; and not wish those who from Adam had for a long while been imprisoned to have now gained their liberty? . . . Wouldst thou not wish that He should descend and redeem such as these?" (Cyril of Jerusalem, *Lecture* IV, p. 22; see also Pannenberg, *The Apostles' Creed*, pp. 93-94).

8. One of the ways available for contemporary theology is provided by the appropriation of Whiteheadian metaphysics in process theology to speak of "objective immortality." See John B. Cobb, Jr., *A Christian Natural Theology* (Philadelphia: Westminster, 1965), pp. 63-79.

9. Thus Pannenberg: "The meaning of the Christian acknowledgement of the conquest of the kingdom of death and Jesus Christ's descent into hell lies in the universal scope of

salvation" (*The Apostles' Creed*, p. 95). See also Hans Urs von Balthasar: "The redemptive act of the cross was by no means intended solely for the living, but also includes in itself all those who have died before or after it." (*Credo*, p. 54).

10. See Helmut Thielicke, *I Believe: The Christian's Creed* (Philadelphia: Fortress, 1968), pp. 130-31, and Jan Milic Lochman, *The Faith We Confess*, pp. 144-46.

11. This is the limitation of Bultmann's notion that Jesus is raised into the proclamation of the community.

12. For a phenomenology of this relation between that which eludes speech and discourse, see my *Beyond Theism*, pp. 53ff.

13. Karl Barth notes the basic issue as follows: "It is of course a notorious fact that the tradition that we have received of this memory of the forty days [the resurrection] is in its details in remarkable disorder, far from satisfactory to the historian. But alongside of that stands the other fact that, in spite of very pressing apologetic needs and although that disorder could not even then be concealed from anyone, this tradition was unconcernedly taken up into the New Testament in this very condition" (*Credo*, p. 100). But it is important to go further in order to identify the meaning of this disorder, to discern, as it were, the order of this apparent disorder.

14. Even if we include the transfiguration of Jesus as a displaced appearance narrative it has an effect similar to the announcement of the resurrection: that of fear (Mark 9:6).

15. One is tempted to make use of Paul's notion of the radical transformation of the body of flesh into a body of glory to account for this non-recognition. But whatever "body of glory" may mean it is not likely to mean that it makes Jesus look like a gardener! The body of glory may indeed be what blinds Paul on the way to Damascus but it will not account for any of the other narratives.

16. "I confess the Cross, because I know of the Resurrection; for if, after being crucified, He had remained as He was, I had not perchance confessed it, for I might have concealed both it and my Master; but now that the Resurrection has followed the Cross, I am not ashamed to declare it" (Cyril of Jerusalem; *Lecture* XIII, p. 83).

17. Karl Barth rightly insists: "The Crucified is the Risen One and the Risen One is the Crucified" (*Credo*, p. 95).

18. For further reflection on this account see "dead and buried" above and "the resurrection of the dead" below.

19. Thus in the *Sectional Confession of Faith* #18, attributed to Gregory Thaumaturgas: "He destroyed death through the resurrection that had in view the resurrection of us all" (ANF VI, p. 45).

20. In this connection we may recall that the forty years in the wilderness was not only remembered as a time of testing, rebellion, and grumbling, as in Numbers 11:1, but also as the time of the betrothal or "honeymoon" of Israel and Yahweh, as in Jeremiah 2:2-3. The forty days of Jesus' wilderness experience may correspond to the former, while the forty days of the resurrection appearances corresponds to the latter image.

21. There is, of course a subsequent appearance in chapter 21, but 20:30-31 indicates that at some point in its composition the Gospel of John did not include chapter 21.

22. "For think not that because He is now absent in the flesh, He is therefore absent also in the Spirit. He is here present in the midst of us" (Cyril of Jerusalem, *Lecture* XIV, p. 103).

23. The question of the identity of the son of man is a vexed one. I have shown that this "New Humanity" is a collective reality for which Jesus is the central figure in "The Martyrdom of the Son of Man," *Text and Logos: The Humanistic Interpretation of the New Testament*, edited by Theodore W. Jennings, Jr. (Atlanta: Scholars Press, 1990), pp. 229-43.

24. So, Cyril of Jerusalem, referring to "Moses' seat" notes: "for it signifies not his wooden seat, but the authority of his teaching" (*Lecture* XII, p. 78). Augustine maintains: "To say that 'God sits' signifies not the position of his members, but his judicial power" (Burleigh, *Augustine: Earlier Writings*, p. 361).

25. Rufinus demonstrates that the seating at the right hand refers to the humanity of Jesus and so belongs to the incarnation (*Commentary*, p. 555).

26. This further confirms the discussion of providence in the first article of the Creed. The assertion that it is the crucified who "is in charge" precludes an abstract and speculative notion of providence which makes God responsible for the mystery of evil in the world. For

us the one who "is in charge" is precisely the "lamb" whose death opens the way to life. This is the way the divine power is exercised in the present.

27. See the discussion in Von Rad, *Old Testament Theology* I:121ff.

28. See Jürgen Moltmann, *The Theology of Hope: On the Ground and the Implications of a Christian Eschatology* (New York: Harper & Row, 1967), pp. 265ff.

29. See the discussion of "dead and buried" above, and of "resurrection of the dead" below.

30. Thus Karl Barth: "He is the content of our time and that not only of our present but also of our future" (*Credo*, p. 119). And in discussing "life everlasting," Barth says: "it is not primarily expectation of something but expectation of the Lord" (Ibid., p. 166). Barth's formulations restrict this future to the future of the Church (pp. 119-20) which, in my view, is impermissible.

31. "The expectation of Christ's coming again to judgment is the foundation of the standard by which the Christian withstands the pressure of ruling circumstances and the tendencies of the spirit of any given age" (Pannenberg, *The Apostles' Creed*, p. 121).

32. The discussion of the "end of history" occasioned by Francis Fukuyama supposes that history has primarily to do with the question of the regnant economic-political system. But even this debate can be supposed to be "over" only if the perspectives of religious communities are discounted. The prophetic traditions expressed in Judaism, Christianity, and Islam have not yet been exhausted. And the future for which Christian faith hopes is by no means identical with the triumph of what is called democratic capitalism.

33. "The Judge Whom we go to meet (or rather Who comes to meet us as our future!) is not [just] any judge. . . . Regard is not paid to the seriousness of the judgment of Jesus Christ if it is not expected strictly as his judgment." (Barth, *Credo*, p. 123). Augustine is even more explicit on this point: "Let us acknowledge our Saviour; Let us not fear our Judge. . . . We have Him as Advocate; would we fear Him as Judge? Nay, rather, because we have sent Him ahead as our Advocate, let us hope that He will be our Judge" (Sermon 213, p. 125).

34. Some ancient manuscripts omit this but it accords well in any case with the point of view of Luke's picture of Jesus.

ARTICLE 3

1. "But great and learned commentators of the divine Scriptures have not as yet discussed the doctrine of the Holy Spirit with the same fullness and care, so that we may easily understand his peculiar character as Holy Spirit, by which he is to be distinguished from the Father and the Son" (Burleigh, *Augustine: Earlier Writings*, p. 364).

2. Matthew uses demons in place of evil spirits in these stories, perhaps in order to avoid confusion with holy spirit.

3. "He is the *Holy* Spirit because He is the Spirit of Jesus Christ" (Barth, *Credo*, p. 129).

4. "God imparts Himself to us, to us men, takes us, so to speak, with Him on this way" (Barth, *Credo*, p. 132). But Barth's own "confessing situation" in the struggle against fascism prevents him from giving full weight to this insight. The freedom of God does not mean the transcendence of God in the sense of a separation between the creature and the creator but rather is expressed in the freedom of God to enter the creature not only in the incarnation of the Son, but also in the empowering of the human through the Spirit.

5. Pannenberg speaks of spirit as the presence of the coming God and the presence of the past of that coming in Jesus (*The Apostles' Creed*, pp. 141-42).

6. Thus Pannenberg speaks of "the church as the field of activity of the Spirit of Christ" (Ibid., p. 145).

7. This is not fully perceived by Karl Barth, who speaks "paradoxically" of the "hiddenness of the body of Christ" (*Credo*, p. 148).

8. So, Hans Urs von Balthasar emphasizes that catholicity designates a movement and communication to all nations (*Credo*, p. 84).

9. Barth notes of the church "that its commission and its life are not two different things but one" (*Credo*, pp. 142-43). But this unfortunately allows him to collapse the commission

into the interior life of the church in such a way as to focus upon an enclosed word and sacrament. Thus, though he agrees that "it will necessarily be a missionary church" (p. 145), it is this primarily because it is above all for Christians and only in this way for all. Pannenberg expands this view: "What is decisive is that the church clings to and pursues the apostles' mission to the whole of mankind" (*The Apostles' Creed*, p. 148).

10. Rufinus notes that the Holy Spirit came upon "each of the Apostles, that they might speak diverse languages so that no race however foreign, no tongue however barbarous, might be inaccessible to their reach" (*Commentary*, p. 542). It is also here that we encounter the view that the Apostles, about to disperse on their mission, agreed on the Creed as a sign or password by which the true proclamation of the gospel might be recognized, thereby guarding the movement against treachery.

11. Christianity is essentially related to the work of translation. This is in contrast, for example to Islam, which maintains its identity through the retention of Arabic as the language of faith. By taking seriously the essential nature of translation for Christian existence we can see that there is no "native tongue" or "native culture" for Christianity. Rather it is always necessarily engaged in translation and so in transformation.

12. "Unless the Christian faith gather men together into a society in which brotherly love can operate, it remains less fruitful. Hence we believe [in] the Holy Catholic Church" (Burleigh, *Augustine: Earlier Writings*, p. 366).

13. See Hans Urs von Balthasar, *Credo*, p. 85.

14. Ivo of Chartres combines the sacramental and trans-generational interpretation: "the truth of the church's sacraments in which the saints who have departed from this life in the unity of the faith have communicated" (McCracken, *Early Medieval Theology*, pp. 326-27). Pannenberg notes the original meaning of the clause as both communion with martyrs and sacraments (*The Apostles' Creed*, p. 149).

15. Niceta of Remesiana, *Explanation*, p. 49. However, Niceta collapses the discussion of the communion of saints into the discussion of the Holy Catholic Church, thus making the church inclusive of those not specifically Christian.

16. Cited in the introduction to *Of True Religion* (Burleigh, p. 218).

17. See Hendrikus W. Boers, *Theology out of the Ghetto* (Leiden: E. J. Brill, 1971), pp. 74-104.

18. Nor is this arbitrary, for Rahab is also known as a pattern for Christians even by the otherwise moralistic author of James (2:25).

19. It has become customary to speak here of latent Christianity or anonymous Christians. But this is incorrect. It is wrong headed to try to maintain that those who are good people are somehow unconscious Christians. There can in fact be no such thing as a crypto-Christian, or latent Christianity. Christianity is constituted by an explicit and public commitment to Jesus as the Christ. That is, after all, why there is such a thing as a Creed. The point of the communion of saints is to talk about the solidarity of Christians and non-Christians, not overt and covert, conscious and unconscious Christians.

20. It is interesting to note that the disciples who protested in this way against those others who were engaged in casting out demons were also the disciples who failed to recognize the meaning of the cross. The cross demonstrates the commitment of God against all powers of division and domination. But the disciples still want positions of privilege in the reign of God without understanding that this motive must be excluded by Jesus' followers.

21. This is the great weakness of Barth's interpretation of this clause which reduces it to the effect of atonement and so makes it a misplaced clause of the second article (*Credo*, pp. 150ff.). But Barth's later second thoughts about baptism in particular and the sacraments in general open the way for an understanding of the forgiveness of sins as something that we are called to do. (See *Church Dogmatics* IV, 4, fragment.)

22. We may also note here the community discipline referred to by Paul in 1 Corinthians 5:1-5, where it is the gathered community, rather than Paul as apostle, which acts to exclude one whose form of life is regarded as coming into contradiction to the gospel. That it is the church as such which has this power and gift is still recognized by Augustine (see Sermon 213, p. 128).

23. In this connection we also recall Matthew's account of the healing of the paralytic where Jesus demonstrates the forgiveness of sins through the command to walk. Of the

crowd it is said that "they were filled with awe, and they glorified God, who had given such authority to human beings" (Matthew 9:8).

24. Hans Urs von Balthasar refers here to "the representative power, conferred at Easter, of forgiving sins in the authority of Christ" and notes: "It is impossible that just somebody or other could say to someone else: I pardon your murder, your adultery, your apostasy." But this restriction is wholly without foundation as von Balthasar is almost driven to acknowledge in the case of emergency baptism lying within the purview of "everyone" (*Credo*, p. 91).

25. Here Barth quite rightly speaks of sin and death as an impossible possibility (*Credo*, pp. 36-37).

26. Thus Ivo of Chartres maintained that the forgiveness of sins refers "not only to those which are forgiven through Baptism but also those which, through humble confession have been cleansed in worthy satisfaction" (McCracken, *Early Medieval Theology*, p. 327). Here Ivo refers to the practice of confession that had been separated from the public worship of the community as preparation for the participation in the mass or Eucharist. While this separation cannot be accepted by Protestantism, it is nonetheless true that the practice of liturgical confession (and absolution) may have an important role to play in actualizing this forgiveness of sins. See my *Liturgy of Liberation: The Confession and Forgiveness of Sins* (Nashville: Abingdon, 1988), pp. 144ff.

27. Moltmann notes that the character of Christian proclamation is *ego te absolvo* (I forgive you). See Jürgen Moltmann, *The Church in the Power of the Spirit* (New York: Harper & Row, 1977), p. 223.

28. See Cyril of Jerusalem, *Lecture* I, p. 7.

29. See Richard Horsley and J. S. Hanson, *Bandits, Prophets and Messiahs* (Minneapolis: Winston-Seabury, 1985) for a discrimination of the various groups that have been incorrectly subsumed under the name of zealots.

30. Thus Lochman notes that the Christian-Marxist dialogue found the resurrection a productive theme for discussion: "Had not Christ's resurrection been understood and attested in practice by many Christians, especially at the beginning, and subsequently in left-wing 'radical Christian' circles as an authorization to rebel against the forces of death?" (Lochman, *The Faith We Confess*, p. 151).

31. The universal scope of the divine mercy is one of the most important contributions of Karl Barth. Although in his *Credo* (p. 171) he stops short of an affirmation of universal redemption, his subsequent work in *Church Dogmatics* II, 2, (pp. 306-506) is far less ambiguous.

32. See Cyril of Jerusalem, *Lecture* XV, p. 105. In keeping with this ancient perspective Hans Urs von Balthasar writes: "Not only will humanity, which is something like the result or the sum total of the created world, be resurrected, but the created world too" (Balthasar, *Credo*, p. 98).

33. Thus according also to the covenant with Noah all life belongs to God. This is the reason given for the prohibition of the eating of blood (Genesis 9:4; see also Leviticus 17:11).

34. "The Spirit confers their future on all created things and thereby gives them life" (Pannenberg, *The Apostles' Creed*, p. 140).

35. "It is because of our resurrection that we believe all that we believe" (Niceta of Remesiana, *Explanation*, p. 50).